Pandora

A NOVEL BY SYLVIA FRASER

Pandora

DRAWINGS BY HAROLD TOWN

McClelland and Stewart Limited/Toronto/Montreal

0-7710-3177-7

The Canadian Publishers
McClelland and Stewart Limited
25 Hollinger Road, Toronto 374

Printed and bound in Canada by
John Deyell Limited

Contents

For Russ.
For Jack. For Harold. For Sheila.

Forthwith there escaped a multitude of plagues
for hapless man —
such as gout, rheumatism and colic
for his body,
and envy, spite and revenge
for his mind —
and scattered themselves far and wide.
Pandora hastened to replace the lid,
but, alas! the whole contents of the jar
had escaped,
one thing only excepted, which lay at the bottom,
and that was
hope.

The Age of Fable,
Bulfinch's Mythology

Home

AND SHE BROUGHT FORTH her fourth-born child out of flesh-heave, mountain-burst, joy-throe, pain-spasm, silt, seaweed, dinosaur dung, lost continents, blood, mucus and genetic hazard, and she wrapped her in white flannel, and she laid her, struggling, wheezing, spewing, in the ragbox by Grannie Cragg's treadle machine.

The twins, age five, stare into the ragbox.

"You promised us a baby *brother*," says Adel.

"Because of Baby Victor who choked," says Ada.

Grannie Cragg's hand flaps like a broken sparrow's wing over the patchwork bunting: "It's not so easy to trap the mandrake root."

The mother convulses between layers of ether and eiderdown in the ebbtide of her breed-stew.

The father rocks in his cane chair, squinting at the world through the narrow window of his rage.

"July at high noon!" grumbles Grannie Cragg. "Most young got the sense to be midwifed by the moon."

Dearly beloved, forasmuch as all men are conceived and born in sin, and that our Saviour Christ saith none can enter into the Kingdom of God except he be regenerate and born anew of Water and of the Holy Ghost: I beseech you. . . .

The twins support their mother, Ada under the left arm, Adel under the right, because she is five minutes older. Grannie Cragg, wrapped in the colours of the earth, carries the baby in satin Christening robes. Adel thrusts her face into the baby's face: "My mother had to cut up her wedding dress to make Christian clothes for you!"

The minister, unrolling his r's like quality yardgoods, pronounces the Order of Baptism:

"O merrrciful God, grant that the old Eve in this Child may be so buried that the new woman may be rrrrraised up in her.

"Grant that all carrrrnal affections may die in her, and that all things belonging to the Spirit may live and grow.

"Grant that she may have powerrrr and strength to have victory, and to triumph, against the Devil, the worrrld, and the flesh."

The minister sprinkles the child with holy water: "Pandora Gothic, I baptise thee in the Name of the Fatherrrrr, and of the Son, and of the Holy Ghost."

The minister gives Pandora to her father.

"And now, let us sing hymn No. 175 . . . Jesu, Loverrr of My Soul."

Joyful notes fly from the mother's mouth to the Christ, in fresco, on the ceiling, and they zephyr His sienna beard, and they curl about His flesh-toned feet, and they lick up His carmine wounds.

The father glares at the Christ on the ceiling. Splintered notes stick in his craw, and he grinds them between his molars as he stiff-arms the spirit-sodden child that is now also animal-sodden. *Cuckold of a deadman!*

Shadows solidify into shapes. Mouths stick to the centre of faces. Hands are explored to their source, in body. Breasts turn to glass.

Pandora graduates to a black crib, imprinted with the body of Baby Victor who choked.

"Mo-ther . . . ."

Pandora's mother is reedy and graceful with chestnut braids bound in a halo round her forehead. Pandora's mother smells of powdered milk and dead roses.

"Fa-ther . . . ."

Pandora's father is tall and fleshy with a bald head and glistering steel-rimmed eyes: Pandora's father smells of blood and rage.

Once I awoke, and there was a teddy bear, with eyes like stars, at the bottom of my crib.

Once I awoke and I couldn't see. I said: "Oh, oh, I am blinded!" but my mother said, "No, the sandman has just spilled his bag. You have styes in your eyes."

Pandora's mother bathes her eyes with Grannie Cragg's eyebright, till light slides in like morning under a dark door.

"Once I was blind, but now I can seee.
'I am so glad that Jesus loves meeeee."

Pandora's mother sings hymns.

Pandora's mother sings hymns as she plies her iron over her scorched ironing-board. Pandora's mother sings hymns as she twists doilies out of butcher's string and clips her frozen bedsheets to brittle lines. Pandora's mother sings hymns as she chops carrots; shreds cabbages; grinds bread; cubes cows, in endless odyssey from icebox to stove to pantry. Her fingers slide over the world, reducing it to smaller and smaller pieces: Her mind is filled with clouds.

"Jerusalem my happy home
When shall I come to thee?
When shall my sorrows have an end
Thy joys when shall I see?"

Pandora beats time on a tin pieplate. She drops her spoon.
"Mother . . . ."

Pandora's mother doesn't hear.
"Mother . . . ."

Pandora's mother doesn't see. Tears, from an onion she is grating, roll down her cheeks. She hurls her passion to
". . . E-TER-NITY!"

My mother has slipped from her skin. My mother has flown out of her body to be with her songs.

Pandora tries to see her face in her pieplate: She cannot.

Pandora tries to see her face in her mother's upturned eyes: She cannot.

Pandora feels herself tumbling backwards through space. She makes herself stiff as an ironing-board. She screams. She feels her name fly up from her body, with her scream. She feels her scream fist-pound the ceiling. Pandora flies through the clouds on her tin skyplate . . . . Up, up, up, to Jerusalem and the Baby Victor!

Pandora awakes on the cold linoleum with a dishrag on her forehead. She sees her mother, her father, her sisters, standing over her. She sees her face in the glare of eight reflecting pools flashing with anger, embarrassment, resentment. It is an ugly face. A twisted face. Pandora knows: *I am bad.*

Pandora's crib is sent to the cellar. She is sent to an iron bed in the attic. Her sun is a naked bulb. Her grass is a slivery floor. Behind the slanting walls are cubbyholes, as dark as dreams, where old ghosts and last year's Christmas balls lie packed in dusty boxes.

Pandora is lonely. *Shirley Temple has a room full of stuffed animals and sunbeams!* Pandora has seen pictures of it in magazines.

Pandora climbs up into her new bed. Over her head hangs Baby Victor, by the neck, in an oval frame. Under her body lies the fever-cradle of Aunt Cora who died in this bed of diphtheria.

Rock-a-bye Baby. . . .

"No! I don't want to go to bed!" *Please let the light last a little longer.*

Pandora squats, naked, on the linoleum. Adel-Ada read The Bobbsey Twins At Home, sentences turnabouts, at the kitchen table. Adelaide tries to coax a flannel "angel" over Pandora's head.

"*No!*" Pandora shoves her mother's hand away. She pokes a finger in her ear: She digs out a grain of sand. She pokes another finger into the other ear: She dislodges a flake of wax.

"*No!*" Pandora shoves her mother's hand away. She plucks a shred of cotton from the crack in her big toe. *This little piggy, that little piggy,* adding five, ten seconds to her life.

"*No!*" Pandora shoves her mother's hand away. She evicts a dot of corduroy from her bellybutton.

"*No!*" Pandora shoves her mother's hand away. She opens her legs . . . *Crack!* Adelaide's palm stings Pandora's cheek. Pandora gapes, her now-guilty hand between her now-guilty legs. A scarlet stain, the shape of a hand, spreads across Pandora's cheek.

Adel stops reading. Ada stops reading. They nudge each other. They giggle.

Adelaide panics: *Crack!* She strikes Pandora's other cheek. "*Don't ever let me catch you do such a filthy thing again!*"

Pandora, sobbing in corrupted innocence, is wrapped in white flannel and laid between cold sheets. She fits her own hands into the red hands on her cheeks: *I hate you, horrible mother!*

"*No, Pandora,*" *chides Aunt diphtheria Cora from inside her mattress.* "*You must love your mother. Your mother cut up her wedding dress to baptise you from sin.*"

Pandora tucks her hands between her legs. It is warm there, not harsh and cold like the steel hole in her Wet'ums Doll.

"*Don't ever let me catch you . . .*"

"No, mother." Pandora explores herself through a moral loophole: "*I won't let you CATCH me!*"

Liquid scalds Pandora's thighs. It gushes through flannel ditches; it deluges concave Aunt *oh you, filthy, naughty, filthy* Cora; then grows cold.

The night is long, dark, wet.

The sun breaks like a fresh egg through Pandora's window.

"*Dear Little Pandora, how did you sleep?*"

"*Terribly badly mother! Heaven knows what was in my bed, but it was dreadful!*"

Then the Queen lifted the braided coronet from her own head, and placed it on Little Pandora's head. "*Dear Pandora, you have felt the pee through twenty mattresses and twenty eiderdowns. You are a Real Princess!*"

The Royal Family bows its head, and the pee ascends in a

*golden chamberpot, up into the sky, and there it shines today,
just under the tail of Sirius, the dog star, unless someone has
stolen it!*

* * *

Adel-Ada won't play with Pandora: They stop reading
Black Beauty, sentences turnabouts, whenever she comes near.
They say she is too young for such sorrow, but Pandora knows:
They don't like me.

Pandora confronts her sorrowing face in her vanity mirror.
She chucks herself under the chin, the way Perfect Strangers
in flowerpot hats do it, and she moues her consolation: "Oh,
what a pretty little girl. . . . An angel face. . . . A fairy child."

Perfect Strangers never tell Adel-Ada THEY are pretty!
Pandora grimaces: *But Adel-Ada can READ.*

Pandora pesters her mother to show her which letters make
which words when she reads fairytales, but Adelaide says:
"No, Pandora, Home & School says it might be different from
what the teacher teaches, and then you'd get mixed up."

Ha! Pandora has learned The Alphabet Song *on the sly!*
She mouths it defiantly to herself in the mirror: A B C D . . .
All but P, which is dirty.

Once she bellowed it to a shelf of alphabet soup, and a lady
with a bird-hat and a bird-beak complained, "That is a very
pretty child with a dimple in her chin but she has a noisy
Devil within!"

Pandora examines her cloven chin. *Adel-Ada are GOOD.
They have KNIT chins like my mother. Adel-Ada go down
the street with their arms linked, like the chain of a sweetheart
locket, with their own pictures inside. The twins live inside
my mother's name.*

Pandora hides her cloven chin with a pretty bow tied from
two golden curls. *Adel-Ada only have skinny brown braids you
can see through, but if the Nazis catch me they will cut off my
curls and make whips of them like they did to Rapanzel whose
name means turnip.*

14

Pandora knows quite a lot about the Nazis.

If the NAZIS catch you they hang you, naked, on a hook, and they shave off your hair, and they whip you. If the JAPS catch you, they stick hot needles up your fingernails and they pull out your teeth for the Tooth Fairy. Pandora learned that at Sunday School from Amy Walker who reads War Comics, inside her World Friends, while the other children nail Jesus to the cross and sing He Loves Me.

Pandora puts her hands over her ears. She closes her eyes. She burrows to the heart of what she knows is her problem:

Adel-Ada won't play with me because . . . they don't like me.
They don't like me because . . . I scream.
Nobody likes me because . . . I scream and hold my breath.
I have to scream because . . . because . . .

The answer comes in a rush: *I have to scream because nobody likes me!*

It is a futile insight, too bitter to sustain. Pandora shoves it back inside her head. She pulls out another.

"Over the meadow and through the woods,
To grandmother's house I go. . . ."

Pandora drops white pebbles in a seam down her backyard. She does not stop to curse out her father's cabbages, or to touch her mother's mimosa and watch it curl its leaves and turn away. She does not work the mouths of twin snapdragons, making them insult each other, in angry sentences turnabouts, or tease the aunts on the peonies. *No time! No time!* Pandora is paying a formal visit to Grannie Cragg, who lives kitty-corner across the alley.

Pandora unlatches her grannie's elder-stick gate, and she hops onto her grannie's first flagstone. She says a Grannie Charm:

My grannie has eyes like two cups of green tea.

She hops onto the next:

My grannie has crooked hickory hands and a crooked hickory cane.

She hops again:

My grannie has mouldy hair, and teeth she can take out.
She hops again.
My grannie grows toadstools in chamberpots, and dead-man's fingers in her bathtub.
She hops again.
My grannie has three gold rings, for three dead grandpas, and three gold wishes.
Pandora is running out of flagstones:
My-grannie-smokes-a-pipe-and-once-she-owned-a-monkey-named-Mike! . . . My grannie snores!
Pandora hops onto the last flagstone:
My grannie speaks to ghosts, and once she spoke to the ghost of Aunt diphtheria Cora, gliding through our cubbyholes with the sound of kissing tissue-paper. My father yelled at my mother, "Get that old crone out of here, and YOU stay in MY house where you belong!"
Pandora knocks three times on her grannie's walnut door. She peeks into her grannie's root-porch: She sees jutebags of hickory nuts and rutabagas and stinging nettles: She does not see her grannie.
Pandora breaks off a piece of her grannie's brittle brown cottage, which everyone knows is gingerbread, and her grannie pokes her head through the frosty sugar-pane, and her grannie says, "Oh, it's YOU, Pandora. Come in my little Chickee, and we shall have elderberry juice, in silver thimbles, and raspberry jam from my Brown Betty jampot!"
Pandora sighs: That's the way it should be, but Grannie Cragg just gives elderberry juice to Adel-Ada because they are five years *elder.*
Pandora stands on one foot. She stands on the other.
She has come to ask her grannie to help her to break the Evil Spell which was put upon her by the Wicked Witch who cursed her out in her cradle before she got her eyes open. Then she, Pandora, will be Good, like her stinky-snot Step-Sisters Adel-Ada, without having to think about it, and everyone will love her. Pandora has brought her grannie a holly-hock-doll in a bur-basket, covered with bleeding hearts: It is

the closest she could get to the crooked root in her grannie's spellbook. She wants her grannie to turn the hollyhock-doll into chocolate, which is Good, as a Sign that she, Pandora, is Good. She knows her grannie can do it. She has seen her grannie turn pollen into yellow Easter-egg dye, and roots into red dolls' clothes, and petals into purple ink, and yesterday her grannie touched her hickory stick to stinging nettle, and turned it into Baker's Sweet Red chocolate for Adel-Ada, despite sugar rationing and The War.

Grannie must be sleeping.

Pandora lays her hollyhock-doll on her grannie's stoop, and somersaults across her grannie's camomile lawn that smells spicy when you crush it. She peels a nutty shepherd's purse. She munches a blade of chive. She ripples her nose through her grannie's wild thyme, for coughs; her sweet rosemarie, for headaches; her catmint, for scaring away rats.

Pandora peeks into her grannie's poison pocket. She spies on the deadly nightshade; the tricky foxglove; the sly monk's hood; the destroying am-an-i-tas that her grannie calls "rain coral." Pandora only thinks their names: To say them aloud would poison her mouth. Even to think them makes her tongue prickle. Pandora crosses her eyes. She spits.

Pandora returns to her grannie's stoop. Her hollyhock-doll is wilting. She is afraid that will melt the spell, not to mention the chocolate.

Pandora skips to the side of her grannie's wood-shingle cottage. She peeks through her philodendron curtains. She sees Grannie Cragg sprawled on her spoolbed, over a pan of male and female liverworts; teeth out, jaw slack, lost in an opiated dream. . . . *Sybil Cragg, a slender maid of seventeen, is being meadow-ravished by a fleet-footed youth she did not marry. . . .*

Pandora raps on the window: "Graaaaa-n*ee!*"

She hits the one note capable of shattering the old woman's dream-crystal. Grannie Cragg starts up, shrieking, from her bliss: "Lordie, Lordie, Lordie!" She glimpses her hag's face in her vanity mirror. "Oh Lordie, Lordie, Lordie!"

"Graaaaaa-n*eeeee!*"

Grannie Cragg shrouds her old woman's body in hopsacking. She stumbles to her root-porch. Pandora, in fresh pink pinafore, looks cruelly young.

Grannie Cragg groans: "As sure as the Lord made pisspots, I might have known it was you!"

Pandora, stridently hopeful, holds out her hollyhock-doll. "Chocolate, grannie?"

The old woman moans: "Go home, Chickee! Leave a body to lie and die."

"Ahhh, Gra-n*eee*! You did it for Adel-Ada."

"Adel-Ada brought me stinging nettles. All you do is pick my burs and bleed my camomile."

"Ahhhh, Gra-n*eee*!"

The old woman opens her walnut door. Pandora creeps inside. Grannie Cragg takes down a package of Baker's chocolate from her pantry. She hacks off a square, chops that into halves, and then into . . .

"Ooooh, grannie! That isn't *any*! I won't be able to feel that in my mouth!"

"Lordie!" exclaims the old woman. "You'd eat *me* if I was chocolate!"

Pandora is shocked. "No, I wouldn't grannie!" *I wouldn't eat YOU, because I LOVE you!*

The old woman breaks off a fresh square. "Now *git*, before my senses catch up with my hands."

Pandora snatches the chocolate. She imagines it curled in her tongue, squashing Goodness into her mouth, forever. "Oh, *thank* you, grannie!"

Pandora runs up the flagstone path, out the elder-stick gate. She unbuttons the pebbles from her own lawn, and crawls under her mother's juniper tree, where Good Spells have the best chance of happening.

Pandora pops the chocolate into her mouth. Her eyes dilate. Her cheeks contract. She spits the chocolate into the dirt. Her face crumbles. *My grannie has given me Baker's bitter-Blue chocolate! . . . My Wicked Step-Grannie has poisoned me!*

Pandora cries into the shaggy fingers of her mother's juniper tree. She knows the Evil Spell has not been broken. She knows — with bitter-Blue resignation — that she is locked inside her thorn-thicket forever.

*   *   *

"Old King Cole was a merry old soul,
And a merry old soul was he.
He calls for his pipe,
And he calls for his bowl,
And he calls for his Fiddlers Three!"
Pandora hums Old King Cole to herself as she sprawls on the Gothics' threadbare rug, colouring in her Mother Goose book.

Adel-Ada read The Bobbsey Twins Keeping House, sentences turnabouts, from a corner of the gaping chesterfield.

Lyle Gothic swoops low, in his cane-bottom chair, over the smouldering wreckage of COLOGNE STILL BURNING FIERCELY, dropping bombs *every six seconds for 90 minutes. . . . Six million pounds from 1,250 planes . . . the greatest bombardment of all time!*

"Ha, ha, ha," he chuckles. "Those RAF boys really know their stuff, but *Pack Up Your Troubles in Your Old Kit Bag* they don't have good songs like they did in The Great War."

Adelaide Gothic is down cellar sifting ashes:
"Chained to the World, to Sin ty'd down,
In Darkness still I lie;
Lord, break my bonds, Lord give me wings,
And teach me how to fly!"
The hymn-notes flutter through Pandora's stomach. They jangle through Lyle's corns. He shouts: "Aaaaaa-*deeee*!"

Adelaide, riding her high-C into Eternity, doesn't hear.

Lyle bellows: "AAAAAAAAAA-DEEEEEEEEEEEEEEE!"
"Then slay my Sins without reserve,
Burn up each lust in me;
Kill, kill my vain rebellious heart,
And I shall live to Theeeeeeee!"

Lyle slaps Pandora's rump with his folded Mill City Clarion. "Get up, *you*! Fetch your mother."

Pandora bristles: She doesn't like that word "fetch." It is a dog's word. She puts down her purple crayon, slowly enough to show resentment but not so slowly as to draw fire, and elbow-crawls to the air vent. She bellows: "AAAAAAAAAA-DEEEEEEEEEEEEEEE!" catching exactly the pitch of hysterical outrage that inflamed Lyle's original.

Lyle is rankled, without knowing why. "Don't *you* call your mother 'Addy'!" he dog-growls.

Pipe-soot descends in a cloud on Adelaide below. The hymn-notes spatter into dry coughs. She ascends through a trapdoor in the pantry, with a rag tied, Milk-for-Britain style, around her forehead. "Did you call, Lyle?"

"Get me some King Cola. With a lemon twist."

Adelaide slips into the kitchen. She returns with a frosted glass.

"*Damn*! I said with a *lemon twist*. If you'd take that filthy rag off your head."

"Sorry."

"And bring me something sweet."

Adelaide goes back to the kitchen.

"Mother *Goose*," sings Pandora. "Mother *Goose* and Old King *Co-la*!"

Adelaide hands her husband three oatmeal cookies and a wedge of lemon on a Tranquillity Rose plate. She sets her lips like Grannie Cragg when she swallows bittersweet. "I didn't have time to bake."

Lyle takes the cookies with a look of deep injury.

He returns to Cologne In Flames.

She returns to last winter's ashes.

"Sun of righteousness, arise.
Shed Thy blissful rays on me;
Kindly listen to my cries,
Try'd by Him who tempted Thee.
Thou my helpless soul defend,
Keep me blameless to the end!"

Lyle rattles his Crossword Puzzle: "Adel! Get me a pencil. One with a sharp point."

Adel jumps up from the right-side of The Bobbsey Twins Keeping House.

"Ada! . . . Get me an eraser — and not one of those idiot sponge things."

Ada jumps up from the left-side of The Bobbsey Twins Keeping House.

"AAAAAAAAAAAAAAA-DEEEEEEEEEEEEEE!"

The hymn ceases in mid-tremolo. Adelaide appears, as if by transmigration, at the living-room door. "Yes, Lyle?"

He holds out his glass: "Refill this."

Adel returns with the pencil. Ada with the rubber. Addy with the King Cola.

Pandora sings her King Cola song with spiralling recklessness: *"And he calls for his Fiddlers Three!"*

"Pandora!"

She ignores her father.

"Pandora!"

She continues to colour . . . *round and round,* inside King Cola's head, in tighter and denser circles.

"Pandora!" Lyle swats at his daughter's rump with his folded paper. She has thoughtfully edged out of range.

"Why, you — "

Lyle rears out of his cane-bottom chair. He scoops up Pandora with his left hand. It is not a real hand. Pandora dangles at the end of her father's steel hook.

Lyle shakes his hook. Pandora's teeth rattle. Her eyes roll.

"You little bugger, I'm going to — "

Pandora knows what he is going to do:

"I'm going to *kill* you! I'm going to spike you through!"

Pandora folds her hands across the bib of her sunsuit and begins to pray: "The Lord is My Shepherd, I shall not . . ."

Adelaide, mobilized by the power of prayer, grabs her by the rump. "Don't you *dare* injure this child!"

Lyle gapes. He is shocked. He is indignant.

"When have I ever struck *any*one in this house? When have I

ever done *anything* to *any* of you, but work my ass off for you?"

He turns to his loved ones for the gratitude he feels is his due. He receives a hostile stare. *Don't the fools understand that . . . ? Oh, shit!* Rage drains from Lyle like a mechanical monster that has shorted its circuit. He is ashamed. He tries to free himself from the soggy bundle hanging from his hook. It has gone through what it remembers of The Lord is My Shepherd, and is tremulously beginning Thank You, Lord, For The Food We Eat, its repertoire being limited.

Lyle is snagged through a teddy-bear's eye. "God-*damn!*" He is the fumbling, foolish focus of attention. The loathesome hook is on cruel display.

Pandora, sensing she has moved out of the trenches, indulges in a little high-church pretension: "Thank you, Lorrrrd, for the birrrrrrrrds that sing. . . ."

Lyle is not a patient man, nor a humorous man. His rage builds swiftly.

"Addy! Grab this kid.

"Adel! Fetch some scissors.

"Ada! You fool, *do* something!"

Adelaide cuts her husband loose with her embroidery scissors. He snatches up Pandora with his good hand. He propels her — *quickly! quickly!* — through the kitchen, into the pantry, down the trapdoor, past the furnace. He opens the winter-storage vault. He throws Pandora inside. He bolts the door: "And don't think you're getting out till I'm good and ready!"

Pandora screams: Nobody comes. She sings hymns, swaddling herself in mother-resignation and the love of Jesus: Nobody comes. She smells mothballs. She vomits into a pair of cleat-boots. Winter coats brush her cheeks. She gropes her way up their dead arms to their necks, pierced through with steel-hooks. It is hot: Pandora's head breeds lice:

When the Nazis catch you, they dangle you, naked, on steel-hooks, and they shave your head, and they beat you red-pulp with hickory sticks, and they feed you a bit of turnip soup and they give you a pick and they say, "O.K., swine, dig your

place!" The Nazis call people "swine," only they say "svine."
Then they make you put your clothes in a dead heap with
your grannie-teeth smiling on top, and they go AKK-AKK-
AKK into your belly, and they jump on you with steel boots,
and you go "AAAAAAGGGHHH!" into the mud, with your
tongue in a green knot, and blood squirts out your ears, and
the bulldozers roll over you, and they plant cabbages. . . .
Pandora isn't positive about the cabbages, but it sounds just
like what the Nazis would do.

Pandora pulls a coathanger from the rack. She pushes her
head through it. She tries to hang herself back up on the rack,
closing her mouth in a stiff line to save the darning-needles the
bother of sewing it up.

And if the red crayon doesn't break her neck in the lemon
twist, I'll tell you more about it tomorrow!

* * *

"I love little pussy,
His coat is so warm. . . ."
Pandora has a friend. His name is Charlie. She found him in
a garbage-can, where all the best things go eventually.

Charlie has rippling fur, like freshly-whipped cream, and a
prideful plume he carries topgallant.

Charlie has an Elizabethan ruff, that he holds aristocrati-
cally high, and Dutchman's breeches that discreetly screen his
lordly nether parts.

Charlie has a red rascal of a tongue, like a swatch of quality
flannel, and eyes like two cups of catnip tea, and a polka-dot
purr with twenty-three spots in it: *Oh, what a remarkable*
beast.

Lyle swats Charlie from the chesterfield with a folded newspaper. "G'way, you stinking fleabag!"

Charlie, dislodged by what he can't help noticing are the
Flats-to-let, heads disdainfully for the front door.

Pandora is aghast. Apologizing profusely for the misunder-
standing over the accommodations, not to mention the gen-
erally poor quality of the cuisine, she scrounges the ragbox

from Grannie Cragg's treadle machine. She covers it with silver-foil, emblazoned with Charlie's crest: The Sleeping Rampant. She layers it with heated flannel scraps, then combed milkweed hair, then — ever so respectfully — Charlie.

Pandora pats, probes, nudges, scratches, rubs, tickles Charlie in his silver-bed, marrying each gesture to the needs of each square inch that he offers up as he rotates like a roast before the fire. Charlie's ears droop in perfect trust. The warm marble under his chin trembles with the gentle exertion of his happiness. Pandora clasps her hands in humble thrall: *To have produced so much high-quality bliss!*

Pandora scoops Charlie from his milkweed bed. She drapes him fashionably over her arm, like a muff, and teeter-wiggles on high-heels past her mother's ironing-board: She is pretending to be Aunt Rosie.

Pandora hangs Charlie round her neck like a fox furpiece. She snake-coils her hair over her ears, and draws her lips into knifeblades: She is pretending to be Aunt Estelle.

Pandora twists Charlie's tail into a moustache, and smiles beguilingly: She is pretending to be Uncle Damon. She waves it flirtatiously in front of her face, like an ostrich fan: She is pretending to be Other Grandma Pearl.

Pandora flips Charlie sunnyside up. She runs her fingers up and down his ribcage, playing and singing a medley of Old Favourites:

"How Sweet the Sound of Pussycat's Name

"Nearer My Pussycat to Thee

"Fairest Lord Pussycat

"Oh, for a Closer Walk with Thee, Pussycat."

"Don't do that!" snaps Adelaide, suddenly alerted. "Don't maul Charlie. Why don't you play with your Wet'ums Doll?"

"Nuts!"

"Pandora! Don't say that *filthy* word!"

Pandora twists Charlie's tail into a pretty halo. "I hate Wet'ums Dolls. They're so . . ." she purses her lips in spiteful mimicry, *"fil-thee!"*

Pandora drags Charlie into the living-room where her

father is listening to Dr. E. T. Salmon talk about The War. She kisses Charlie noisily on the nose.

"Get that tom from your face!" growls Lyle. "You kiss that dirty thing again, and he's going to the pound for gassing!"

Pandora snatches up Charlie. She drags him back to the kitchen, pouring endearments on his battered tom's head.

Adelaide pounds her ironing-board with more fervour than is necessary: *It is galling, oh it is galling! This extravagant foolishness. It seems so . . .* Adelaide confesses it for the first time *. . . so insulting, somehow. There seems to be such a lack of proportion, in this house, between actual worth, actual service, and the loving return.* Adelaide burns her hand. *Darn!* She sucks it, giving vent to a mother's special fear: *It isn't even as if Charlie were a "nice" cat!*

It is a long, hot, Charlie-flawed summer; his fondness for garbage-pails; his uninhibited use of tomcat spray; his fleas, his fights, his burs. . . .

Adelaide works over Pandora's head with a fine-tooth comb, disentangling blonde hair from its bur mattings; twisting, gouging, yanking, threatening. Pandora works over Charlie's prostrate hide, performing a similar service, but so *unremonstratively,* so hair-by-hair solicitously, that Charlie's dreams are not so much disturbed as improved, causing him to yawn, to snort, to exude tangy odours from his many orifices, while Pandora illustrates, for *all who have eyes to see,* what Motherhood would be in a Perfect World.

Adelaide's nostrils twitch: "What's that stench?" She yanks Pandora's hair. "Is that *you,* or is it that blamed cat?"

Pandora lowers her lashes with a Madonna's humility: "It is I."

Afterwards, Pandora is dismissed with a threat-and-a-whollop while Charlie is laid to rest in his silver-bed, and gently prayed upon:

Charlie suffereth long, and is kind: Charlie envieth not; Charlie flaunteth not himself, is not puffed up. . . . Faith, Hope, Charlie: these three. But the greatest of these is Charlie. Charlie never faileth.

Hickory, dickory, tic toc. . . .

Pandora twists herself free of the humid sheets. She pads across the attic floor, trying not to think about the ghost of Aunt *diphtheria* Cora who moves through secret places with the sound of kissing tissue-paper. She sits on a three-legged stool, covered with patches from Grannie Cragg's dead children, inside a gable window that bulges like the eye of a frog, and she looks over the roofs of houses filled with cracked linoleum, and the greasy remains of old suppers, and she contemplates the Universe through a shiny lens ground from her secret yearnings:

The stars are very far away, too sharp, too bright, too beautiful to hold, like the twinkling of a distant Christmas you know will break your heart. And yet . . . and yet . . . If I could turn myself into a happy thought, I'd float up, and up, and up, and maybe one day I could nibble at the moon!

Pandora sighs: The same indiscriminate rays which beautify the shivery treetops, beatify her father's cabbage patch. *Maybe when I'm allowed out of the backyard . . . Maybe next month, when I go to school. . . .*

Street

September, 1942 to August, 1943

The twins take Pandora to Laura Secord Public School, Ada holding her left hand, Adel holding her right because she is five minutes older. Grannie Cragg sews a teaspoon of coriander into a secret pocket in Pandora's jumper, for good luck. Adelaide embroiders "Lest We Forget" in purple on a hanky, to remind her not to use the back of her hand. Lyle gives her two new pennies to "spend wisely" at the candy factory.

Pandora is in Room 1. It is the biggest room she has ever seen, with a floor as shiny as a pond, a lake, *an ocean!* There are fifty other kids. They sit on little chairs in a big circle, and they sing Jesus Loves Me, holding onto their liferafts as the floor pitches and their parents sail out the doors and windows. Some of the other kids cry, but *The Steadfast Tin Soldier considered it wasn't done to cry out when she was in uniform.*

Pandora's teacher is Miss Potter. She has hair like butterscotch-ripple icecream, and a moonstone ring that goes *clicketty-click* when she plays the piano about Autumn *plinketty-plunk* Leaves.

Pandora moulds with plasticine, and is asked to stop humming. She is given blocks that go one way in a box, and if you don't get them in the other kids march past, singing. She is sent home down the stone fire-escape, which is steep, like a mountain. One boy is whipped for swinging on the rail. He was warned.

Pandora just goes to school in the afternoons. She feels

29

gypped: Everyone calls her "kindy-garden baby," and no one will teach her to read. At recess, all the kids in her room have to stick together in the crook of the fire-escape, like a bunch of sheep with burs on their coats, watching the Big Kids play, fondling a favourite toy they are too shy to bring out of their pockets, and collecting more than their share of insults.

Pandora enjoys learning the new songs about the seasons, and the pretty things she makes out of coloured paper. But sometimes, she feels the water run very swiftly under the floorboards, and the waves swell and crest and spume, and the rain slash against the windows, and she must stand very stiff, on one leg, in her paper boat, with her heart leaden in her hands, and the shore and the lighthouse a very long way off.

Pandora lives at No. 13 Oriental Avenue, which was named for the ginkgo tree on its States Avenue corner.

In the mornings, Pandora sits on her front steps, with her chin in her hands, and her elbows on her knees, and her skirt pulled down to her Sisman scampers, and she participates, new-member, in the life-and-politics of her street.

Usually she is up by eight. That's so she can stick out her tongue at the girls who wiggle-waggle past on their way to Thor Munitions with their hair in metal-curlers and their bad teeth smeared with purple lipstick.

Then she waits.

She waits for the breadman: *You should pet his horse and sometimes he gives you broken tarts.*

She waits for the vegetableman: *All the ladies fight because of the rotten peaches under the netting.*

She waits for the iceman: *He lets you suck ice, but you should only suck the "pure" kind you can see through.*

She waits for the junkman: *He calls "adeetse!" and keeps his money in a goat's bladder.*

She waits for the popman: *His bottles explode ping, ping, ping! in hot weather.*

She waits for the hoot, honk, whistle, clang, of every wagon, truck, cart, van, summoning the matriarchs of Oriental Avenue to their doors and curbs, with their baskets and bags, for a squeeze of the produce and a touch of conviviality. *Oh, life is wonderful on Oriental Avenue!*

Pandora lives in a sour-cream frame, three up from St. Charles Place, in a row of peaked houses set like the teeth of a saw, with their verandahs forming the handle.

Mrs. Newton is Pandora's neighbour-lady to the left. Mrs. Newton is scrawny, like a pullet chicken, with periscope eyes that turn in their sockets, and a needle nose, for poking into small places, like between the slats of her venetian-blinds, where she sits with her canary, Hennypenny, and the lights out. Mrs. Newton has carroty hair nobody knows is dyed, and a ruby mouth that she holds in an O of continual wonder as she walkie-talkies up and down the street, picking up bits and snips through the squint in her rhinestone glasses. *Mr.* Newton fixes clocks.

Mrs. Lawrence is Pandora's neighbour-lady to the right. Mrs. Lawrence has hair like toasted meringue, and fleshy arms that flap more than the sheets she puts on the line. Once she opened a chicken gizzard and found a pearl!

Old Mr. Grandby sits on the Lawrences' verandah, and rocks and shakes, and shivers and sweats, and he complains about the weather but he is always one season behind. Old Mr. Grandby's bones snap, like dry twigs in a fire: Old Mr. Grandby is dying.

The Diceys live next to the Newtons.

Mrs. Dicey has a face like boiled spinach, and she beats *Old* Mrs. Dicey, chained to her bed with a bicycle lock. Mrs. Dicey has the only chestnut tree in six blocks. She chases the kids with her broom. Mrs. Newton phones her to tittle-tattle, which is the only time they speak. *Mrs. Dicey poisons cats!*

The Barkers live down from the Diceys. They run Barkers' Groceteria. The Barkers have a choice of faces, marked paid and unpaid, depending on whom they are talking to, and thick grey hair Mrs. Barker rolls up like her nickels.

The Stintons live in the snooty house on the corner. It has a false-stone front, and a brass nameplate, and a doorbell that chimes The Bells of St. Mary's, and oval windows like dead-men's eyes. Mr. Stinton is an undertaker. Mrs. Stinton is a snob. She pretends their house faces States Avenue. Stinky Stinton carries coffins. Stinky Stinton stinks of corpse juice.

Pandora sees Lucy Spittal rocking on the opposite curb. *Lucy has a face like a horse, and her mother collects horseballs for her roses.*

Lucy waves.

Pandora waves back. "Yah, yah, Luc*ee*! Your mother eats horseballs!"

Lucy throws a stone. Pandora kicks it off her step: "This is *my* property!"

Lucy sticks out her tongue.

Pandora thumbs her nose. "Your mother tapes your belly-button!" That's to keep Lucy from flipping it.

"Ha-ha! See your pants!"

"Li-ar!" but Pandora can't help sticking her head up her skirt just to check.

"See the sights! See the sights!" chants the victorious Lucy.

Pandora makes donkey ears, a sly reference to the fact that Lucy goes to dum-dum school. "Shame! shame! shame!"

Lucy's mother calls. Lucy leaves, with little reluctance.

Lucy's mother is a widow-lady. Mrs. Spittal has a beard that she shaves off, and the other ladies say she shouldn't, and a moustache that she doesn't shave off, and the other ladies say she should. Last Hallowe'en *Mrs. Spittal* went out, in men's clothes, collecting candykisses, while *Lucy* stayed home and handed out the apples! Pandora heard the ladies of Oriental discussing it:

"Oh, there's more here than meets the eye, and you can tell *that* to the preacher!" exclaims Mrs. Newton, imperiously rattling her *Spic and Span, Life Can Be Beautiful* garbage-cans. "Why, I have seen that Spittal person — with these my own two eyes — promenading New York Avenue in *men's* trousers with a *fly* — " Mrs. Newton rolls her rhinestone eyes in Pandora's direction, and makes a moue with her mouth, that is like an open secret. "It's a *fact*, I don't mind saying, no person has ever seen *me* in trousers of any sort, nor at breakfast excepting I was combed and with my face on."

Oriental Avenue is just a working-class street, and yet it is also a street where — Mrs. Newton is quick to inform newcomers along with a plate of *butter-wouldn't-melt-in-her-mouth* cookies — certain standards are scrupulously maintained.

Standards of Social Congress and Exchange: Despite continuous social contact, the women of Oriental Avenue rarely address each other by their Christian names. They never enter each other's homes without knocking (in the winter) or yoo-hooing through the screendoor (in the summer). They do not gossip about their husbands, whom they refer to as "my spouse," "Mr. X," "my mister," "my hubby," but never as "my old man." More information is exchanged by clothesline than by telephone wire: The ladies of Oriental have an easy conversational range of three backyards.

The men of Oriental Avenue address each other by their Christian names or not at all. They refer to their wives as "the wife," "the better half," "the little woman," "the good woman," but never as "my" anything, or by her Christian name. The men of Oriental Avenue do not socialise beyond "Is it hot/cold enough for you Bill?" Oriental is a street of women, and that has nothing to do with The War.

Standards of Dress: Housedresses, aprons, laddered stockings, are acceptable for an Oriental matron as far as the grocery store, but slacks, bare legs, bandanas, curlers, kimonos are not. A woman, who is going uptown, is expected to put on a hat or hairnet, almost run-less stockings, corsets and her earrings. Hair should be curled or neatly rolled, not loose on the neck. Powder, lipstick, rouge, toilet water are optional, according to one's upbringing and religious beliefs. Mascara is "cheap." Hair bleach is "hard." To point out that a woman wears mascara is to question her taste. To point out that she uses peroxide is to question her morals.

Though a man is entitled to come home sweaty and dishevelled from work, he is expected to wash, shave, and apply talcum powder before he is seen again. Though shorts and undershirts are tolerated for watering grass at the back of the house, they are not acceptable for watering grass at the front of the house. Overalls, coveralls, or any form of workman's uniform are considered déclassé for home chores. Better to wear once-good trousers with a pin in them.

In general, the men of Oriental Avenue dress "down" to go to work, and "up" for the evening, as opposed to men on a middle-class street who dress "up" in white shirts for work and "down" in sports clothes for their leisure.

Standards of Street Deportment: Saturday is a male day, Sunday a female one. No conspicuous or dirty work should be performed on a Sunday and there should be no boisterous child's play.

Food should be consumed indoors, or at a designated picnic area. Music, noise, entertainment should be contained within the walls of the sponsoring house. Use of alcoholic beverages should be concealed, and that includes the wrapping of "empties" for the garbage.

Standards of Maintenance: Weeds should be pulled, leaves raked, snow shovelled. Where treeroots make it difficult to grow grass, one must illustrate, by word and deed, that one feels guilty about it.

Conspicuous moves upward, such as the change from frame to insul-brick, should be disguised as sots to practicality: "I like the *wood* misself, but my hubby's getting so his back's not so good for doing the painting."

Standards of Difference: As with most people who agree on practically everything, the residents of Oriental Avenue pride themselves on their differences: Radical experiments with trellises, hose nozzles, lawn ornaments are judiciously noted and commented upon. The new is preferred to the old, the shiny to the dull, the fussy to the simple, but the residents of Oriental lack the cash to indulge themselves.

Standards of Competition: A well-established rivalry exists between the westside of Oriental Avenue and its mirror image, the eastside of Oriental Avenue. At first, the advantage would seem to be on the eastside, where the homes are set farther back from the street, allowing for greater display. However, the eastside suffers three handicaps: the Reading Railway, running behind it; the National Binder-Twine Co., on its north corner; St. Cecilia's home for Cripples and Incurables on its south corner. Though the latter two enclose the eastside in elegant green brackets, this cannot make up for the stigma of a) being zoned Commercial, b) all that misery-in-wheelchairs tucked, with the Catholics, behind the bushes.

The westsiders' handicap can be summed up in two words: The Clays. They live — if that is the word for it — in the corner house, once-identical to the Stintons'. There all similarity between the two families ceases. The Clays are not snobs: They do not pretend they live on St. Charles Place, though everyone wishes they would. The Clays are *slobs*, pure and simple. The parents quarrel and breed: You can hear them curse each other out, as far as the Newtons' porch (not to mention in the centre of the Clays' stinkweed suckers where Pandora has often seen Our Lady of the Rhinestones lurking). The brattish Clay children, all with runny noses, spread pestilence up and down the street: They sass, they spit, they swear — but then, what can you expect from a welfare family that summons the beerwagon right to its unpainted frontdoor?

The ladies of Oriental Avenue do not like to gossip; they do not like to judge; but, all you have to do is to look at the Stintons, in splendour, on one corner, and the Clays, in squalor, on the other, to know how strongly God Himself values decent Protestant burial over unbridled Catholic breed.

Standards of Decency: In spite of the fact that the first impulse of any west/eastsider, when faced with a problem, is to wish it over onto the other side of the street, the residents of Oriental are good neighbours united by the tough virtues of honesty, industry, sobriety, and the certain knowledge that life is short, difficult, unpredictable, and likely to get more so. Their worst faults arise from those niggling fears, common to diligent people who are just able to make it if everyone pulls his own weight, and so despised by those who have more or who care less.

They worry that another family, of the cut of the Clays, will move into the vacant Hennicot place, thus threatening the ever-precarious quality of life on a working-class street. They worry that certain of their number will succumb to war-time pressure to rent rooms and convert to duplexes. They worry that more foreigners will move in from Mediterranean Avenue, though Mrs. Niobe is clean and quiet.

They worry about change: insidious flea-bite change, such as a two-cent rise in the price of eggs, and those glossy indulgences which elected men call "progress" and which are supposed to be the good flip side of The War. They worry about everything that loosens their grip on the things they know, and their sense of what they can control through honest work.

They do not talk directly about their worries: They telegraph them in sighs, shrugs, pursed lips, frowns, unfinished sentences.

They do complain — openly and continuously — about Oriental Avenue per se: its potholes "the size of sewer covers"; its crevices "wide enough to swallow a pocketbook."

"Oh, it's a disgrace, no two ways about it," complains Mrs. Lawrence, mopping sweat with her window rag. "The junkman's horse went lame in one of them just last week."

"It's a disgrace, all right," agrees Mrs. Newton, poking her flowering crab with a bamboo rake, "but what's the choice? If your City Works moves in here, they'll widen us into a speedway, plain and simple. It gives me the migraine just to think about it!"

"If they widen, we'll lose our trees," laments Adelaide. "Look . . . they're starting to turn colour already."

The ladies gaze reverentially up at their trees: two rows of them, with their centres hideously gutted to accommodate the hydro wires with which Mill City is lavishly gridded.

"Yes, we'd lose our trees," affirms Mrs. Lawrence darkly. "Not to mention our dogs and our children."

Mrs. Newton fixes Adelaide with a look of aggrievement:

"There are *some* pets I wouldn't mind seeing the end of. Like those that makes their wee-wee in other folks' gardens!"

"A *disgrace!*" exclaims old Mr. Grandby, bursting into palsied life from his rocking chair. "A *disgrace*, with all the potholes, not to mention our dogs that wee-wee our children!"

"Now, pa," chides Mrs. Lawrence, gently tucking him under his Boer War blanket. "Don't het yourself up. It just gets you mixed."

Mrs. Niobe, black-shawled, hollow-eyed, erect, crosses Oriental Avenue to mail a letter.

"Any news?" asks Mrs. Lawrence.

"Nothing. . . . We write. . . . Nothing."

"Poor soul," sighs Mrs. Lawrence.

"I feel so sorry for that brave woman."

"Yes . . . one son gone, and now . . ." Mrs. Newton clicks her metal tongue: "Still . . . it must be a comfort to have four sons left. I think when you just have the *one*, you make so much more of him, don't you? If they ever took my Willie. . . . Course he's 4-F."

Mrs. Barker, in grocer's smock, with freshly waved blue-cheese *49 cents a pound* hair, nods efficiently to the housewives blocking the sidewalk.

"Anything special today?" asks Mrs. Lawrence.

"Nescafe. A 4-ounce tin for 57 cents — that's two cents less than at Loblaws." Mrs. Barker runs drily down her shelves, then bows to pressure: "We *are* getting some salmon in." She casts a tart glance at Mrs. Newton. "*One* tin to a *steady* customer."

Mrs. Barker, ever-conscious of the passage of time-means-money, forces herself to stop and chat with the ladies. The ladies try to reach out beyond their White Naphtha *Guiding Light* soap, and Ivory *Against the Storm* flakes, for the sort of conversation that will show her they, too, can come to grips with the issues when they have a mind to.

"If you ask *me*, it's the British housewives who are the real heroes of this mess. . . ."

"Yes, well, the Jews have suffered, too. *Eighty thousand*

killed in Poland, the man on the radio said. That's *a lot*, for one time!"

"Eighty thousand," cackles old Mr. Grandby, from the stubble of his understanding, "*and* the sheeney who went lame in the pothole!"

"Pardon?"

"The potholes in the street," explains Mrs. Lawrence. "Pa lags a mite in conversation." She trumpets into his almost-good ear: "Don't het yourself up, dear. They took him to the vet's."

There is an awkward silence during which Mrs. Barker distinctly hears three pennies drop. She checks her Westclox watch: "Twenty-eight of twelve! Mr. Barker will wonder where I am. Those munitions girls would steal the counter, if it wasn't nailed down!"

Mrs. Newton follows her with a resentful look. "Poor thing! It's a pity she never had children." She puts down her bamboo rake. "But mercy me! I'm missing my Road of Life."

The screendoor slams. Adelaide sighs. "I wish all *I* had to do was listen to those soap-suds things!"

"Ha!" snorts Mrs. Lawrence. "You can listen from 11:30 Road of Life to 5 p.m. When a Girl Marries, and never be the wiser."

The two ladies go inside to make lunch and to listen to Road of Life.

Oh, where does all the time go?

Pandora waits for the noon whistle. She sees Mrs. Goodfellow toss and pitch up the eastside, between two Zeller's bags. "Hi, Mrs. Goodfellow. Can I help?"

"Thanks, dear," wheezes Mrs. Goodfellow. "I was O.K. till I slipped off my shoes on the bus. Then, by golly, my feet all swoll up!"

Mrs. Goodfellow is Arlene Goodfellow's mother: Arlene has spatter-paint freckles, and crinkly copper hair, like Kurly Kate fresh from the package, not tarnished like Mrs. Goodfellow's frizzle. Arlene is Pandora's bestfriend, even though she is two years older.

Pandora carries Mrs. Goodfellow's shopping-bag to her house, then into her yellow kitchen. She hears Sydney Goodfellow, home from school with measles, playing Barcarolle on his violin.

Sydney is a year older than Arlene. Sydney has a round gopher's face, and a hearing-aid that he wears in a bulge over his heart. Mr. Goodfellow makes Arlene practise the piano, but when Sydney plays his violin, he yells. . . .

"Cut out that god-damned screech-racket, willya? Can't you *hear?* I'm trying to get some bloody sleep!"

Mrs. Goodfellow bustles into the living-room to make sure Sydney has his hearing-aid on and *can* hear.

Mr. Goodfellow is a policeman, which is why he sleeps in the afternoon. He chases Arlene and Pandora with the hose, laughing for fun, but he turns it right on Sydney — bullet, into his face — and Sydney cries, and Mr. Goodfellow swears. . . .

"Cut out that fucking racket down there!"

Mrs. Goodfellow flushes Pandora, with thanks, out the backdoor.

Pandora is in no hurry. She dawdles in the shade of the Goodfellows' humble orchard — rotten apple, buggy peach, wormy plum, blighted pear — recalling the highlights of her life since the Goodfellows came into it two months ago.

Once we made birdhouses out of pablum boxes! Once we made a walkie-talkie out of soup cans with a "nosy" extension for Mrs. Newton! Once we made a pulley for secret messages out of Mr. Goodfellow's tobacco pouch and the laces I stole from my mother's hee hee hee brassiere!

Arlene has seen Sydney without any clothes on! Arlene has touched her father's gun with bullets in it!

Pandora wanders out the Goodfellows' side-alley, and heads home via the gutters.

Once we made a peepshow out of an Agnew Surpass shoebox, with a window in the top, and a roll of comics, with Popeye blasting the slimy slant-eye Yaps and spraying himself afterwards with insect powder. We charged everyone a penny-a-peek, and we made twenty-seven cents, and we pasted a War Savings Stamp on the school poster of Hitler with his face in a pig's snout!

Sydney has a War poster under his bed with a naked woman being whipped by the Nazis, and bible words:

Oh Lord, Deliver Us From Evil.

Pandora finds a Player's box in the gutter in front of the Stintons', and strip-mines it of its tinfoil. *Sydney has a silver wad as big as a baseball, but there was a girl in the paper with one as big as herself, and she made it into a bomb, and she sent it to some pilots, and they painted her name — MARY — on a REAL bomb, and they blasted the dirty Jerries out of their holes, flying low so they could tell her how many bodies she got! Sydney is going to twist his tinfoil into a tommy-gun, which is bigger than his father's police-guns, and he is going to give it to the Marines to blast the Jap-scum out of their stinking jungles. . . . DIE, FILTHY SLANT-EYES! . . . AKK-AKK-AKK. . . . AAAAAGHHHHHHHH! IN THE GUTS!*

The Japs are worse than the Jerries. Everybody says it: *The Japs go straight to Hari-Kari with Fu Manchu and their Honourable Ancestors. The Japs fly planes they can't jump out of, and when they crash onto a ship it's like dropping a tin of spaghetti.*

Pandora flies a noisy human plane up the street. She crash-dives into a telephone pole. She pretends she can read the notice, tacked to its side. *Anyways, I know what it says:*

WANTED: one thousand tons of paper, flattened
and securely fastened.
DON'T put out cellophane, waxed, carbon or
tarred paper.
DON'T put out garbage.
CANADA NEEDS ALL YOUR WASTE PAPER!
The Citizens Committee for Troops in Training

Ha! This paper-drive I'll put out Adel-Ada's Honour Di-
plomas and Perfect Papers that my mother shows off to the
neighbours. Then maybe I'll get a COG button, too! Adel-
Ada have COG buttons (Collector of Goods) for Distinguished
Civilian Service. They used to collect every Saturday till they
found the boys on their truck were adding stones to make the
sacks heavier. Adel-Ada didn't think that was right. *They're*
sooo good!

Pandora sees Adel-Ada walking, arm-in-arm, toward her,
with Davey Clay taunting them: "Tweedledum-Tweedledee!
Priss-priss-priss!"

It serves them right for not liking me!

Pandora follows Adel-Ada inside: Their mother is listening
to Big Sister and sorting socks. Pandora sits down at an oilcloth placemat, and pretends to say "grace." Really she is
humming Whistling Down the Road I Go, which Arlene
taught her, one finger, on the piano.

Adel-Ada spell giggling messages in their alphabet soup.
They ignore Pandora.

Pandora is relieved.

Pandora is disappointed.

She went to considerable trouble that morning to slip two
fat tomato-worms into the pencilcases they won for Perfect
Attendance, and then to squeeze them, Adel's under the right
thumb, Ada's under the left: It wasn't the sort of thing you
could miss on opening your pencilcase.

Adel-Ada baffle Pandora. They hate her, but they don't
tattle on her. They have picked her out of their lives the way
you would dispose of a dirty kleenex. Pandora would love to
do the same to them but . . .

"Darn it, Pandora! You're so *greedy!* Why don't you ever
take the *closest* piece of cake and leave the *biggest* for someone else? Adel and Ada always leave the *biggest* piece even
when it's *closest!*"

Adel-Ada stare stonily into their soup bowls.

Pandora cries into her crumbled cake: *Yeah! They always*
fight for the SMALLEST piece!

Today Adel-Ada renounce cake altogether in exchange for

the intimacy of licks, turnabouts, of their mother's chocolate beater: *I wish it would TURNABOUTS and cut off their tongues!*

Pandora is the first in her kindergarten class to learn to tie her shoelaces.

Hola! — as Wonder Woman would say — *I can even do a double bow.*

She practises, at recess, with the other kids, in the crook of the fire-escape where they are confined by law. Ruth-Anne Baltimore, who is rich, has buckles on her shoes.

One, two, buckle my shoe. . . .

Ruth-Anne Baltimore cheats.

Every day, after school, Pandora casts herself, with the other kids, onto the warm, black bosom of the street. *The street:* so pocked and fissured it has almost been abandoned by traffic. *The street:* the centre of urchin anarchy. *I am the King of the Horseballs! I am the Lord of the Flies!*

The gang rolls from child-bearing house to child-bearing house, bawling names and adding bodies.

"LU-CEE!" who flips her bellybutton.

"STINK-EEE!" who stinks of corpse juice.

"NO-NAME!" who moved into the Hennicot place, and hasn't been given one yet.

"SHEL-LEE!" one of the Clays, who tells fibs and has a runny nose.

"NEL-LEE!" another of the Clays, who tells *bigger* fibs, and has a *longer* runny nose.

"BIL-LEE!" who tells/has   bigger/longer.

"GOR-DEE!" who ditto ditto.

"DA-VEE!" who ditto-the-ditto same.

"AA-DEL!" A pale head appears at an upper window.

"AA-DA!" A pale head joins it.

"Wonna? . . ." Adel-Ada shake their skinny braids: "No thanks."

The kids take off like gangbusters for the Binder-Twine front lawn. They open negotiations, in formal street argot:

"What-ul-we-play?"

"Les-play-bazeball."

"Dicey-ul-holler-an-weel-hafta-gw'in."

"Les-play-Hide-un-Seek."

"Nahh. . . ."

"Yeah. . . . Les-play-Hide-un-Seek."

The ginkgo tree is chosen, as always, as the homefree tree. Rules are laid, with a maximum of spirited bickering.

"No-gw'in-o'er-the-trax."

"No-gw'in-ina-yer-own-propty."

"No-gw'in-ina-thu-Cripples."

Sydney fist-fans eleven pine needles. Shelly draws the short one.

"You pushed that ina-my-hand!"

"Did *not*!"

"Poor sport! Poor sport!"

Shelly ungraciously blinds her eyes against the Chinese temple tree: "Ten-twenny-thurdy-fordy. . . ."

"*Pee*-ker! *Chea*-ter!"

"Bug-ger! Am not!"

The hiders scatter — into the ditch by the railway tracks; behind the Stintons' ornamental yew; under the Clays' broken porch. The hiders know every nook and niche, plus the tolerance of every owner for trespass-and-trample. The seeker hasn't a chance. It is really a game of tease and torment.

"*Las*-cots-it!"

Shelly catches Lucy Spittal (as always) and the no-name newkid.

Sydney frees them. Shelly punches him. They grapple in the crinkly fans under the ginkgo tree.

Shelly's brothers pile on. Arlene geronimos out of the Stintons' yews. Pandora gallops around Mrs. Niobe's bridal-wreath hedge. It is Everyone Else vs. the Clays: The sweating, cursing pinwheel rolls over and over under the spreading ginkgo tree.

Stinky Stinton runs home.

A Clay head pokes from the human coil: "Yah, yah! Has to save his cof-fin hands!"

The Clays are repulsed, fist-length by fist-length, to their own property on the westside. Everyone Else retires, cater-corner, to the Goodfellow steps. Bruises, the colour of purple hearts, are compared. Scratches, as wide as trenches, are licked.

"Boy! Didja-see-what-I-did-a-that-rinkydink-Gordie?"

"I-musta-busta-Shelly's-arm."

Gordie and Davey Clay, wearing family honour like a row of glittering medals, swagger toward the Goodfellows'. They cross to the eastside, their gaunt cheeks working like terrible medieval war-machines.

They spit: *Spit and run!*

Everyone Else stares palely at the rich, phlegmy stain: All the Clays have permanent headcolds.

"Yah, yah! *Missed!*" shouts Arlene, rallying her side.

The Everyones fill a brown bag with good eastside mud and a lot of dark threats.

They approach the Clays'. They wheel. They fire.

Bull's-eye! Not that you'd notice a little extra dirt on the Clays' front steps! *Not* that you'd notice a little extra mud on the Clays themselves!

There is a fruity exchange of insult, broken by the occasional giggle.

Giggles proliferate.

It is time.

Ten straws are plucked from the Clays' porch broom. They are held by Stinky Stinton, who has slunk back as a low-caste neutral.

The Clays pick three-out-of-five of the short ones.

"Yah, yah!" taunt the Everyones, savouring the dying moments of battle. "*You* hafta Speak First!"

Gordie Clay, still starchy with conceit, swaggers forward. He mumbles through chapped lips: "Hello."

"Louder!"

"HELL-OH!" Then, once more shunting and coupling his words: "Les-play-Kick-thu-Can."

*   *   *

"How about the playground this aft?"

Last time Pandora went to Civic Playground, beside the

44

jail, the tough boys from Baltic Avenue twisted her dizzy on one of the swings, and dunked her into the horsetrough, and rolled her over the terracotta earth, and made her eat dust.

"Let's go to Paradise Park."

"It's gonna rain."

"No, your mother's hanging her clothes out. So's Mrs. Niobe."

"Well . . . O.K."

Arlene wheels out the most slendiferous possession on the block — her golden tricycle, taller than Pandora, with a silver wheel that captures the sunlight and flings it in fiery splinters at the ants on the pavement below. "It's *your* turn to pedal us."

"No, Arlene." It is important that Pandora not be intimidated by this gaudy display. "*I* pedalled to the petshop to see the monkey, *as you very well know.*"

Paradise Park, on Boardwalk Ave., is a magnificent ten-acre greensward bequeathed to Mill City by its first residents, the Gormly Family, along with a suitable sum for upkeep in perpetuity. As Arlene and Pandora cycle through Wayfarers Arch, they are greeted by the Gormlys themselves — Sir Edward Arley, dignified, granite-jawed, standing, finger on frockcoat-button, with his bull-mastiff Thorvald resting on his polished toe. Forever by his side is Lady Eugenia, one arm extended in marble welcome, the other arced around the Gormly scions: Hannah, Harriet and Arley Edward.

A bronze plaque, one of many throughout the park, by which the Gormlys chat with, and chide, their guests, reads:

ꟿᴇʟᴄᴏᴍᴇ ꟿᴀʏꜰᴀʀᴇʀꜱ

Welcome: pedestrians, wheelchairs, perambulators, tricycles, canines on leashes, horses with sanitary facilities.

Unwelcome: motorized vehicles, bicycles, horsedrawn vehicles, canines at large, horses without sanitary facilities, other.

Rest on Our Lands. . . .

Drink, Ye, of Our Waters. . . .

A tin sign hastily tacked to the bottom reads:

> CAUTION: Do not drink park water. Toxic.
>   Mill City Parks Board.

The grass in Paradise Park is groomed to golf-green speci-
fications. A panzer division of gardeners rumbles over it on
sprinklers, seeders, aeriators, rollers. Portions of turf judged
inferior as to colour or texture are replaced by the yard, like
broadloom.

Arlene and Pandora sweep westward around the cinderpath. Though no sign actually says **Keep Off the Grass**, this
velvety path, lined with white curbstones, makes it clear where
the Bequeathing Family expect their Wayfarers to go. Stone
benches, at measured intervals, mark the route, each dedicated
by a bronze plaque: "In loving memory of . . ." Paradise is not
a picnic park. To attempt to draw two benches together would
be like desecrating tombstones.

The trees lining the path deserve special mention: The Bequeathing Family seldom planted a green-foliage one when
they could plant a red one, or a non-flowering one when they
could plant a flowering one. More remarkable — all are symmetrical. The effect, as the eye passes from one perfectly bal-
anced silhouette to another, is of that same disturbing serenity
created by the symmetrical faces on Egyptian sarcophaguses.

Arlene and Pandora have never seen Paradise Park off-
season. It is a summer place: rich, ripe, realised. Flowers burst,
overnight, into blossom, and are replaced at first-wilt. Fall
never happens. Leaves remain glued to Paradise trees long
after they clog gutters over the rest of Mill City. At first snow,
black gratings are drawn across all park entrances as if a proud
and beautiful woman were to take the veil as her winter
descends.

Arlene and Pandora stop at the lavatory: It is almost a com-
mand performance. There is only one **Wayside Station** in all of
Paradise, and that so hideously stenched and stained on the

inside, and so coyly over-wistaria'd on the outside, that first-time guests to the park have frequently suffered more than one would think compassionate. It is the Bequeathing Family's one grudging concession to the mortality of others: In all else, guests are expected to improve themselves.

Arlene and Pandora cycle past Joy Fountain, with its cabbage-leaf tiers held aloft by garlanded maidens: "To Blessed Eugenia From Her Loving Edward Arley. . . . *Flow Gently, Sweet Afton.*"

They wheel down a connecting lovechain of pools to Iron Fountain, with three dragons balancing a cannonball: "To Blessed Edward Arley From His Loving Eugenia. . . . *Fight the Good Fight.*"

They meander through the perfumed arbours of Hannah's Rose Bowl, where the elite of Mill City hold their ladyfinger teas, and play croquet through silver hoops in the sunlight: "To Hannah Dear, Who Loved Beauty."

They peek through thorn hedges into Harriet's rival Blind Bowl, where blind bowlers, in dark glasses, crash their tinkling balls, past midnight, terrifying the sighted with their piercing cheers as they claim dark victories with the lights out: "To Harriet Dear, Who Loved Service."

They pedal past a generous stone sandbox, plaqued with a dog's profile: Thorvald's Comfort Station. Here is the promised respite for canines-on-leashes who did not, as repeatedly beseeched, Befoul the Promenade. Pandora giggles uncharitably: A small child, who can't read Old English, is playing in the sandbox.

There are no baseball diamonds in Paradise Park, no swings, no slides. In this the Bequeathing Family reflects conventional wisdom: Grass, the medium of parks, is not yet considered the medium of child's play. Dust is; gravel is; asphalt is. Civic Playground, with its brick walls iced in broken bottles, is a Mill City showplace.

Perhaps all this is why Arlene and Pandora don't often come to Paradise. They feel a little unwelcome here, as if in the presence of a dowager aunt who showers them with sweets at the same time she lets them know she doesn't like children with sticky hands.

One nook in the park is different: Wilde Corner. In Wilde Corner, the powermowers stop, as if by sacred trust, a full five yards on either side of a babbling brook. In Wilde Corner, boulders — roughhewn, unwhitewashed — clog the flow of admittedly-translucent water.

It is at Wilde Corner that Arlene and Pandora plan to drink their pop and to eat their mayonnaise jar of brownies.

Arlene, however, is in a mood. She is tired of pedalling, and she wishes she were at Civic Playground. She notices — out loud — several places where powermowers have encroached on the official Wilde fringe. She is suspicious — and says so — that some tidying up has been done among the boulders of the babbling brook. She stops, in disgust, after finding *seventeen* four-leaf clovers in the first clump she looks into!

Arlene points, rather churlishly, to the plaque she and Pandora have agreed to ignore: "Wilde Corner: To Arley Edward Dear, Who Loved Nature." She asks, pointblank: "Do you think any of this is really real?"

Pandora admits it: "I've wondered myself, Arlene."

It is an important point of belief: Is Wilde Corner a single Act of Creation, spontaneously unfolding? Or is it but the preordained product of Immutable Law, which, when seen through the Veil of Our Ignorance, only appears Wilde?

Arlene and Pandora — without exactly putting it that way — instinctively harken to the more romantic Creation Theory.

They imagine — as an Act of Faith — the Bequeathing Father, frockcoated, granite-jawed, standing, unruffled by the wind, at the top of yon hillock. They see him smite the earth, with his gold-knobbed cane. They see water gush from green nothingness. They see it ripple downward, like the humps of a crystal serpent, to meander for a few yards before arching its back and plunging, once again, into green nothingness.

"Well?"

Arlene and Pandora sprawl on either side of babbling

brook, and they try to see upstream, past its shimmering Veil, to the Source itself.

Arlene thinks she sees the arm of a waterpump. Pandora thinks she sees the foot of a filtering system.

"It looks real to me," says Arlene, feeling guilty for raising the question.

"Yes, it's really real!" says Pandora, who would still sooner be here than headfirst in the horsetrough at Civic Playground.

They take their pop from the wicker carrier. Arlene spreads her red raincoat as a blanket. She opens the mayonnaise jar of brownies.

"What did the mayonnaise say to the refrigerator?" she asks.

"I don't know."

"Shut the door, I'm dressing!"

Pandora, taken by storm after such a solemn mood, is convulsed: It's the funniest thing she's heard all week, *and it's been a good week!* "Arlene," she reminds her friend, "that's *dirty!*"

Each takes a brownie.

They notice the man.

He is slouched against a catalpa tree, whose pods never open, watching them through bloodshot bull's-eyes.

"What *big eyes* he has!"

"He must be a soldier. Look. He's wearing an army coat."

"He's no soldier. His boots are dirty, and he's hairy."

"You can be hairy in the navy."

"Nope. He's a German spy! Look at his ears. They're as big as cabbages from listening too much."

Arlene gestures zip-the-lip: *Let us not be responsible for giving away Our Country's secrets.* She reaches for her Stubby orange. "Rats! Guess what."

Pandora reaches for her King Cola. "Nuts! We forgot the opener."

The man gestures from the catalpa.

"Maybe *he*'ll open them." The girls exchange glances: They've been taught to run from Strange Men who don't wash; who don't shave; who look funny; who look *at* them funny; who stagger; who smell; who offer candy; who wear clothes that don't fit. This Strange Man arouses suspicion on several accounts, but he is also, like themselves, a Guest of the Gormlys in a park which their mothers have repeatedly told them is the safest place in the world for children to play.

The man beckons again.

Arlene and Pandora do what most people do when confronted by two pieces of conflicting dogma: They ignore the most inconvenient one.

"He's calling *you*," says Arlene.

"No, he's calling *you*," says Pandora.

"Let's go together," says Arlene.

The girls approach, swinging their bottles in feigned nonchalance. The man, fitting one cap under the other, snaps his wrists. The caps spurt off.

"Golly, *thanks* mister!"

Arlene and Pandora retreat, in hasty dignity, to Arlene's red raincoat.

"What *big hands* he has!"

"What *big teeth* he has!"

"He's gone," says Pandora.

"No. He's behind the bushes."

The man beckons from his mockernut covering.

"He wants *you*," says Pandora.

"No, he wants *you*," says Arlene.

They are helpless in their indebtedness.

"We'll go together," says Pandora.

They shuffle, hand in hand, to within a few yards. The man, grinning, urges them forward. They shake their heads.

The man steps from behind the mockernut bushes.

Ohhhhhhhhhhhhh!

Arlene is first onto the trike. Then she remembers: "It's *your* turn to pedal." She jumps off. Pandora jumps on. "Hurree! He's getting his pants on!"

Pandora pedals. Arlene pumps from behind.

"Fas-*ter*!"

"I can't! You're pulling my hair! Get *off*, Arlene!"

"I can't! My teethbraces are caught!"

The cinderpath unrolls like a wolf's tongue, flanked by white-boulder teeth. The faster Pandora pumps, the more it seems to unwind.

"Hur-*ree!*"

The two girls tumble off the golden trike at Wayfarers Arch, at the feet of the Gormly Family. The man is nowhere in sight. Arlene untangles her teethbraces from Pandora's hair. "My father says a girl shouldn't go out at night without pepper in her pocket!"

"It's broad day!"

"Yeah, but it's a *park*. That's like a *woods*."

"Paradise Park?"

Arlene gapes at Pandora.

Pandora gapes at Arlene.

The absurdity of the shocking incident, when viewed from the security of Sir Edward Arley's polished toe, overwhelms them.

"Did you see," gasps Arlene, "how big . . . ?"

"As big," gasps Pandora, "as . . . ?"

"Oh, *bigger!*" gasps Arlene. "*Ten* times bigger!"

"Ten times!" gasps Pandora. "Yes! As big as . . ." She points recklessly up into the Bequeathing Father's Marble Crotch.

"Shut the door!" quips Arlene. "I'm dressing!"

Arlene and Pandora cycle past the stately homes of Boardwalk, with the silver wheel of the golden tricycle once more spinning out the seconds in fluid tranquillity.

Arlene shivers: "It's chilly."

"Yes," agrees Pandora.

But it isn't: They are pursued by the WASPish granite gaze of Sir Edward Arley, Bequeathing Father. They are reproved by the marble glaze of Lady Eugenia, Bequeathing Mother.

*   *   *

"PAN-DOOOOOOOOOOR-AH!"

Adelaide cleaves the air right up to the jailhouse.

"PAN-DOOOOOOOR-AH!"

Pandora is rather proud of her mother's voice. It has pitch, range, power, but Elsie Thwaite, who has a voice like a tinned crow, gets all the solo work because she is the minister's wife.

Pandora lays down her skipping-rope: "COOOOOOOOOM-IIIIIIIING!"

Adelaide is waiting on the verandah. "I want you to go to the butcher shop. Here's your rationbook. Use the Brown Spare A No. 5's."

"Ahhhhhhh. . . . Not the *butcher* shop!"

"Honestly, Pandora, I don't know what gets into you!"

"I *hate* the butcher shop!"

"You hate too many things. If you hurry, you can spend a nickel at the candy factory."

Pandora trudges past St. Cecilia's Cripples' Home, over the railway tracks, kicking dead leaves and chanting: *Meat, meat, I hate to get meat. Bloody, stinky, slimy. . . .* She tries not to think of the slaughter-cars that shriek down these rails, trailing the bleats of the doomed and the stench of death: *It's not MY fault. It isn't fair to blame ME!*

The butcher shop on Baltic Avenue is a cream-plaster building, moulded by a giant with dirty thumbs and trimmed in maroon (or, as Pandora would have it, in dried blood).

"Yes, Mrs. Stinton. May I assist you to some spareribs? They're choice." The butcher holds up a strip of bloodied piano keys. "Three pounds for . . ."

Pandora draws an angry face in the sawdust with the toe of her shoe.

Thud! The butcher's cleaver severs flesh. *It's mean of Arlene and the Clays to blame ME.*

"Good day, Mrs. Newton. How about some calves' kidneys? Just like ripe plums, with the bloom still on them."

Pandora stares up into the whirring fan.

ZZZZzzzzzzzz. . . . The butcher's electric blade slices through something she conjures up as warm, and woolly, with a tender voice and a terrified heart. Her teeth ache from clenching them. Her nostrils clot with the smell of blood.

Pandora's eyes spiral reluctantly, yet inevitably, down a coil of flypaper to a row of red-splotched porcelain trays. They move from one . . . to another . . . to another. . . .

Mary had a little lamb chops, 55¢ a lb., grazing on a meadow of cemetery grass.

This little piggy went to market with parsley stuck in his smashed splish-splosh snout.

The sheep's in the meadow, the cow's in the uck-guck round steak minced, 41¢ a lb.

Humpty-Dumpty sat on a Grade A large, 45¢ a doz.

Higgly-piggly my black hen with its eyes poked out and its head bashed in.

"Next, please?" The butcher drops his tone of unctuous servitude. "Oh, *you*, Pandora."

ZZZZZzzzzz. Thud. Splat.

Pandora watches the ball of string unwind down to the pink parcel, warm with blood, that she will have to hold in her hand.

"Here."

Gouts of flesh hang from the butcher's nails. He leaves a bloody thumbprint on Pandora's rationbook, right over her own name: That is with his right hand. His left hand is a meathook. "Wait! Take some codfish cuts. They're in the freezer."

Lyle Gothic smiles at his next customer. "Ahhhh, Mrs. Finney. How about a nice turkey. Just feel that breast. . . ."

The freezer window is hoary with frost. Pandora gropes inside. *AAaaaaaaaaahhhhhgggg!* Her hand touches it: a white bunny, pierced through one eye with a meathook. The other eye stares, glazed and accusing. His belly is scooped out. His puff-tail hangs by a tendon.

Pandora bows her head: *My father has killed the Easter bunny. He has killed the Easter bunny, and one day he will kill Charlie-puss, just as he says. He will steak his heart. Then he will kill me. He will sneak up into the attic, under a sheet,*

and he will scoop out my belly, and he will hang me on a hook.
Lyle Gothic prickles inside his starched white shirt. He can
feel the pierce of his daughter's curse-green eyes. A tolerable
day has become intolerable: *One bad penny can blot out the
sun.*

Lyle returns to his syllables of exaggerated concern:
"Tough, Mrs. Dicey? Surely not!" He feeds curses, and stew-
ing beef, into the meat-grinder: *Bitches! All of them!*

Pandora's mother is leaning over a cauldron, ladling tomatoes into scalding water, and pushing grapes through a sieve.
"Now, that didn't take long, did it?"

The tomatoes squeal as their skins split. The grape eyes
weep, then pop. Her borrowed butcher's apron is richly mottled in red juice.

*My father kills the animals, and my mother kills the fruit.
They drink their juices, with purple running down their
faces, in bed, in the dark. They have done it to Adel-Ada.
They have squeezed out their juices, and that is why they're
so pale. They do it to Jesus, they drink His juice, and they will
do it to me. They will squeeze the juice right out of me, and
they will drink it, together, in the dark.*

Pandora runs from the house. She stands on one foot, and
she bangs her head to drive out the wicked lies she has made
up about her mother and father in her double-crown, where
the Devil touched her, and her hair won't lie flat.

Pandora sweetens her mouth with blackballs, one in each
cheek. She concentrates on guessing what colour each will be
without taking them out.

She has six left. She jiggles them in her pinafore pocket, and
strolls up Oriental Avenue looking for a little action.

The skipping-game has broken up. Arlene and Shelly Clay
are wheeling Baby Scotty in a rusty buggy, with Nellie Clay
holding onto the side. Spotty, the Clay mongrel, trots behind.

Baby Scotty is crying. Shelly feels inside the shabby flan-
nelette. "Maybe he's got a pin stuck."

Pandora and Arlene playfully nudge each other up and down the curb. Pandora slips Arlene a blackball.

"I *saw!*" snips Nellie.

"Gives-divs!" snipes Shelly.

"*You* never share."

"I would if I ever had some!"

A bargain is struck.

Nellie tosses a stick into the burning bush in front of the Cripples' Home. Spotty takes off, licketty-split, after it. Arlene, Pandora, Nellie, Shelly and Baby Scotty take off after Spotty.

They possess the centre of the burning bush. Nellie mounts guard. Shelly takes off Baby Scotty's napkin. Arlene and Pandora have a look.

"That's not much," complains Arlene.

She and Pandora exchange a smirk of sinful experience.

"*Twenty* times bigger!" whispers Arlene.

"Because he was a *Nazi!*" giggles Pandora.

"Hurry, eh!" Shelly snatches at the blackballs. Pandora buries them in her pocket.

"I had my fingers crossed."

"You did *not!*"

Shelly pulls Pandora's hair. Nellie hits Arlene. Scotty bawls. Spotty barks.

Old Mr. Grandby, shivering and shaking, looks over at the burning bush, which is shivering and shaking, and the two sets of tremors coalesce like two warring flocks of angels, and old Mr. Grandby's world — for the first time in ten years — stops trembling. "*Oh Lord!*" he exclaims, half-rising from the trenches of Paschendaele, "*I look into the gates of Paradise. I wait to see Thy Face.*" Spotty leaps out of the burning bush. Old Mr. Grandby stubbornly reseats himself, and prepares for a long siege: "*Lord, I am NOT going to Heaven!*"

Pandora nurses a scraped elbow, Arlene a bruised thigh. They wander toward the jailhouse, bouncing Arlene's India-rubber ball.

"If Baby Victor hadn't choked, I would have charged the

Clays, and it would have been a better show, I'll bet," confides Pandora.

"No, Baby Victor would have been *older* than you. He would have shown *your* thing in the burning bushes."

"I don't have a thing," says Pandora. "I have 'insides,' which are neater."

"But," says Arlene, putting the whole thing into maddening perspective, "*Sydney* doesn't have to squat."

Pandora whispers giddily into Arlene's ear. *Shut the door, I'm dressing!*

* * *

The days get shorter and darker. Leaves shrivel. Snow falls. A terrible enchantment falls upon the earth.

Pandora's legs are the first to disappear. She loses them inside a pair of brown stockings attached to an elastic harness. To these are added flannel leggings, three pairs of socks, two sets of red mitts, a red snowsuit and a fleece-lined red helmet. Pandora waddles, arms stiffly extended, down the street: *I am a red coatrack!*

On a particularly spiteful day in December, a large red scarf is wrapped round Pandora's nose, lined in front with kleenex. Thenceforth, all season's greetings must be mailed to her through the eyeslot between red scarf and red helmet: *I am a red mailbox!*

Now the days are so short the streetlights turn on before supper. Pandora is not allowed out on the street after school. She feels as if the freedoms she so painfully earned last fall have all been stolen from her. A grey eyelid has closed over the world, and strain as she might, she can't shove it up again.

Miss Potter goes blind. Pandora was afraid she would: She could see the bones pushing through the tips of her fingers as if they were trying to be eyes when she played the piano about Winter *plinketty-fumble-plunk* Wonderland.

The snow falls, and is shovelled. It all falls down again, and is shovelled up again. It falls again, and — *hola!* The eyelid slits just when Pandora has given up hope. The winter melts, in a noisy gush, down the sewers. Pandora's clothes flow into the storage closet. She sprouts, two inches, with the crocuses.

Pandora reclaims and expands her territory.

"LU-CEE!"

"STINK-EE!"

"JONES-EE!"

Pandora parts the sunflowers, where Sydney birdwatches through his philatelist's magnifying-glass. Arlene pushes the secret flap Sydney cut in the board fence. They crawl cautiously from Goodfellow property onto Binder-Twine property.

It is like passing through a time tunnel.

A dozen rotting carriages lie strewn about the Binder-Twine lot, testifying to a time when the nation's entire economy was tied up with binder-twine. Arlene and Pandora climb the wheels. They bounce on the creaky leather seats. They poke their fingers into broken lanterns. They wrap themselves in newspaper shawls, and mince and curtsey the way they are sure "olden ladies" did it.

They jungle-crawl to the factory itself — a crumbling brick building turned blindly in upon itself like a fortress. They pry off a cellar grate. They sniff the spicy odour of liquids ripening in barrels. They listen to the whine of machines in perpetual motion. They ponder the mystery of the Binder-Twine Factory:

Not once have they ever seen anyone enter or leave it except for the front gardener and the nightwatchman. Nobody has. Everybody on the block asks: "What do they do in there?"

Some say it has to do with the Nazis.

Some say it is the Martians.

Some say. . . . *"What-the-hell are you brats doing here?"*

It is Old Fowley, the watchdog gardener!

Arlene and Pandora dart, flea-footed, around the building. Fowley drags after them, cursing their good legs along with his gimpy one. They wriggle through the flap in the sunflowers. Old Fowley hoves into sight.

He peers myopically.

He curses.

"It's the quairest thing," he tells Smith, the nightwatchman. "Them kids are *there*, then, fast as your eye, they're *not* there. . . . A ten-foot board fence. . . . Ain't no way over it. Ain't no way through it. . . . I'm beginning to think it ain't *kids* at all. I'm beginning to think. . . ."

Maybe it's the Nazis!

Maybe it's the Martians!

Old Fowley takes a swig from his pickled milk-bottle. "Oncet I saw something back there, by that fence, you wouldn't believe. . . . An *eye*, as big as yer fist, an eye, all by hisself, staring up from the middle of the sunflower patch!"

Smith, the nightwatchman, shakes his head: *Poor Old Fowley, mad as a tick, and getting worse.*

Smith is a lucky man: He has never looked through a fog of rubbing alcohol into a sunflower patch and seen Sydney's eye, staring up at him, unblinking, through his philatelist's magnifying-glass. But then, Smith is an unlucky man: He has never lain, on a bed of rags, and been tickled, insensible, by twelve naked virgins with fingers like harpchords and tongues like hummingbirds' wings.

Old Fowley takes another swig and prepares himself, giddily, for sleep.

Pandora stands on St. Charles Place, opposite a four-storey building that used to house Minerva Knitting Mills. Its glass face, past which spindles of scarlet, emerald and sapphire used to whir, was recently painted black, as an air-raid precaution. Now, instead of sparkling like a stained-glass window, when fired by the sun, it glows like a marble tombstone, inscribed with ten-foot gilt letters: THOR MUNITIONS, LTD. The new name has been painted over the old in such a way as to co-ordinate the N, I, T and N of MUNITIONS with the N, I, T and N of KNITTING: It is this sort of brutal efficiency which makes the difference when a nation — however unwillingly — finds itself at War.

The eight-to-four shift is just ending: Workers in coveralls pour through the electrically-charged fence. Pandora is waiting for her Aunt Rosie, who works on the TNT line. Rosie's real name is Rosalind, but since she's been at the munitions, everyone calls her Rosie, for Rosie the Rivetter. Everyone but Lyle Gothic and Aunt Estelle. They call her Rosalind.

Pandora sees her Aunt Rosie wheeling her carmine bicycle, wrangled on priority by a cute guy at the StreamLine Bicycle Company. She is surrounded by a half-dozen male workers. Natch. Pandora's Aunt Rosie is a Glamor Girl. She has a beauty spot, as black as a tealeaf, on her cloven chin, and henna hair she used to wear in a pompadour, just like Ginger Rogers, with waves down her back, just like Rita Hayworth, till she feather-cut it to please President Roosevelt, who asked Veronica Lake to do something about her hair because of girls getting it caught in the machines.

Rosie is very patriotic.

She doesn't even wear bobbypins since Myrna Loy proved she could get divorced without them.

Myrna Divorced in 'Victory Bob'

Reno (AP) — Actress Myrna Loy, 36, was granted a divorce from Arthur Hornblow, 49. Miss Loy's hair was done in a new Victory Bob "designed to conserve hairpins."

Rosie draws up alongside.

"Hi, Pandy!" She brakes with a sling-back foot. She grins Fatal Apple: "Climb on kid. I'll ride you."

Pandora climbs onto the bar, that girls aren't supposed to have, and they leave the curb the way Rosie walks — wiggily, then gaining momentum.

"Didja see that cute guy I was with? He's a Greek. He escaped from a concentration camp in a goat-cart. I got a date with him for Friday." Rosie giggles: "Estelle and your old man would have a *fit* if they knew, but this is the Modern Age, kid, and unless we learn to live in it, it's gonna be the last Modern Age there is."

Rosie talks that way because she poses for War Worker pictures, and makes speeches about Stamp Out the U-Boat with War Savings Stamps, and once she was voted The Girl I'd Most Like to Be Torpedoed With by a corvette that was torpedoed, a week later, and went down, all hands.

"Or," as Rosie puts it, thumping her spectacular bosom, "down all *hearts*. . . . They were my buddies, *one sweet bunch of guys*, and now, where were they?" Rosie brakes in front of Barkers' Groceteria. "That's when I could see there was no running away from this thing. It was *eating* me, but what could I do? . . . I couldn't just grab a gun and go after the Jerries, the way a *guy* would. I knew I'd have to settle for the homefront stuff. *That's* when I started winning Quota E Certificates — four in four weeks, more than anybody had ever got. *Proud?* Sure I was proud, but I knew it wasn't *me* that deserved the credit. I know it was *those* guys who, by *their* sacrifice, had given *me* the heart!"

Rosie thumps her spectacular chest. Mr. Barker, in blushing confusion rings up NO CHARGE. *Mrs.* Barker thrusts him aside.

"A package of Wrigley's, please . . . Ahh . . . Juicy Fruit.

"Those guys were in back o' me, inspiring me to do other things, too . . . Things so *small* I feel sheepish mentioning them.

"Yeah . . . and a pack of Sweet Caps." Rosie wriggles her hand inside her coveralls. "Where was I? . . . Oh, yeah. . . ." She collects her purchases and they head for the door. "*First* I started taking my coffee *black*. Then I ripped all zippers and domefasteners — every scrap of metal I could find — off my clothes and I sent the stuff to salvage. *Not much*, you say? No, but enough metal for, say, a *clip of cartridges* for a Lee Enfield, and if *that's* not enough for *you*, just ask yourself how *you'd* feel if one of *our* boys pulled the trigger, with a bayonet coming at him, and no *bullet* came out because *you* were wearing it to hold up your skirt!"

Rosie offers Pandora a stick of gum, folds another into her mouth.

"And don't forget, while I'm talking about zippers as *scrap metal,* the zipper itself is a Vital Commodity providing Vital Service."

Rosie mounts her bike. Pandora slides onto the bar.

"Did you know that *123* items of *Actual Combat* are closed by zippers? *I* didn't know it either till the ZIPPON ZIPPER people told me, so from now on, if you can't get your favourite ZIPPON ZIPPER, remember, *ZIPPON ZIPPER has Gone to War! . . . Right into the Frontlines! Right onto the backs and sides of Our Fighting Men!"*

Rosie stops for the traffic cop at the corner of Oriental. "Wanna get ZIPPON back? You bet your sweet aspidistra you do! And *I'm* gonna tell you how! *Buy War Bonds!"*

She pauses to grin at the cop. "*That* way, we'll get Our Fighting Men — *and* ZIPPON ZIPPER — back home again!"

That's the speech Rosie is going to make at the next ZIPPON ZIPPER Bond Rally. She practises the first part again as she wiggle-waggles, very personally, across the intersection, gesturing with even more oomph, almost breaking down completely at the part about the sweet bunch o' guys that went down, all hearts, but recovering in time to re-dedicate her mouth, with Revlon's Fatal Apple lipstick, at the Gothics' front walk.

Pandora is deeply impressed. "Won't you be *scared,* Aunt Rosie, up in front of all those people?"

"Naaahh, kid. You get used to it." She kisses her mouth on a kleenex. She examines the valentine smudge self-critically. "I shouldn't wear so much. It isn't patriotic, but you sort o' need it when you're in the public eye." She runs her pointy-tongue, remittingly, over her lips. She giggles: "Harper's Bazaar says it's my *Red Badge of Courage!"*

Rosie snaps shut her compact. The hinge breaks. "Nuts! These plastic thingies are useless." She hands it to Pandora. "Here, kid. Take it."

Wow! Pandora examines the airforce-blue case with the RCAF crest. "Gee, *thanks,* Aunt Rosie!"

Rosie winks. "Keep Your Powder Dry," she says with new significance. She pushes off from the curb. "Oh yeah. . . . Tell your ma I'll drop in at the end of the week — if I don't do something *rash* like run off and join the Marines!"

Join the Marines? Oh, Wow! But surely Aunt Rosie meant the WACs?!

* * *

Arlene and Pandora climb the wire fence at the end of the Goodfellows' backyard. They wave, cordially, to three men working the Reading Railway cinderbed: As taxpayers' daughters, convinced that railway property is public property, they value good relations with their employees.

They immerse themselves in a twitch-grass river flowing parallel to the tracks. They scrounge for rusty spikes, hanks of rubber, squiggles of tin, to be sold to the adeetse man for twenty-five cents from his goat's bladder.

They watch a passenger train materialise out of a puff of smoke, and receive the gloved salute of royalty.

They set out across the tracks — eight of them, strewn with freightlines. Even idle, the boxcars give off the reek of power, legend and destiny. Their black sinews ooze oil. Their wheels gleam with a patina of speed. Their side-doors whisper of hoboes, their side-ladders of the flights of desperadoes.

Their graffiti partake of the Early Brazen Age: Arlene and Pandora know only that some of the words aren't very nice.

Arlene and Pandora descend into the Ravine, a jagged green fault, which successive city fathers have tried hard to correct through the excavation of gravel and the dumping of garbage. This portion, running parallel to Oriental, on the far side of the tracks, is much the way the last Ice Age left it: a virgin gorge, cleft with one mighty heave from a Cyclopean ice-axe.

"Shall we take Narrow Path or Steep Path?"

"Let's take Crooked Path."

The Ravine is not a pretty place: Its soil is wet and mouldy; its air, dank and clammy — a throwback to that time when Earth had not quite separated from Water, or Water from Air, or Day from Night; when the continents were still slipping like bars of soap around their salty bath and Time was registered by the rise and fall of mountains.

The Ravine's vegetation also dates back to that more primitive age: fern, fungus, lichen, scrub, and a sprinkling of scruff-conifer. The hardwoods have not yet taken hold here, and certainly not that reckless explosion of colour and form made possible by the evolution of the flower.

Here, the monotony of coarse-green and shag-brown is broken only by clusters of poison berries. Here, the ground life is reptillian; the air life, insectian.

Arlene and Pandora keep an eye peeled downward for scuttle, slip, hiss as they clamber over Sulphur Rock and Chinese-Trickle Falls. They swat their way past Hornet Tree and Cess Pool, with its toad-water the colour of licorice. They dart by Teeter Rock, suspended *heavy-heavy hangs over thy head* like a judgment, and Blasted Tree, thrice God-cursed by lightning.

They descend to a trench at the bottom of the Ravine. The sun is directly overhead. It is day here, for an hour or so.

"I betcha it's open."

"Betcha it isn't."

They pass under a decaying red gate that says Good Luck in Chinese, through waist-high grass, to a dance pavillion — now boarded up, now overhung with mock-orange. They rap on a window, tin-plastered with Coca Cola signs: *Will it open?*

Just when they have given up hope, the window cranks down and a ravaged head pokes out.

"One!" says Arlene, thumping her nickel on the counter.

"One!" says Pandora.

No point in saying one of what: The old crone is both blind and mute. *Life is one big lottery down here at the centre of the earth!*

Arlene gets cream-soda. Pandora, grape.

"Oh, boy!"

They are terrified some day they will get a flavour they don't like, though each is hardput to say what flavour that might be.

Clank clank clank: The Coke window closes. The old crone drops, like a fortune-telling mannequin, back into her rocking chair, waiting to deal out Fate the next time a coin is slotted.

Arlene and Pandora sit on the warped dancefloor, under a ceiling that was once midnight-blue and star-spangled. They eat their peanutbutter sandwiches, wrapped in waxpaper transparent from reuse, and arrive at a guilt-ridden agreement to "forget" their brown bags.

There are two ways up the far side of the Ravine: a muddy path, and a flight of steps built at a time when the pavillion was a roadhouse specializing in bathtub gin (which, some say, is how the old crone got to be the old crone).

Arlene and Pandora do not dare take the steps. You see . . . nobody knows for sure whether there are 365 or 366 of them. Who can resist counting? No matter how careful, Arlene and Pandora always lose track. What choice is there? Down they go again, counting backwards. Still wrong. Up again, rolling their numbers in a ball ahead of them, panting, heaving, adding a step at a time. Still wrong. *Bounce bounce bounce* — their lopsided tally rolls to the bottom. They follow, *step, step, step,* trying to pick up the numbers.

Once they landed at the bottom, with knees too leaden to lift. They tried bumping up on their behinds, but someone had ground glass into every third step.

It grows dark. It starts to rain. They cling together, crying on the 103rd (104th?) step.

Thump thump thump. . . . Footsteps. . . . *Heavy* footsteps. Men — in uniform. *OURS, thank goodness!* Two policemen. They carry Arlene and Pandora home, slung over their shoulders like sacks of potatoes, with glass slivers in their behinds, and all the Clays laughing.

The steps are out of the question.

Arlene and Pandora start up the far side of the Ravine: *One, two, three.* . . . By the time Pandora is saying "twenty," Arlene is on the same step saying "twenty-one.". . . What choice is there?

Pandora passes out of kindergarten. Only one girl in her class failed. She couldn't get her blocks back into her box, while the others marched past singing.

*   *   *

Lyle Gothic sits on the verandah in his wicker chair, which is his summer cottage, from June through September, and he swabs his bald head, which he says got that way because of the helmets in The Great War, and he reads about the new War, now growing old. . . .
Ruhr Devastation 'Terrifying'
Sub Massacre May Mean More Tea, Coffee, Sugar
Goering 'Very Ill'. . . . His devoted wife Emmy sits by his side.

Adelaide sits by Lyle's side on a rusty porch swing, tying coloured thou-shalt-knots at the back of her embroidery hoop. Pandora sits on the top step, looking at a Wonder Woman comicbook.

Adelaide's swing-chain grates.

"Can't you stop that damned noise?"

"Sorry, I didn't know I was doing anything."

Lyle puts down his paper: He can no longer see to read.

Adelaide can no longer see to sew: "I think it's time you went to bed, Pandora."

"Ahhhhhhhhh. . . ."

Lyle goes through the screen door first, then Adelaide, then — dragging her feet — Pandora.

Lyle is a big man, over six feet. His lightly-haired flesh, though not excessive, fits him like a poorly-tailored suit. It is soft flesh, a child's flesh. Now it is scored from his cane chair. The marks are not visible, but Adelaide knows they are there. She thinks, with a blinding stab through the temples, how the flesh will look. She wipes her mind clean with the first biblical text she can think of: *And the Lord set a mark upon Cain.* . . .

Pandora trudges upstairs to bed, taking Wonder Woman to look at under the covers.

Lyle deals out Monopoly deeds to himself and Howard Hughes, his guest opponent. By eleven, Howard is down a cool three mill. He has to sell his tool company, not to mention Jane Russell and his Hollywood studio. "Guess I'll go up. . . ."

Pandora hears her father moving awkwardly about the room below. She hears him drop something heavy, then curse.

Pandora hears her mother wind the alarm clock. She hears her go into the bathroom. She hears a deep shuddering groan, which is the sound the tap makes when you screw it the wrong way. She imagines her mother's corsets lying, still warm, in a pink pool, by her bed, *with the laces and steel staves and hooks and hooks and* . . . Pandora stuffs her head under her pillow. *I have seen my mother's corsets by moonlight.*

On Fridays, when Grannie Cragg is feeling up to snuff, she takes Adelaide and Adel-Ada and Pandora to the Ventnor Theatre to see a cartoon, a picture, another picture, then the first picture all over again. Pandora likes Tom & Jerry, and the Dead End Kids, and Walt Disney, and Sherlock Holmes. Adelaide likes Clark Gable with a love story, but Grannie Cragg likes westerns with Chill Wills who, she says, is the dead-spit of Grandpa Two who exploded down a mine before Aunt Cora died of diphtheria and Uncle Basil was hit by a falling pawnball.

Sometimes they go to the Ventnor Ice Cream Parlour first, and they order sundaes, for fifteen cents. Pandora likes chocolate with a cherry, but she doesn't like it when her mother says "grace" over the melting sundaes, or when Grannie Cragg puts her teeth in her purse, or when Aunt Estelle (who is her father's sister and sometimes comes along) washes her change in the waterglass. "You never know where it's been, or who's touched it, and what have they been doing with their hands? Where have they placed them?"

Pandora sits on her front steps, with her chin cupped in

her hands, and her elbows propped on her knees, and her seersucker skirt pulled down to her Sisman scampers, counting all that is left of a fortune that once seemed inexhaustible: *Only ten more days of vacation, and no one to spend them with.*

Arlene and Sydney are at a cottage.

The twins have the mumps, Adel in the right cheek, Ada in the left.

Lucy Spittal is at dum-dum camp.

The Clays are helping the Minister of Labour pick black currants:

> "YOUR Nation needs YOUR help.
> FOOD is vital to VICTORY."

Still, Pandora is impatient for the day to begin. She has worked out a surprise. She is waiting for the milkman. She is waiting for the breadman.

Clip clop clip clop. . . . A horse and wagon turns onto Oriental Avenue.

"Sheridan's Bread, Tastes like lead!" shouts Pandora.

The breadman laughs, and waves.

Pandora skips round her side-alley. She returns with a shiny pail, glued with a picture of a horse. That's the surprise! Pandora heard it on the radio:

"Attention, Animal Lovers! The Humane Society is appealing to kindhearted citizens to aid in giving horses water this summer. Anyone interested in helping Those Who Cannot Speak for Themselves When Thirsty, is requested to telephone Society Headquarters, and a pail bearing the Humane Society name, to be filled with water every day, will be promptly delivered."

Molly gulps down the refreshing liquid. Pandora pats her sweaty mane. She fishes an apple from her sundress pocket, and lays it flat on her palm. Molly's fat lips graze greedily over it, smacking, drooling, tickling, till Pandora, laughing, wipes the foam onto her underpants. That makes the breadman laugh.

"What's *your* name?"

"Pandora."

"Want a ride, Pandora?"

"On the wagon?"

"Will your mother let you?"

"Sure!" Pandora is indignant: *"I'm* allowed on the street, *Mis-*ter!"

Pandora climbs into the trap. *Clip clop clip clop.* The breadman delivers two loaves to Mrs. Dicey. Pandora raises and lowers his horsestop. "Hi, Mrs. Niobe! Hi, Mrs. Barker!" *Clip clop clip clop.* The breadman delivers an orange cake to Mrs. Stinton, and turns onto States Avenue toward the railway tracks. *Clip clop clip clop.*

"Want to drive?"

"Sure!"

"We'll cut along by the tracks. I don't want some old biddy phoning the company."

Molly balks at the railway cinderbed. The breadman flicks his whip. Molly lurches forward: *Clippetty cloppetty clap.* The cinders change Molly's plodding rhythm into something less predictable. Pandora shivers. *Hi ho, Silver! We are practically outlaws!*

"Here, take the reins."

Pandora moves between the breadman's knees. He puts his two hands over hers. She feels the slow, grumbling rhythm pass up through Molly's flanks, and along the reins.

The breadman lays his whip on Molly's withers. She plunges forward. *Clippetty cloppetty clippetty cloppetty.* Pandora loses her balance. The breadman presses her body between his knees. Pandora doesn't like to be squeezed. She calls, "Whooooah!" and tries to wriggle free.

The breadman tugs the reins. *"Hooo-*back!" They are in a stand of slippery elms. "What's the matter? Can't you take a little excitement?"

The breadman has pointy teeth, like the whale that swallowed Pinocchio. Pandora can smell his breath. She puts her hands against his chest, and pushes. She remembers her manners. She drops her hands. "I had a Good Time, Mister Breadman, thank you, but I guess I'll go. My mother shall be calling me."

The breadman is disappointed: "That's a real shame. I thought we'd have a picnic." He pulls down a box of cherry tarts. He slides his finger through the cellophane.

"Well. . . ." Pandora hesitates, one Sisman scamper on the steelstep. She moves back inside the trap. "Maybe if I'm not *too* long."

Pandora sits primly on the leatherseat. She takes the nearest cherry tart, which is also the biggest. They munch companionably. Juice sticks to the breadman's moustache. Pandora averts her eyes: *It is not polite to stare when people are chewing.*

The breadman laughs: "Your old man got a moustache?"

"My father doesn't have *any* hair."

"Does your boyfriend have a moustache?"

"I don't *have* a boyfriend!"

"A cute girl like you. . . ? Ahhh, I bet you do! I bet he's got a moustache."

The breadman's thumb rests lightly on a box of chocolate eclairs. Temptation makes Pandora coy. "I don't know *any*body with a moustache except. . . ." She counts them on her fingers: "Uncle Basil, who got killed, Uncle Damon, who ran away, and uh. . . ." She knows there's another. *"Hitler!"*

The breadman laughs: "That's rich!" He presses his thumb — ping! — through the cellophane. Pandora expects he will offer her an eclair, guests first. Instead, he takes one himself. "Mmmmm . . . *good!*" He licks cream from his moustache. He grins. "Ever been kissed by a guy with a moustache?"

Pandora ducks her head.

"Know what it feels like?"

The breadman swings Pandora up on the seat. He shoves an eclair into her mouth, and runs his moustache against her cheek. "See? It tickles!"

Pandora, embarrassed, munches her eclair without tasting it. The breadman runs his fingers up and down her arm. He tickles her neck. He sticks his fingers into her bellybutton. He thrusts his hand up her skirt. He yanks at her button pants. He tries to rip them off.

Pandora punches the breadman with both fists. He slaps her. She sucks in her breath, to scream. He jabs her in the stomach. She loses her breath in a swoosh. She bursts into tears.

"*Stop* that! Whatsa matter? I was just *tickling!* If I knew you were a crybaby, I'd never have asked you!"

Pandora is confused: She doesn't know why she is being scolded. She doesn't know what she has done wrong. She isn't sure what the breadman has done wrong. She tries to remember what he did. She tries to remember what Mr. Goodfellow does to Arlene when he tickles her.

"O.K. Stop crying, and I won't hold it against you." The breadman wipes Pandora's face with a soiled hanky. "Stop crying, and I've got something for you."

Pandora rubs her eyes with her fist. "What?"

"A surprise. I got it in my pocket, but you have to stop crying."

Pandora dabs at her eyes. "I'm *not* crying."

The breadman puts his hand in his pocket. He jiggles it, the way her father does when he has coins for candy. "You have to put your hand in and get it."

Pandora eyes the pocket. She doesn't want to touch the breadman. She doesn't like the breadman.

"I don't want to."

"It's something real nice!"

"Noooo. . . ."

"I guess I'll have to give it to another little girl." The breadman chuckles: "*All* little girls like what I've got."

"Ahhh. . . ."

"What's the matter? Here, don't be afraid. Maybe it's a little doll. Would you like that? Maybe it's a dollar! What would you buy if you had a whole dollar? Would you buy pretty ribbons?"

The breadman circles Pandora's wrist with his fingers. He coaxes her hand into his pocket. It is a big pocket. It is ripped.

. . . It is a while before Pandora realizes how cruelly she has been tricked. She tries to pull out her hand. The breadman holds it tight. "What's the matter? Don't you like the nice puppy? Pat the nice puppy. Play with the nice puppy. Does your father have a nice puppy? Take out the nice puppy. Take the nice puppy out for a walk. He wants to show you how he can jump. He wants to play. . . ."

Panic clogs Pandora's chest. It explodes through her throat. The breadman clamps his hand over her mouth. He jams the scream back into her body. She convulses.

The breadman panics. He sees three railwaymen down the tracks on a jigger. His hand is wrapped around Pandora's throat. He presses his fingers into the chords of her neck. She begins to choke.

The breadman loosens his hand. He lets Pandora catch her breath. He snarls: *"Shut up,* and *maybe* I'll let you go."

Pandora forces herself to calm down. The breadman takes his hand from her mouth. He yanks her head back by the hair. He thrusts his face into hers. "If I let you go, what are you going to say?"

"Th-thank you?"

"No! What are you going to tell your old man?"

"N-nothing."

"You better not!" hisses the breadman. "Because if you're lying, *I'm coming to get you!"* He pulls Pandora's hair tighter. Her eyes water. Her head aches. He reaches for his whip. "See this? You tell *one word,* and I'll whip you till the flesh falls off your bones!"

The breadman feels tremors pass through Pandora's body. Her terror excites him. He draws her body over his knee. He runs his hands over her chest, her thighs, between her legs. Pandora makes herself very still, the way a small animal, cornered in a bush, humbly assumes the posture of death as a sop to death.

The breadman grunts. He takes his hands from Pandora's body. She jumps past him, down the steps, out of the trap.

She runs. She runs and runs and. . . .

Pandora hides.

She hides in her cubbyhole.

She hides in the dark.

She hides in a wedge of cheese, as black as fear, where the floor meets the sky and the ghost of Aunt *oh you naughty, filthy* Cora moves with the sound of kissing tissue-paper.

Pandora is afraid, but she cannot name her fear. Pandora is ashamed, but she cannot name her shame. Fear and shame gorge like buzzards on her burden of guilty knowledge, leaving only a few twisted bones:

"I don't like the breadman. He stinks. He beats Molly with a whip till her skin falls off!"

"Don't say those things," scolds Adelaide. "You're getting as bad as Mrs. Newton with your gossip."

"It's *true!*"

"It *isn't* true. Mr. Pluman is a nice man. A little forward, for my tastes, but a decent enough sort."

Pandora looks at her naked body in her dresser-mirror: It is covered with roller-skating scars and bruises from jumping out of trees. She weeps: She is heartbroken.

Pandora sits in the cellar watching her mother prod sheets through the rubber lips of her wash-wringer, and listening to the sucking sound the dirty water makes as it runs down the drain.

"I don't understand what gets into you sometimes. You've been under my feet for four days now. Why don't you go outside where it's nice, and play, instead of moping around in here?" Adelaide adds bleach to her washwater. "It's always the same with you, isn't it, Pandora? You're all bushy-tailed with enthusiasm one minute, and five minutes later you've lost interest. You wouldn't give me a moment's peace till I phoned up about that Humane Society pail, and now where is it? You haven't even brushed Charlie-puss this week, and you know what your father will say if he finds more cat hairs on the chesterfield!"

Arlene and Sydney return from the beach. Arlene gives

Pandora a pink seashell you can put to your ear and hear the ocean roar. Sydney gives her a purple-satin pillowcase with "Hi Sweetheart" in gold on one side and "Bala" on the other.

Pandora puts the seashell and the purple pillow into the dresser-drawer, where she keeps things. She says to Arlene, "I don't want to play with Sydney anymore. I don't like Sydney. Sydney stinks."

Arlene tells Sydney.

Sydney puts on his stilts, which make him taller than his father, and he gouges out Pandora's front lawn.

School: Them

September, 1943 to June, 1944

Pandora rolls her ankle socks with the exaggerated precision of the very young, the very old, the very drunk. It is the day after Labour Day. Arlene is calling. The two girls skip, in gum-cracking animation, to Laura Secord Public School, a red-brick battleship on a rough sea of asphalt at the corner of Baltic and Boardwalk.

Laura Secord is Victorian-Gothic, with Neo-Classic pretensions. Its two-storey face is peaked in the middle and square-turreted at either end. Its front portal is arched and Ionian-columned. To its right is a flagpole flying the Union Jack, donated by the Westminster Chapter of the Imperial Order Daughters of the Empire. To its left is a monument to Laura Secord and her cow who, in 1813, warned British troops of an American border attack, thus naming a chocolate company. Over the school's brass-ringed oak-door — reserved for teachers, inspectors, dignitaries of the IODE and executive members of the Home & School — are the Armorial Bearings of the Dominion of Canada: the Lion, the Unicorn and other heraldic sundries in stone, *A mari usque ad mare.*

It is 8:25. Fifty Downstairs Girls — starched, curled, beribboned — stand in line outside their door.

"Hi Janis!" calls Arlene to a girl who is sixth. "Can me and my friend get in?"

"Yes. Behind Wendy. She asked first."

Arlene and Pandora shoulder their way into line behind

Wendy. A lanky, buck-toothed girl, behind Pandora, jabs her in the ribs with her ruler. "Who said *you* could get in?"

"*I* did," vouches Janis, dead-to-her-rights. It is an unwritten rule, among Downstairs Girls, that one person can let in three others: Dispensing such favours is the whole point in coming early.

The buck-toothed girl tramples Pandora's white socks. "Butt *out!*"

Pandora — insecure because she is only a friend-of-a-friend — drops back: "Let the baby have her bottle!"

The buck-toothed girl elbows Pandora, now behind her. Pandora topples against the girl behind her, and the whole line goes *plop! plop! plop!* like dominoes.

"Quit-yer-shuvin!"

"It's not *me!*"

"*You* horned in."

"*I* let her in."

Janis, Wendy, Arlene shove back against the buck-toothed girl. Pandora, now well-supported, shoves forward.

"*Shuv! shuv! shuv!*" chants the line, instinctively siding with the power-Establishment closest to the door.

The buck-toothed girl is forced out.

"*Shame! shame! shame!*" chants the line, as she slinks back to the end.

A teacher heaves open the door. It is not a "hurray" situation but a ripple of relief passes down the line.

"Single file! Straighten up! Left, right!"

Pandora marches up air puddles worn in the steps by a million marching feet.

"Hands *off* the banister!"

Pandora stuffs her hands into her pockets. Though she can see Room 3 — her new room — immediately opposite, she knows she must walk the length of the hall, past the Coronation picture of King George VI and Queen Elizabeth; past Jacques Cartier Erecting the Cross before a band of awed Indians; past the teachers' room at the bottom of the hall, then back up the other side, past Northern River by Tom

Thomson, Awarded to Miss M. D. Larkspur and her Triple Trio, 1929.

The shadowy band of students slides around the wall like fish around an aquarium. Light-globes glow overhead, distant suns seen mistily through layers of water. The teachers — killer crabs — lurk at the mouths of their numbered caverns.

Pandora knows all the teachers by reputation (Nice, Crabby, Strict-but-Fair) and trademark eccentricity. Now, as she passes each of the twelve, she does what generations of children have done before her: She reduces each teacher's authority to an idiosyncrasy she, Pandora, can possess and control: *Miss LaStrobe wears glasses-on-a-chain. Miss Sissons has a bad odour. Miss Fen clicks her teeth. Miss Macintosh's slip shows.*

She stops outside Room 3. She re-rolls her ankle socks.

"Move along!" orders a dumpy woman, primitively moulded out of grey plasticine.

Pandora stares vengefully at the place where this person's neck should be: *Miss Warner has no neck, and no waist, and hardly any legs, and once when she was giving the strap her pants fell down to her ankles!*

In sum, *Miss Warner is Crabby.*

Room 3 is a beige square with windows down one side, blackboards along two others, and a cork bulletin-board across the fourth. A tasteful frieze of alphabetical letters holds the whole thing together. *At last somebody is going to teach me to read.*

Pandora hangs her khaki coat on the Girls' side of the cloakroom, concealing it under a pretty green one so no one will switch it to the Boys' side to tease her.

She re-rolls her socks.

She tries to see herself in the mirror on the door, but it has been tilted so that Miss Warner can spy on the cloakroom from various tricky angles and has nothing to do with primping.

A dozen boys and girls already hang about the periphery of Room 3, gazing at six rows of desks, bolted to the floor and chained to each other. If the first kid had taken a seat, the others would have. Now it requires an act of courage. Pandora is tempted, but she has already been bawled out twice. She fingers her drawstring pencilcase, trying to look as if she were deciding which seat is best: In fact, which seat *is* best? *By the windows? By the blackboards? At the front? At the back?* Pandora is shrewd enough to see the lures and pitfalls of each piece of real-estate, but not experienced enough to balance them off.

She remembers some of the kids from kindergarten, but none warmly enough to risk a snub by speaking first.

"What a super pencilcase! My uncle has a tie like that, only it's blue with a Spitfire!"

Pandora recognizes Ruth-Anne Somebody.

She beams with pride over her pencilcase, painted with a Hawker Hurricane. Then she notices Ruth-Anne's Jack-and-Jill pencilbox: It has *three* drawers!

The bell rings.

Miss Warner shuttles jointlessly to the front of the room, her body lumpy inside her grey suit, her shingled grey hair framing a face whose features all run pessimistically downhill.

She pauses amidst the trappings of office: an oak desk, with one drawer that locks for her purse and the strap; a dinted green-metal wastebasket; a walnut coatrack hung with a grey worsted coat and charcoal derby; a windowledge pencil-sharpener with the sign, "One at a time"; a Union Jack; a framed scroll reading, "One Flag, One King, One Fleet, One Empire," angled like the mirror to serve as auxiliary eyes; a wall map of the world, with Neilson's chocolate bars in every ocean; an erratic intercom wallphone with metal earmuffs.

Miss Warner prints her name on the board.

"Good morning, class," she says in a voice that knows it never could be.

There is a raggetty answering chorus.

Miss Warner taps her name with a metal-tipped pointer: "Good morning, *Miss War-ner*," she says, in a joyful, respectful, childish lisp.

"Good morning, *Miss War-ner*," replies the class, wisely accepting this second interpretation.

"Now then." Miss Warner returns to her own baleful thoughts and sounds. "I'll seat you in alphabetical order until I find out how smart you are." She points to the AaBbCcDd EeFf frieze. "Everyone stand under the letter that begins his, or her, last name, except those with physical handicaps. You stand under X."

No one stands under X. Miss Warner singles out Jessie Christie, with glasses as thick as Coke bottles, and Lillian Brill, with squint, and Bertie Brown who is too fat for all but the dum-dum seats. "Under the X, please. How can I help you if you won't help yourselves?"

Danny Lido doesn't know where his last name begins in the alphabet. He thinks L M N O is Elemeno, the way Pandora used to sing it in The Alphabet Song.

"If you don't know where you stand in the *alphabet*, perhaps you'd better stand in the corner," quips Miss Warner.

Danny turns around, and there is a patch the size of a toilet-seat on his brown breeches. Everyone laughs, but Miss Warner cracks her pointer on the chalk-trough. "You shouldn't laugh at people who are *poor*, as long as they are *clean*, but I won't put up with *dirtiness* in this classroom, and I most certainly will *not* tolerate anyone bringing *nits* in here!"

Everyone looks at everyone else: *Nits? Knits?* They eye Danny Lido: *What are gnits?*

Pandora is given the second seat in the second row, behind Jessie Christie, whom she doesn't like, and beside Ruth-Anne Baltimore, whom she does like. She runs her fingers over her desk's pitted chocolate surface, flipping its inkwell lids and learning, very quickly, how to poke up their glass-liners. She examines the art nouveau scrollwork at the sides of her desk, and rocks contentedly on her flip-up seat.

Pandora is given a fat licorice pencil, and a ruler with a metal edge for jabbing buck-toothed busybodies in the back, and — hola! — a shiny blue reader.

She dusts her desk with her "Lest We Forget" hanky, still fresh from having been forgotten all last year, and arranges her possessions inside: She is no longer a kindergarten squatter tossed by Fate from one baby chair to another. Pandora looks

— and feels — like what she is: a woman of property.

The noon bell rings.

Pandora flutter-kicks down one side of the hall, and up the other:

Miss Frisby eats peanuts. Miss Whimple has a dimple. Miss Horowitz has big . . . elbows.

Grannie Cragg is sick. She has rented out her cottage, and come to live in Adelaide's sewing-room. Pandora gathers stinging nettles for her from the mouldy leaves by the Pollywog Pond. Pandora sits by her spoolbed, and — with all the newest methodology at her tongue-tip — teaches her grannie to read. "Aaaaaaa . . . AAAA . . . You see, grannie, sometimes the vowels talk hard, and sometimes they talk soft. They're the generals, and the other letters can't say anything without them, not even a single syllable."

Grannie Cragg holds the blue primer in her gnarled hands. She squints at the Arrogant A, the Elegant E, the self-Important I, the Obdurate O, the Unctuous U, and all their hangers on, both upper and lower case.

"They wouldn'ta helped where I been, Chickee, and they aren't gonna help me where I'm going."

The book slips from grannie's dozy fingers . . . Grannie *Here Lies Sybil* Cragg is turning to parchment.

Twice a day the girls of Room 3 march, in more-or-less random two's, out to the Downstairs Girls' playground — upright, at a medium pace, inner hands joined, outer arms swinging, fingertip-distance fore and aft — as required by Recess Drill Section III, Subsection A, Clause i of the Laura Secord Public School Criminal Code. Since they have more-or-less become acquainted, they more-or-less play together, clustering around a girl with a tennis ball, or a skipping-rope and clamouring, "Choose me! Choose me! Please, can *I* play?"

Nobody ever chooses Lillian Brill, who is shy with squint, until Pandora, exercising power in the belief it is compassion, says, "Lillian Brill, we'll let you skip with us in the mornings, but you've got to be an ever-ender."

Lillian Brill, snuffling through tears of gratitude, donkey-hitches herself to the skip-rope and donkey-turns, in perpetuity.

It is a difficult situation to live with: Lillian Brill, so wretchedly thrilled to be included on any terms, reveals the playgroup for what it is: not an accidental assortment of care-free girls who like to skip, but a jostling selection of anxious girls in the process of forming a society. Lillian Brill wears nakedly on her face the fear of exclusion that the others are not prepared to acknowledge. When the girls of Room 3 skip, they turn their backs on Lillian Brill.

Cecily Battersea, with the confidence of ownership, speaks the collective resentment: "I don't want Lillian Brill turning the end of my rope. She gets it all sweaty."

Pandora accepts her responsibility: "Lillian Brill . . ." She twists the rope from Lily's fingers. "You won't be able to turn anymore. Georgia Brooks has hurt her leg, so she will be ever-ender today. You can't have two ever-enders — there wouldn't be any game."

The girls of Room 3 find ways of congratulating Pandora without ever acknowledging anything has happened.

Pandora earns 10 out of 10 on her first Honour Card. She receives perfect marks the next week, and the next: *So it is settled: I am smart like Adel-Ada.*

Miss Warner re-organizes the class, according to the now-official smartness rating. Pandora is assigned the seat by the door. This means she gets to close the door; to answer the door; to run messages unchaperoned through the halls; to collect the milk tickets. It is a position of considerable power and responsibility.

Pandora re-classifies: *Miss Warner is not Crabby. Miss Warner is Strict-but-Fair.*

It is two minutes to the final bell, but hardly anyone is seated: Most of Room 3 is in the cloakroom splitting two-ply kleenex.

Today is Thursday: Thursday is Health Day.

That means Miss Warner patrols the rows, checking to see that all of her pupils have handkerchiefs or kleenex; sniffing their breath; examining their fingernails; looking through their hair in her relentless search for germs and other vermin. If she finds anyone who is "unhealthy" she pastes a black germ-hand on his/her row for a week. Danny Lido has had dirty elbows *twice*. Miss Warner says, "Dirty Danny, if this happens again, I'm going to get the boys in your row to help clean you up!"

When Danny goes home to lunch, he is soaking wet, and crying, because Jessie Christie and two Big Boys have washed his head in the toilet.

"That's *mean*, Jessie Christie!" scolds Ruth-Anne Baltimore.

"You aren't even in his row," chides Pandora. She turns to Horace Ghostie and Godfrey Trumps: *"You* aren't even in our grade!"

"Dirty Danny has nits!" sniggers Jessie.

"Cooties, too!" says Horace.

"I squashed one!" says Godfrey. "It had *ten* legs!"

Ruth-Anne recoils: "Nits!"

Pandora recoils: "Cooties!"

Oh well. It is not necessary for poor children to be dirty.

Aunt Rosie has a dog.

He is an English bulldog, named Winston, with a khaki coat and a tin helmet, and sometimes they pose for War pictures together. When you show Winnie a Union Jack, he stands on his hindlegs and salutes, with his right paw, which is more than Phyllis Grove will do.

Phyllis Grove won't salute the flag. Miss Warner has put her in a dum-dum seat at the back of the room so she can go into the cloakroom while the other children are pledging allegiance. After school, Jessie Christie yells, "Tokyo Phyllis! Tokyo Phyllis!" and Lucy Ford, whose uncle lost his legs, says: "Spy! Rotten spy! My friend's aunt's bulldog is going to bite your bottom!" Meaning Pandora, and Aunt Rosie, and Winnie.

Phyllis Grove has slanty eyes. Pandora knows it's just because her mother pulls her braids too tight: *Phyllis Tokyo Rat-scum!*

*   *   *

The intercom wallbox clears its rusty throat, rids itself of a few electronic burps, and *buzzzzzzzz.* . . .

Miss Warner, holding the metal earmuffs at arm's length, hisses into the mouthpiece: "Yessssss?" There is a long, testy silence during which she is *not* tricked into putting on the earmuffs. "ATTEN-SHIIIIIIIUN!" blasts the voice of Col. Percival Burns through the earmuffs. "You shall proceed, division by division, in orderly fashion, to the auditorium, for one-hour-forty-minutes of School Spirit."

Miss Warner claps her hands three times. The pupils of Room 3 arise *flip flip flipping* their seats in noisy forgetfulness. They are ordered to reseat themselves. They rise again, in regulation silence, and set forth, two-by-two, into the streaming halls, behind Rooms 1 and 2, with the shortest in front of the tallest, and the girls in front of the boys, and each teacher leading her own contingent *hup! hup! hup!* beating 4/4 time on the hollow floors with the cuban heels of her black oxfords . . . leaving civilian life behind them.

The line turns left and down, into the basement, past the Boys' and Girls' washrooms, under a grid of steam-bleeding pipes, past the plaster cavern where Janitor Frank Foukes, twisted with shrapnel from The Great War, keeps the home fires burning.

"Compan-*eeeeeeee*, halt!"

Now each class proceeds separately, behind its teacher, through the auditorium door, under the buffalo head donated by the Odd Fellows.

"Eyes left!"

It passes the reviewing stand, draped in midnight velvet, donated by the Mill City Players' Guild.

"Eyes front!"

It files between rows of folding chairs, donated by the Home & School.

"At ease!"

All rooms are now in place.

Col. Percival Burns — his black brows knit in a V-for-Victory, his black hair polished like a pair of new boots — announces: "The Winner — Room 10!"

A well-ordered squeal arises from Miss Orpheus' room, which has just won the bronze plaque for the gaudiest display of discipline.

"The Losers — Room 8!"

A ragged groan arises from Miss Macintosh's room which has just won two weeks' drill-practice.

Col. Burns gestures for silence.

Sydney Goodfellow marches on stage, from the right, in his Cub Scout uniform. Fat Flora Thwaite, the minister's daughter, marches on stage, from the left, in her Brownie uniform. Sydney and Flora pinch the upper-outer corners of the Union Jack (donated by the IODE) and the Red Ensign (provided, before last election, by the provincial government). Each sidles three paces inward. The flags unfurl.

Sydney and Flora snap a salute.

The student body snaps a salute.

"I pledge allegiance. . . ."

Miss Orpheus pitchpipes a G: *"God Save Our. . . ."*

Sydney and Flora retire from the platform.

A slight, button-nosed man in clerical collar takes their place. He folds his white-kid hands across his chest: *"Our Fatherrrrr, which arrrt in Heaven. . . ."*

Rev. Thwaite fixes his audience with fierce, pale eyes. "How many here are Papists?" There is an uneasy silence, while the students suspiciously eye one another.

Rev. Thwaite, ever-resourceful, rephrases his question: "How many here are of the Roman Catholic persuasion?"

Now several dozen hands poke uncertainly upward.

Rev. Thwaite's reassuring smile takes in both the self-confessed and their now-hostile witnesses: "We are *all* Chrrrrrristians here," he says, resmoothing the waters he has just troubled.

Rev. Thwaite moulds his hands into the finger-bristling gesture that means he is going to be Contemporary Controversial. He delivers a brief work of Ecumenism entitled "What matters if they kiss the rrrrrring?" carefully holy-rollering his r's to comfort the conservative.

Col. Burns clasps the slender neck of the microphone.

"It is my proud duty to announce the winner of last week's Basket Drive. . . . Keep up the good work, *Room 7!*

"It is my proud duty to announce our Red Cross Thermometer is almost over the top. . . . $1.27 more and we'll have a gusher!"

Col. Burns lashes the microphone cord around his ankle. "And now, for a few *less pleasant* observations.

"Once more, I am informed that certain unruly elements are walking over the lawns of private citizens on their way to and from school. This has got to cease.

"Once more, I am forced to announce that the noise level on the playground during the recess allotment has gone beyond the level of tolerance. This has got to cease.

"Once more, I must remind all students that no one is allowed in this building before or between classes, except by written permission, including the use of washroom facilities. This has got to cease.

"Once more . . . Once more . . . Cease! . . . Cease! . . ."

Miss LaStrobe's class recites the Beatitudes, Matthew 5:1-12, responsively with Miss Sissons' class.

Miss Frisby's class sings D'ye Ken John Peel in three parts.

Rev. Thwaite moulds his hands across his chest in Traditional Incontestable: "May the Lorrrd watch between Thee and me . . ." adding the occasional "verrrily, verrily" for no other reason than to plump up his part.

The pupils march back to class — two-by-two, with the boys preceding the girls, the taller preceding the shorter, and each teacher bringing up the rear *hup! hup! hup!* with her cuban heels marking 4/4 time through the hallowed halls.

The line turns up the basement stairs. Miss Sissons, from Room 9, is standing overhead on the first landing. Pandora, in her first independent act of the morning, risks a peek, from the military ranks, up Miss Sissons' skirt. She is rewarded by a flash of navy-blue bloomer. She alerts Georgia Brooks, who alerts Ruth-Anne Baltimore, who alerts Jill Peters. Room 3, heads now held blissfully high, giggle-hups up the stairs. Pandora trips. There is a dreadful pileup. The whole line has to halt, right down to Miss Brinks, of Room 1, just coming out from under the Odd Fellows' buffalo head.

Pandora is trampled.

Miss Warner prints "OW" on the board. "What sound do these two letters make?"

No one raises a hand.

"Pandora. . . . What would you say if you stuck your finger in the O, and got it caught there?"

Pandora thinks of the time the plumber had to saw her finger out of the hot-water tap. She stands up on the right side of her desk, which is for answering questions: "OOOO-OOwwwwwww!" she wails.

"That's right," says Miss Warner. She raises both hands like a conductor. "All together, class, please."

"OOOOOOwwwwwwwwww!" wails Room 3 from the right side of its desks.

"Again, please."

"OOOOOOOOOOwwwwwwwwwww!"

Pandora sits by the rope-lashed spoolbed: "OOOOO-wwwwww," she wails to the arid head on the pillow. "Altogether now, please."

"Ahhhhhhooooowwwwwa," sighs Grannie Cragg.

"OOOOOOOOOOwwwwwwwww," prompts Pandora.

"Ahhhhhhooooowwwwwa," moans Grannie Cragg.

Pandora puts her ear to Grannie Cragg's sour mouth: She can hear the vowels rustling like locusts in her throat. *The more letters that Grannie Cragg swallows, the dryer she seems to get!*

Miss Warner's oxfords recede *sluffetty sluff sluff sluff* down the hall. Miss Orpheus' impeccable spikes advance *click click click.*

Miss Orpheus — youthful, vibrant, slim as a flute — explodes through the door of Room 3. With her mouth in a perfect whole note, she sings, "DOOOOOOOOOOH!" biting off the end so sharply the class pitches forward into the vacuum.

Miss Orpheus taps her baton.

With teeth, and blank spaces, barred like the keyboard of a grand piano, Room 3 replies: "MEEEEEEEeeeeee!"

Miss Orpheus: "SOOOOOOOOOH!"

Room 3: "DOOOOooooooh!"

"That's the spirit, boys and girls. Now, do the whole scale, and when you get to the top, hold it. Let the music pour out. Let the sound tickle your tympanum! Let your skull s-w-ell till it feels like the dome of St. Peter's!"

Miss Orpheus blasts Middle C on her pitchpipe.

Room 3 lays waste the scale.

"That's the spirit, boys and girls! Now . . . a deep breath. Again, please!"

Miss Orpheus tramps the aisles, her staccato heels beating as efficiently as any metronome. She freezes. She frowns. She lays a cupped ear alongside Jessie Christie's mouth. Then Lillian Brill's mouth. Then Cecily Battersea's mouth. Then Flora Thwaite's mouth. "Aha! *You* there girl! Up on your feet, Miss Bullfrog!"

Flora Thwaite stumbles to her feet and, you know, with her fat belly, dirty white sweater, green blazer and bulging eyes, *Fat Flora actually looks like a bullfrog*! The class bursts into startled laughter. Miss Orpheus — fresh from pedagogy school — lets it go on long enough to prove she, too, can take a joke, then taps her baton for silence. "Let's be constructive, boys and girls! Let's help Miss Bullfrog turn into Miss Canary."

She blasts her pitchpipe.

"I want you to solo on White Coral Bells. Got the note?"

Fat Flora opens her mouth: No sound.

She tries again: No sound.

"You're holding your diaphragm too tight. Here, open your jacket."

Flora clutches the blazer she wears to hide her fatness.

"Don't be shy, girl!" Miss Orpheus' sensitive artist's fingers probe Flora's fat coils. "Ahhhh . . . *here* we are!" She raps Flora's diaphragm. "Relax!" Flora's belly heaves out in a gassy rush of air. The class titters. "Steady, boys and girls. Let's concentrate on being helpful."

Miss Orpheus blasts her pitchpipe.

This time Flora makes it as far as "upon a slender stalk" before breaking down.

"*Now*, you're relaxing too much. You're flapping like a sheet on the washline. Let's take it again, my girl, and this time let's *both* of us try!"

Again.

"That's a little better."

Again.

"You're losing it, I'm afraid."

Again.

"Come on, Miss Bullfrog, lift those notes. *Again!*"

Room 3 ripples with silent hysteria: Fear, embarrassment, shame, mingle with the high-tension pitchpipe notes *quivering, quivering, quivering*, against the windows like supersonic sound trapped in crystal, leaping from nerve-ending to nerve-ending, tightening, twisting, tuning the cords of each nervous system into an instrument of unbearable sensitivity.

"Oh dear!" sighs Miss Orpheus, in discouragement. "Hop back to one of the listener's lilypads at the back of the room, and we'll have another go at it next day."

The word "hop" is most unfortunate: Fat Flora has been so transmogrified by Miss Orpheus' persistent frog imagery that she squats, quite miserably, quite literally, on her heavy haunches, dirty-white belly thrust through green blazer, and she hops *plop! plop! plop!* down the aisle in search of a lilypad.

Room 3 gasps.

"Gar-ump! Gar-ump!" croaks Jessie Christie.

Room 3 explodes.

Pandora jams her head in her desk. Ruth-Anne stuffs her mouth with a hanky. Lily Brill screams.

"Order!" commands the panicky Miss Orpheus. *"Order,* children, *please."*

It is much too late. *"Garump! Garump! Garump!"* intones Jessie Christie, rhythmically stamping his feet. *"Garump! Garump! Garump!"* intone a dozen others.

Fat Flora flees the room, down, down, down to the basement.

The recess bell rings.

The pupils of Room 3 lurch, lunge down the steps after her: They are sick all over the washroom floors.

Miss Orpheus is mortified. "I don't know how it happened. They just seemed to get away from me. I guess I'm just too easy on them. I do so want them to enjoy the music!"

"There are tricks to every trade," nods Miss Warner, not unkindly. She opens her speller at page 3, and prepares to weave a few enchantments of her own.

*　　*　　*

Pandora can read: In fact, she does it so well she no longer needs the letters. She recites Fun with Dick and Jane instead of her prayers. She hums it at the supper table as she mashes her turnips and plants rows of peas.

My name is Dick.
I have a dog.
See, see, see my dog.
Look, see my dog.
His name is Spot. Run, Spot, run. Run, run, run.
My name is Jane.
I have a cat.
See, see, see my cat.

Her name is Puff. Run, Puff, run. Run, run, run.
Who is this?
It is my father!
See, see, see my father.
Hear him yell.
Hear him yell, yell, yell.
Run, mother, run.
Run, run, run.
Run, Adel, run.
Run, run, run.
Run, Ada, run.
Run, run, run.
Yell, run, yell.
"Pandora!"
Sit, sit, sit.
"Pandora, I'm talking to you!"
Sit, sit, sit.
"If you feed that cat once more under the table I'll . . ."
. . . cut him up for meat, meat, meat.
"You think I'm fooling?"
Run, Puss, run.
"PANDORA!"

Lyle Gothic smashes his fist down on the yellow oilcloth.
Dishes clatter. Milk spills. "Sit up, *you*, do you hear? Sit up
and EAT!" He whips the air with his tinfork. "Do you have
any idea what it costs to feed you for a week, eh? *PAN-
DORA*!!! Sit up and *EAT!*"

Two fists smash down on the table. Dishes clatter. Milk
spills.

Pandora finds her left fist in her Tranquillity Rose turnip
garden, and her right one in her lemon jello.

"I want dessert!" she screams at her mother. "I want Kre-Mel
Caramel Dessert!"

Lyle Gothic's face white-bloats. He swipes Pandora from
the table with his hook. He staggers backward over Charlie-
puss' tail. Charlie rises, howling, to the ceiling.

"God-damned . . . I'll kill that . . . I swear I'll kill . . . *kill.* . . ."

Pandora rocks on her haunches, in the cellar-closet, amidst the crumpled cottons of summer, with her rump planted in a pot of hyacinth bulbs, and she recites all of A Doll for Jane, What Sally Saw, and Puff Wants to Play, not forgetting the periods and the commas.

"Now, class, you've heard the story. Take out your exercise books and answer these questions."

    1. *Why wouldn't Pandora eat her supper?*
        A. *Not hungry.*
        B. *Doesn't like vegetables.*
        C. *Needed it for her turnip garden.*
        D. *Was saving it for the starving War Orphans.*
    2. *What did her father say he would do to Puss?*
        A. *Feed him meat.*
        B. *Cut him into meat, meat, meat.*
        C. *Give him Kre-Mel Caramel for dessert. . . .*

The closet door opens.

Charlie-puss is shoved inside.

The closet door closes.

Pandora strokes Charlie-puss from the points of his ears to the end of his tail, not forgetting the proud lonely hair at the tip. *Charlie fills his skin, and he is happy in there.* Pandora strokes her hair, her face, her chest. She tries to find herself in her skin. *Sometimes I am so big I burst my head. Sometimes I am so small I rattle in the end of my big toe. I wish I could get out of my skin. My mother gets out through her mouth. She slides out on her treble clef when nobody is looking. My father explodes his skin. He splatters everyone with hot skin, and then he grows another. My father sucks in all the air in the room, and everyone else has to squash themselves against the wall, and rub off their noses so as not to prick him!*

Pandora feels her father in the closet. She feels him sucking the air from her lungs. She feels him pressing against her chest, like a big black boot. Pandora stuffs her mouth with hyacinth bulbs, and she would surely have choked if Puss had not reached out a reassuring paw from his nest in her mother's galoshes.

"Ho, ho, ho!" laughs Puss, fixing the Giant boot with one green eye. "That is very good, but then, it is no trick at all for you to make yourself into a big black boot, or a pink dragon, or a white elephant, since you are so big anyway. Why don't you try something tiny, like a mouse, or is that too difficult for you?"

"Fee fie foe fum!" thunders the indignant Giant, and, waving his steel wand, he turns — presto! — into a bald mouse.

Before you can say Kre-Mel Caramel, Puss-in-Galoshes is onto him, and he gobbles him down, every bit, except for the Giant's steel wand, which he uses, happily ever after, as a toothpick.

(TO BE CONTINUED)

* * *

"What a friend we have in Jesus,
   All our griefs and pains to bear. . . ."

Every Sunday, Pandora has to go to St. James Sunday School, with fat Flora Thwaite, the minister's daughter, and her mother Elsie, who sticks pictures of Bible people on a flannelgraph board, and curses out Adam and Eve, and Lot's salt wife, and Cain, and Jacob in the name of God. Then she makes a church steeple with her hands, the way Rev. Thwaite always does when he is about to pass the plate for the mortgage, and they sing Dropping, Dropping, Hear the Pennies Fall, with Mrs. Thwaite playing the piano, with the tune different than at any other Sunday School because Mrs. Thwaite has two fingers missing on her soprano hand and she just leaves those notes out. Pandora found *that* out when Arlene, who has perfect pitch, went with her, and laughed and laughed and laughed.

On Tuesdays — though not so regularly — Pandora has to go to Mrs. Penfield's house with Adel-Ada. Mrs. Penfield is as stout as a battleship papered in cabbage roses, with hanging chins, and a knot of auburn hair, stuck through with an amber hatpin.

Mrs. Penfield stands in her living-room, with its clutter of dainty, tinkling things, and she holds up a brass tray, with a teacosy on top, and she lifts the teacosy to reveal a crystal bottle containing something red and slithery. "What is this?"

Adel-Ada reply in unison: "It's a piece of liver, Mrs. Penfield."

She lifts another teacosy to reveal a peanutbutter jar containing a rubbery white hunk. "What is this?"

Pandora says: "It's a piece of liver, Mrs. Penfield."

Mrs. Penfield points to the crystal bottle. "Why is this piece of liver soft and red?"

Adel-Ada say: "Because it's in water, Mrs. Penfield."

Mrs. Penfield points to the peanutbutter jar. "Why is *that* piece of liver so hard and white?"

Pandora says: "Because it's in alcohol, Mrs. Penfield."

Mrs. Penfield lays a pudgy finger alongside the jar with the white liver. "*This* is what happens to the liver of people who take Alcoholic Beverage."

Mrs. Penfield embraces the bottle with the gooey red liver. "But *this* — this is *your* liver, *yours* and *mine*, just as fresh and sweet as the day the Good Lord made it!"

She turns to Pandora: "Name the Five Senses that are destroyed by the taking of Alcoholic Beverage."

Pandora sticks her finger into her eye: "The sense of sight." She holds her nose: "The sense of smell." She tugs her earlobes: "The sense of ears." She snaps her fingers: "The sense of touch." She sticks out her tongue: "The thenthe of tathte."

"Now then. . . ." Mrs. Penfield fixes Pandora with baleful solemnity. "If you, Pandora — God forgive! — should ever Take to Drink, what else would you be in danger of losing?"

Pandora grimaces: She *knows* the word, but it is the longest she has ever had to say, and she has trouble getting her tongue around it. "I might lose my . . . my . . . eeee-kwa-lib-reee-um!"

"Yes," says Mrs. Penfield. "Your equilibrium. When you see a man stumble, you know that he has already *fallen*. You know that he has been taking Alcoholic Beverage." She smiles around her little group with grim compassion. "When you see such a man, you should never mock him. The Evil is *not* in the man. The Evil is with the Devil, in the bottle."

One Tuesday, Mrs. Penfield passed out pink cards engraved in gold. "I want you children to study this card, and if you think, with God's help, you can live up to this pledge, I'd like you to sign it."

Pandora reads:

> "God helping me, I promise,
> Not to buy, drink, sell, or give,
> Alcoholic Liquors, while I live.
> From all Tobaccos, I'll abstain,
> And never take God's Name in Vain."

Pandora is positive about the Liquor, *almost* positive about the Tobacco, but she is not so sure about God's Name in Vain, which she suspects has just been dropped in to get the rhyme.

Adel signs.

Ada signs.

Pandora does not want to disappoint Mrs. Penfield.

pandora

In His Service

Mrs. Penfield — beaming — collects the cards. "Adel! Ada! Pandora! You have made a promise to God, and now I shall make a promise to you: As sure as the Lord made sweet milk, and the sun to shine, if you don't ever take that *first* drink you will never, never, become an Alcoholic." She closes her eyes. "Let us pray for strength to resist Temptation for the week to come. Then we shall have chocolate cake."

Since then, Pandora has signed two pledge renewals — one in robin's egg blue and one in mint green.

Mrs. Penfield has a parrot named Polly who can recite the Lord's Prayer. *St. Paully wants a wafer!*

Jessie Christie, Horace Ghostie, Godfrey Trumps buffet Dirty Danny across the slushy playground. They force-march him across Baltic Avenue to the vacant lot behind the Mill City Works Department.

Jessie shoves Danny into a snowbank: "Dirty wop!" He washes his face with soot and snow. "Wop-coward!" He makes Danny eat a picture of Mussolini.

Horace Ghostie packs Danny's leather helmet with slush, then puts it back on his head. Godfrey packs his frayed pockets with snow. Danny is crying. Godfrey jams his mouth with frozen coal.

Jessie pinions Danny's arms. Horace unbuttons his breeches. Godfrey stuffs them with dog-poop and snow.

They drag Dirty Danny to a telephone pole. They tie him to the pole with his red scarf. Jessie Christie puts his hand-prints in the snow. He blackens them with cinders.

Pandora sees Dirty Danny tied to the pole. She recognizes him, from behind, by his red scarf, which is the only decent thing he owns. She sees the black germ-hands, and she knows: *That's MEAN, Jessie Christie! Dirty Danny isn't even dirty. He scrubs himself raw, so he won't get his face washed in the toilet with poop in it. His elbows aren't dirty. They're just purpley-brown and chapped, like some of the rest of his skin.*

Dirty Danny can't see Pandora: Raw clots of suffering wretch, like vomit, from his throat. They curdle in Pandora's stomach. She clamps her hands over her mouth to keep from being sick.

Pandora can't bear to approach the telephone pole. She doesn't want to risk getting pieces of Dirty Danny's humiliation stuck all over her. She can't bear the intimacy of Dirty Danny's trembling gratitude.

Pandora's feet freeze, so close to the germ-hands that if she bent over they would be her own. *My mother wants me home early today. . . . Dirty Danny isn't even in my row!*

* * *

Pandora slides over the linoleum on her rump, dusting legs, and no mean task, when you consider there are eight under the table, and eight more under the buffet, and four more under the cabinet, and twenty-four under the chairs, *all twisted into knobs, and held together by crossbars.* Adel is dusting tops — under the doilies instead of around them, and then up along the platerack. Ada is setting out widowed saucers for ashtrays, and draping doilies over the worn spots in the chesterfield. Adelaide is laying out silverplate on the lame-legged cardtable in the kitchen. Adelaide's cheeks are flushed with pleasure, her forehead is puckered with concern: The Duchess of Gloucester Chapter of the Mill City Home Front Auxilliary is coming to sew ditty bags for Canadian soldiers expatriated by War.

"Mother!" squeals Adel from her guard position at the right of the living-room sheers. "They're coming!"

"Mother!" squeals Ada from her guard position at the left of the living-room sheers. "They're here!"

The Duchess ladies file in — in two's and three's and then in a bunch — bringing the world to No. 13 Oriental Avenue.

Pandora shivers in the draughty hall as they unlace velvet galoshes; remove taffeta shoe-protectors; straighten lyle/crepe/silk seams; hitch at garters and girdles; polish steamy glasses, swab drippy noses, stuff lacy hankies down/up bosoms/sleeves; primp hair, pat powder, dab lipstick, dot rouge; adjust their V/round/square/sweetheart necklines; smooth their draped/pleated/tucked/gathered/gored skirts; tug at their peplums, square their shoulder pads, refasten their brooches, and greet each other in the living-room as if they hadn't just shared the same dressing-room facilities.

Pandora staggers upstairs under armloads of coats, hats, gloves. She buries her face in the glossy fur, and sniffs the sophisticated powder perfume of the satin linings. Occasionally, she puts on a funny hat, but that is just for ease of carrying: Pandora is too well-schooled in the sanctity of private property to actually try anything on.

Pandora returns to the living-room, already twanging with high-decibel conversation, and she sits down on a hassock in a position to be noticed. Pandora always does very well with strangers: The Duchess ladies, in particular, play with her curls, and flatter her outrageously. Pandora, for her part, blushes, stammers, and even, on one occasion, hid behind her mother's skirt, so shy was she in the presence of all that flattery. Pandora is almost sincere. After years of playing the "heavy" she is overwhelmed by the novelty of being treated as a polite little girl whose goodness is assumed. She resents the skepticism with which her mother and sisters greet the blossoming of this modest little charmer. Whenever possible, for old-time's sake, she sticks her tongue out at Adel-Ada.

But ... Pandora has now gone through all ten verses of Lord Randal, all fifteen verses of Lord Randal's Daughter, and she has sung Little Children are the Jew-els three times, the last time without being begged. The Duchess of Gloucester ladies are becoming restless.

Mrs. Brownley takes her regent's chair. "Now then, girls, let's get down to brass tacks." She shoots a brisk look at Pandora, who jumps off her hassock and runs away.

Not far.

She settles in the kitchen, ear glued to the heat vent. This, like so much of the romance of spying, is pure gimcrackery: Pandora could hear the ladies, working their high registers, almost any place in the house. *The problem*, as a grumbling Lyle is quick to point out, *is not to.*

"The November meeting of the Duchess of Gloucester Chapter of the Mill City Home Front Auxilliary came to order sharp at 7:03 p.m., EST, with Mrs. J. F. Brownley presiding. It was moved by Mrs. K. S. Gallsworthy, and seconded by Mrs. L. H. Storey, that our Comfort Box Euchre Night had been a gala success, with proceeds of $16.23 to go for Comfort Boxes for Our Fighting Men. Our Comfort Box Committee, spearheaded by Mrs. J. C. Winston, our War Convenor, decided that each Comfort Box should contain: one shaving brush, three razor blades, one package of cigarettes, one chocolate bar, ten toothpicks, three pipe cleaners, and a Sunshine poem penned by Mrs. O. Groat, our own Poet Laureate, on behalf of the Duchess of Gloucester Ladies. It was further moved by Mrs. K. S. Gallsworthy, and seconded by Mrs. L. H. Storey, that a note of thanks be penned to the Cheerio Glee Club for their part in our gala Comfort Box Euchre Night, and that a round of prolonged applause be given to our hard-working Comfort Box Euchre Night Convenor. Carried and executed.

"Mrs. N. P. R. Thackery, our Wool Convenor, informed the ladies that there was still some unclaimed wool in the Wool Box. She also complained that some of the squares she had received were not square, and she reminded the ladies that a proper afghan component should be thirty-seven stitches down and thirty-seven stitches across, with eight-inch ends for joining. 'Now don't be proud, ladies!' Mrs. Thackery warned us jocularly. 'Use your glasses if you need them!'

"In response to the pleas of Mrs. R. W. Wayne, conscientious editor of our Patriotic Patter, Mrs. S. Lawrence agreed to submit seven of her favourite Meatless Recipes, including her prize-winning Leek Casserole. Mrs. T. Young, our Avon representative, was prevailed upon to draw up a list of DO's and DON'T's for Cosmetic Conservation.

"A suggestion by Mrs. L. Gothic that we send flowers to a Mrs. ??? Niobe, a neighbour of some of the ladies present, on the recently reported loss of her son, was carried, with a vote of sympathy.

"Mrs. W. W. Thoreau reminded the ladies it is not too early to start planning our Spring Violet Luncheon.

"Mrs. D. C. Dickens, our Coffee Convenor, suggested that in future we 'stretch' our coffee, served at fund-raising events, as part of an intensified War Effort. She stated that her Coffee-Stretching Fact-Finding Committee has found in a report, now in her hands, that double-dripping increases yield by only thirty percent, whereas one-half ounce of chicory added to one pound of coffee will produce one-third more brew while altering the taste only slightly. She further suggested that BYOS, meaning 'Bring Your Own Sugar,' be added to the bottom of invitations as was currently fashionable with trousseau teas. Mrs. W. W. Thoreau wondered how this would affect the sale of tickets for our Spring Violet Luncheon. Mrs. D. C. Dickens replied that we couldn't concern ourselves with people so selfish as to stay home because of a little chicory when there was a principle at stake. Mrs. K. S. Gallsworthy wondered about the rumours she had heard about chicory staining the teeth. Mrs. Thackery said she didn't think it fair to members of the public, all of whom had paid the same price, to stretch the coffee and not the tea. Mrs. Gallsworthy thought the suggestions re Bring Your Own Sugar went well beyond the jurisdiction of the Coffee-Stretching Fact-Finding Committee. Mrs. R. T. Fitzgerald said that, although she had the greatest respect for the Committee, she didn't think it fair for it to be chaired by someone who neither drinks coffee nor uses sugar in her tea. Mrs. D. C. Dickens arose to defend her position as a neutral. . . ."

"Ladies, ladies!" exclaims Mrs. Brownley, as the printed dispute bubbles heatedly off the page. "I see once more we have stubbed our toe on the rock of controversy. Let us get down to brass tacks and settle this once and for all. . . ."

The ladies sit, paper-napkins afloat on flowered laps, little fingers hooked out from unadulterated teacups, talking, talking, talking with sugar on their rosebud lips.

Pandora and Adel-Ada pass among them: *Tea? coffee? milk?*

"The girls they hire nowadays are beyond belief. Ned says they just sit at their desks, putting on nailpolish. Half of them don't even know how to type."

"It's their boyfriends that bring up my gorge. How anyone could be seen on the street with those zoot-suiters is beyond me! They should pack the whole kit-and-kaboodle off to France!"

"Now, Effie, I think the kids today are kinda cute. They got more gumption than we had."

"Gumption?! That's what they *don't* have. They've had things too good. It's The War. It breaks down moral fibre."

Hands flutter like plump hens over brownies and fudge-cake.

"Oh, dear, I shouldn't. . . ."

"Don't mind if I do. . . ."

"If you insist. . . ."

"*You* don't have to worry, Edna. You eat like a *bird*!"

Pandora stands at Mrs. Thwaite's elbow with the sugar bowl.

"If you ask me, it's the working mothers that are going to be the big postwar problem," says Mrs. Thwaite, reaching for a spoon. "You see those factory girls lounging against the bus-stop, lunchpail in one hand and a cigarette in the other. As Virgil said just last week at his Fireside Sermonette, 'When femininity goes, the home goes.' Rev. Thwaite and I have always been liberal — *too* liberal as some would say — but when I see — " Elsie Thwaite sees Pandora straining forward with greater intensity than she has ever shown at her Sunday flannelgraph lessons. She breaks off. She purses her lips. . . .

Adelaide twists the sugarbowl from Pandora's helping hands. She marches her to the stairs. "Bed. And no hanky-panky."

"*Ahhhh.* . . ." Pandora flounces up the steps, stuffing her mouth with various meringues, macaroons, peanutbutter cookies hidden about her person, and speaking wickedly in tongues, with her mouth full: "Oh, dear, I shouldn't. . . ." "Don't mind if I do. . . ." "If you *insist*. . . ." "*You* don't have to worry, Edna. You eat like a *bird!*"

Now that she is no longer a part of the Duchess ladies' conversation, it gives Pandora a headache: What started at the bottom of the steps as a broad-beamed yammering, has narrowed to a high-pitched whine that pierces Pandora's temples like a hot wire. . . .

It is well after midnight when the other sound starts — a thick reverberation that roils up through the floorboards. It pitches Pandora's bed: *AAAyyyyyyyy*. It rattles the frosty windows: *EEEeeeee*. It moans through the cubbyholes: *OOoo-hhhhhoooo*.

It is coming from Grannie Cragg's room.

It *is* Grannie Cragg.

She is vomiting up the vowels: *AAaaayyeeeeeiiiioooo-uuuuuuu*. . . .

Pandora hears them collect on the landing below: *All* the letters, upper and lower case, with the shorter in front of the taller, and the vowels in front of the consonants.

She hears them climb the steps *hup! hup! hup!*

She hears them cross the floor *hup! hup! hup!*

She sees them tramp her bedclothes *hup! hup! hup!* She feels them stamp her chest. . . . 'A' is wearing cleat-boots. 'O' is carrying a rope. O *is* a rope. He is Cecily Battersea's skipping-rope, twisted into a hangman's noose.

O coils around Pandora's neck. 'I' twists the rope.

"U can't play with this rope," he says. "U get the ends all bloody!"

Pandora hides her face under the covers: "Dear God/Jesus/Holy Ghost . . . I helped my mother tonight. I . . . uh . . . I gave Arlene a piece of yellow chalk. . . ."

'I,' smiling, tightens the rope.

"God Bless Mother! Father! Adel! Ada!" Pandora twists her bedsheet into a string of wet beads. "God Bless Grannie Cragg and Other Grandma and Aunt Rosalind and Aunt Estelle, and Arlene and all the starving War Orphans and all the soldiers bleeding in The War, and . . ." Pandora has run out of bed-sheet. She barters her future: "I won't complain about wearing braids. I won't complain about wearing brown stockings. I promise to . . ."

O yanks Pandora, by the neck, from her bed.

The Nasty Vowels grab Pandora's golden curls. The Nazi Vowels shave her head. The Vowel Nazis drag her *bump! bump! bump!* down the attic steps, and *hup! hup! hup!* out into the snow. The Foul Nazis strip off her nightie, with their black germ-hands. They force her, naked, against a telephone pole.

"It wasn't *my* fault," sobs Pandora.

O has turned into Dirty Danny's red scarf. He ties Pandora to the telephone pole, with enough of himself left over to spell I.O.U. in red, across the snow.

Now U is a horseshoe. U slashes Pandora with his whip.

Pandora's skin falls in red strips from her bones. She screams. U scolds: "Don't be such a baby." U stuffs her mouth with Baker's bitter-Blue chocolate. "I'm just tickling U."

The corners of U's mouth droop in sorrow. U turns into a bristly moustache. U kisses Pandora. U clings to Pandora's lips. U turns into a black caterpillar. Pandora vomits fear and bitter-Blue chocolate.

U drags Pandora *clippetty-clop* across a field of bread-dough studded with pools of blood that pretend to be cherry tarts. A pair of Black Hands graciously beckons them toward a black car parked at Pandora's house. *It is the Stintons' deathcar!* The windows are slatted like the sides of an animal-slaughter car. The headlights weep. The bumper moans with the cries of the doomed and the dying.

The Black Hands force Pandora into the deathcar. It is packed with other girls, all with shaved heads. The stink of fear, as the car lunges through the night, forces everyone on the sidewalk to bury their heads in their armpits.

The deathcar stops, and unloads, at the Downstairs Boys' playground. Pandora is shoved *bump! bump! bump!* down a stairwell, and force-marched *hup! hup! hup!* through steam-bleeding pipes to a cavern. The sign overhead says BATHS, but Pandora knows it is the Boys' washroom. "*I'm* not dirty!" she shrieks. "It's not *me*. It's Dirty Danny!"

The Black Hands give Pandora a cake of coal and a paper towel. The Kindergarten Rhythm Band is playing great tunes from The Great War, such as Pack Up Your Troubles in Your Old Kit Bag, and We'll Meet Again, Pussycat. Pandora recognizes herself, as her younger self, playing flute in the third row. They wave to each other as she is shoved, with a thousand others, through the washroom door.

The door is shut, bolted, sealed. The Black Hands push Pandora toward one of the toilet bowls. "Nooooo!" she howls. Then she sees it has been planted with pretty flowers. Too late, she smells *mothballs*! Her mouth prickles. Her tongue burns. Too late, she recognizes the tricky foxglove, the sly monk's hood, the destroying angel. Her tongue is a hot red pepper. It bleeds fire. Water is available: It has Jessie Christie's poop in it.

Fire scorches Pandora's lungs. She hacks her way, through retching bodies, to the ventilator shaft. "ATTTTTEN-SHIUN!" shouts the black grating. "You shall proceed, in orderly fashion, to the auditorium for one-hour-forty-minutes of School Spirit."

Pandora's lungs explode. There is a reek, like when her mother pulls the guts out of a chicken. Her eyes bleed, then pop, first the right because it is five minutes older. She is part of a mass of melting flesh and crumbling bone that is stamped-ing toward the metal door. Bodies hurl themselves against the door, but not always the right head with the right body, or the appropriate arms with the appropriate legs. They pile against the door in a clammy red pyramid, with the bits and pieces clawing and shrieking, even in death! "I'm here first. Who let you in?"

Pandora, of course, has made it to the top of the blood pyra-mid. A smashed face, under what she believes to be her foot, moans: "You'd eat your own grandmother if she were choco-late!"

Two blank Daddy Warbucks eyes stare at Pandora through the slot in the metal door. "If only you had been grateful. . . ."

The eyes are attached to a grappling hook. It daintily spears Pandora. It tosses her into Mr. Foukes' fiery furnace, rifling her teeth, en route, for lead fillings, which it swallows in a goat's bladder. The grappling hook straightens itself out as best it can: "HEIL HITLER!"

Pandora awakens.

She is shell-shocked, but she doesn't know why: The images of her dream have bleached from her mind like nightmare film exposed to sunlight.

Pandora can hear Grannie Cragg snore-groaning in the room below. She feels shame, guilt, horror. They congeal into a single emotion: foreboding. . . .

Pandora can't shake her sense of foreboding: It settles in a cold, white egg in the pit of her stomach. At noon, she is afraid to go home from school. She buries her head in her desk, but Miss Macintosh, who teaches Grade 2, sees the legs hanging from the desk without a head, and she says, "Hadn't you better go for lunch, little ostrich? It's not so good to get black marks against your name at Christmastime."

Pandora trudges home, across Baltic Avenue, across the railway tracks, hopping on peoples' lawns when she can't be sure where the cracks are.

Pandora stops behind the board fence around the Cripples' Home. She is afraid to go around the corner. She sits in the slush, being careful not to break the cold white ostrich egg inside her. She takes off the rainbow mitts her mother knit out of leftover bits of wool, and she closes her green-tea eyes, and she pushes her eyeballs around in her head so she can see inside her thoughts and know why she is afraid.

It is hopeless, hopeless. *I cannot see in the dark.*

Pandora puts on her rainbow mitts, and she creeps around the board fence.

She stops.

A half dozen neighbours stand around her front steps, staring the way children stare when a new person is moving into the neighbourhood or an old person is moving out. A black car, with venetian blinds, is parked at the curb.

It is the Stintons' deathcar.

"Graaaaaaaaaaaaa-*neeeeeeeeeeeeeeee!*" Pandora runs across the street as two white men carry a stiff white cocoon down her front steps, with her mother behind, crying.

Mrs. Lawrence sees Pandora. She runs toward her, her meringue hair whipped into stiff peaks. She covers Pandora's face with her apron. "No, dear. Come home with me."

The holly wreath on Pandora's frontdoor has been exchanged for a black-crepe one. The pinetree has been stripped of its tinsel and thrown, one week early, into the trash can: Santa Claus does not visit the same house as the Angel of Death.

Grannie Cragg is in the living-room, where the piano used to be, in a pink-satin bed heaped with red and yellow and white and blue flowers.

My grannie doesn't like flowers. My grannie likes WEEDS!

Pandora draws herself up the side of the coffin. Her grannie is wearing a lavender dress fastened with a blue cameo. Pandora has never seen her grannie in anything but brown, black, green. . . .

They wrapped my grannie in a white cocoon, and she has come out a lilac butterfly!

Grannie Cragg's face is the colour of parchment. Her eyes are like marbles sunk in whirlpools of flesh. She looks very old and very mysterious. *My grannie would have liked me better if she hadn't always been so old.*

Pandora looks at her grannie's hands. A gardenia has sprouted between the rooty fingers. Pandora marvels at its fleshy white eyelids, with the tears still on them. She reads the card: "To Grannie Cragg. . . . Eternal Love, from Adel, Ada, Pandora."

Pandora looks into the gardenia. Its heavy scent draws her down into its sweetish core. She stares into the white bowl, brown-stained around the edges. She steadies herself against the coffin.

Pandora has left a trail of fingersmudges on the polished wood. She examines her thumbprint, which is whorled like a chocolate rosebud. She looks at Grannie Cragg's face, which is whorled like a chocolate rosebud. *I wouldn't have eaten you, grannie! I wouldn't have eaten you because I love you.*

The cold egg shifts dangerously in Pandora's stomach. It presses, hard, against her ribcage.

The neighbours come and go — Mrs. Newton who is nosy, and Mrs. Dicey who is crabby, and Mrs. Spittal who is crazy, but today they are neither nosy nor crabby nor crazy. Today they are just a long black murmur in hats and galoshes: "How peaceful. . . . How natural. . . . How lovely the flowers. . . ."

The relatives knot in the kitchen. It is warm there, and busy. There are sandwiches to make, and tea to pour, and dishes to wash. Pandora tries to be helpful. Adelaide pats her head: "Poor Pandora, now you will have no one to say your vowels to."

Tears trickle down Pandora's cheek. Great Aunt Gertie, from Boston, scoops her up in her great doughy arms, and presses her against her great doughy bosom.

"Poor lamb," she croons. "Poor lamb."

Pandora's tears fall on Great Aunt Gertie's warm bosom. She feels it swell under her cheek, under the coarse black dress, like bread-dough under a tablecloth. Sobs wrack the giantess body. Pandora feels herself slipping down the cleft in Great Aunt Gertie's bosom, trapped inside Great Aunt Gertie's body, locked inside the heaving flesh, unable to breathe, panicking, choking, then stopping the struggle, falling backward into the humid folds, trapped but warm, locked but safe, inside but then not outside, absorbed but absolved, content, without sharp edges, dissolved in the unexpected joy of this common sorrow.

Great Aunt Gertie releases Pandora. She dabs at her eyes. She smooths her gollywog hair. She picks up a box of Smiles' n'Chuckles chocolates. "Here, dear. Have a chocolate."

Pandora, in the ebbtide of surrender, takes one without even checking flavours. Great Aunt Gertie, still dabbing at her eyes, stands with the box extended. Pandora hesitates, then takes another. Great Aunt Gertie, swabbing her nose, jiggles the box. Pandora, nonplussed, takes another. She gives Great Aunt Gertie a disbelieving smile. Great Aunt Gertie smiles absently back. Pandora, overwhelmed by this sign of approval, empties the box.

Aunt Estelle sets down the Tranquillity Rose teapot with a heavy clink.

"I'll pour," says Great Aunt Gertie. "How's that, Addy? Too weak?"

"No, that's fine." Adelaide's eyes moisten. "You know how mother was about her cup of tea. She'd make tea out of anything she could get into her billie."

Great Aunt Gertie smiles: "And every colour of the rainbow, too! Some of those purple and green concoctions must have turned her gullet the colour of Joseph's coat. I used to say, 'Land's sake, Sybil, you're not drinking *that!* That's for painting walls.' And she'd say, 'Bide your tongue, Gertie. The artist's got his palette, and I've got mine.' "

Everyone smiles. Pandora grins. She doesn't understand the joke, but she is happy that they are happy.

Adel, emboldened, says: "Once I was gathering nettles with grannie down the Ravine, and a *wolf* was sitting in the greenest patch. He had fangs down to *here.* Grannie chased him away. She said, 'No mangy wolf's going to stand between me and my morning cup of!' "

Everyone smiles again.

"*I* was there, too," ventures Ada. "Grannie just waved her hickory stick and that wolf took off, licketty-split, down the tracks."

"*Dragging his tail behind him!*" chants Pandora.

The grownups chuckle. Pandora's trance of happiness deepens.

"Grannie certainly had her ways," sighs Adelaide. "She liked her toast hard as flint. She said it helped grind the food in her gizzard." Adelaide's face darkens. "I'd just made mother some tea. I thought, 'I wonder if she'd like some dry toast.' I heard a choking sound. I rushed into her room and . . ."

Adelaide's hazel eyes overflow. Adel-Ada avert their glance. Aunt Gertie clears her throat.

The sharp change of mood takes Pandora by surprise. She feels the warmth of shared remembrance slipping from her before she has properly experienced it. She wants to hold the mood, to secure it.

"Mother. . . ." Pandora snatches at a tag-end of recent laughter. "Mother. . . . Why did the Little Moron chase the cow around the block?"

Adelaide flinches.

Adel-Ada set down the cream-sugar.

Great Aunt Gertie stops pouring.

Aunt Estelle pauses, mid-air, with the sugar tongs.

They stare at Pandora.

Aunt Estelle, her lips set in a thin glassy line, advances on her with the sugar tongs. "Pandora, you are the coldest, most unfeeling child I have ever met. Your grandmother lies dead, in the other room, and all you do is stuff your face with chocolates, and defile her coffin with your sticky fingers, and defile her memory with your heartless laughter. If I had my way, I'd pack you off where no one had to look at you until your grandmother is safely buried in hallowed ground."

Adelaide weeps.

Adel-Ada sniffle.

Great Aunt Gertie comforts them with the warmth of her bread-dough arms.

Aunt Estelle stabs the sugarbowl with the sugar tongs.

Pandora strides to the kitchen window. She squashes her face against it. Her eyes burn into the frosted glass like two hot pennies: *He wanted to hear the Jersey Bounce. He wanted to hear the Jersey Bounce.*

Pandora's tears freeze, then fall, with a clink, into the pockets behind her eyes. She walks stiffly through the warm kitchen, past the perfumed living-room, up the stairs, past Grannie Cragg's deathbed; up the attic stairs, through her bedroom, into the narrowest cubbyhole, back, back, back, through the dust and packing boxes and the ghosts of Christmas present, crawling, crawling now, to that darkest wedge where the splintery floor meets the wallpaper sky.

It bursts. The cold white egg inside Pandora bursts. *I didn't eat you, grannie!*

Pandora vomits fear and Smiles'n' *Ha ha* chocolates.

It is snowing.

The world outside Pandora's window is white — without sunlight, without shadow, without dimension. It is coarsely veiled in black branches from Pandora's maple tree. It is black-bordered by her window.

They have taken my grannie away. They have stuffed her, bedfirst, into the earth. They have sprinkled her with red petals. . . .

Adelaide says, "Grannie Cragg has flown up to Heaven to be with God and the Baby Jesus," but Pandora knows that isn't true. *My grannie has gone into the cubbyhole to be with Aunt Cora, who died of diphtheria and Baby Victor who choked.* Pandora can hear the vowels swarming like locusts in her throat. Pandora can smell . . . gardenias.

New people move into Grannie Cragg's cottage. They rip up her camomile lawn. They tear out her wild thyme, for coughs; her sweet rosemarie, for headaches; her catmint, for chasing rats. They insul-brick her wood-shingle cottage, and turn her root-cellar into an aluminum porch for a wash-machine and a baby buggie.

"No more pencils, no more books!
No more teachers' dirty looks!"

Pandora passes first in her class. She gets an Honour Diploma, a Health Certificate and — everyone loves a winner — even a Deportment Recommendation.

Pandora sprints home, tight-fisted, with her loot. "Mo-thur!" The kitchen is empty. She remembers: *My mother is at the cemetery singing hymns.*

Pandora stores her diplomas in her dresser-drawer. The Health Certificate, entwined with grapevines, crumples in the closing. Pandora smooths it on top of her dresser.

Dirty Danny didn't get a Health Certificate. Dirty Danny didn't even pass. Dirty Danny was dirty, so they dragged him away. They put him in a room with the Eskimos, where it is always winter, and they tied him, with his red scarf, to the bed in the whistling wind. Jessie Christie was right. *Dirty Danny has dirty lungs.*

Pandora, buoyed up by a promise of summer and the certification of her own good health, decides to send Dirty Danny a Get-Well card.

I will twist it with grapevines, and I will send it to him in the "Sand."

Pandora ransacks the house for a grape crayon. She finds some grape pop, instead. She drinks it. She forgets about Dirty Danny.

God

Summer, 1944

Summer summer summer — *hola!* Two months! A green eternity.

Arlene and Pandora weave dandelions through the spokes of Arlene's splendiferous tricycle, and they hold a Dandelion Festival, and they charge everyone an inflationary five cents apiece.

They hang a hose over the Gothics' clothesline, and they prance through the spray, trying to hold up their stretchy, mother-knit bathing-suits, giggling, experimenting with every water-texture from rainbow-mist to the unforgiving bullet, letting the rivulets beat against their caps with the echoing thunder of a private Niagara, then taking them off, filling them up, and chasing each other around the junipers as if it mattered whether they got more water on themselves or not.

They invite Lucy Spittal and the Clay girls to come, bring their nozzles, so that now they have a dazzlement of possibilities — an orange whirligig that flings crystal circlets! a fan that flaps like a silver wing! a halo with waterspouts that you can set on your head like a Christmas candle-crown! Every time Lucy Spittal goes near the water, Nellie Clay jacknifes the hose, and then Crazy Lucy looks into the nozzle, and then Nasty Nellie lets go of the hose, and then — *hee hee hee* — Shelly, to be smart, sits on the halo as if it were a chamberpot, and she smothers every waterspout but the one shooting up between her skinny legs, and Mrs. Newton who happens to be watching through her venetian blinds, phones Pandora's mother to complain about galloping corruption among our youth today, and the water is cut off, at source, and everyone is sent home.

Arlene and Pandora make bubble-pipes out of chives. They lie in the Goodfellows' ferns, with the split shaft pointed to the sky, turning every breath into a shimmering dirigible that wobbles two, three seconds, in its own iridescence, before daring lone blue flight. *Ping!* The bubble explodes in a soapy sunburst a handspan from its place of birth.

Arlene and Pandora pitch camp in the Gothics' backyard, in a tent created by stretching canvas over Adelaide's swing-frame. They stock it with all those things a tent should have — Wonder Woman comics, bug jars, a pack of Old Maid cards and, after much tortured pleading, two bedrolls. Now it is no longer a game. They study weather predictions for a week — especially the comings and goings of the shifty witch in the barometer cottage on the Goodfellows' piano. One balmy summer's eve, when all authorities agree there is no possibility of rain, they pack a flashlight, a box of Cracker Jack, two bottles of pop and deliver themselves up to the infinite night. They lie under the stars, their feet in the tent, their heads in a velvety potpourri from Adelaide's flower garden.

It is the time of the Perseids. Meteors rip like a swarm of angry firebees from a radiant north of the constellation Perseus. Arlene and Pandora, sailing the post-midnight hours for the first time, think this must happen every night, and they clutch each other in frog-eyed wonder, watching the formerly immutable stars fight each other for a piece of the heavens, converging, diverging, firewebbing the sky, until Arlene, hugging the stuffed puppy she brought as a last sentimental gesture, starts to cry, and has to phone her father, on the nightshift, to come and rescue her, sobbing so hard he can hardly hear her, because the night is so much longer than she had ever thought possible, and she is homesick and she wants to come home. . . .

Arlene and Pandora tire of eating around the hereditary

114

inadequacies of the Goodfellows' rotten / buggy / wormy / blighted apples / peaches / plums / pears.

They turn brigand.

They smear their cheeks with pollen from the spotted throat of the tiger lily. They hook cherries over their ears and daggers into their shorts-bands.

They rape the Diceys' domestic plum.

They gorge on the fat fruit, noisily sucking sunlight from plush pockets under the indigo skin.

Hola!

Mrs. Dicey's broom appears at an upstairs window, then her arm, like a hairy turnip, then her face, like boiled spinach. "G'wan, you brats! I'll call the police!"

Arlene, emboldened by her thief's regalia, sasses from a tree fork: "My father *is* the police. He says you're a *stupid bitch!*"

Arlene and Pandora sell lemonade, five cents large, three cents small. That is to cover the Diceys' property damage. Other damages were claimed; other penalties were enacted.

Arlene and Pandora restore self-respect by baiting himey Mrs. Barker (from the rival emporium) with a silk purse, yanked on invisible wires into the bushes.

They leave a black box, with a peephole ringed in shoe-polish, inside Nosy Newton's milkbox.

They wire a Dead End sign to the Stintons' hearse.

They stud a pile of hot horseballs with fake pearls, then watch Mrs. Spittal and Lucy *oh hee hee hee, that was a good one!*

Arlene and Pandora disappear over the railway tracks into the Ravine. They look for a stump of phosphorescent wood to smear over their bodies so they will glow in the dark the way The Lone Ranger and his kemosavi terrified desperadoes one week in the funny papers.

They grow an inch apiece.

They get burs in their hair.

Adelaide is incensed.

"This is the *last* time, Pandora. I'm going to have to braid it."

Pandora is incensed.

The act of sitting, with bowed head, while her mother's bone fingers part, plait, bind and wind her hair, as if it had no more personal destiny than the bits of string she twists so endlessly into doilies, is an unbearable humiliation.

Pandora sniffles.

Adelaide instructs. "Braids are *neat*, Pandora. They make you look like a sensible little girl, instead of a wild Indian. Aunt Rosalind likes them, too. She says they're real cute."

"Ouch! You're hurting."

"Sit *still!*"

"I can't *see!* You've pulled my eyes wonky!"

"Honestly, Pandora! This is ridiculous. *I* wear braids. I don't complain. Adel-Ada wear braids. *They* don't complain."

"They *should!* They look like skinned rats!"

Adelaide thwacks Pandora with her thimble. "That's enough from you, Miss Smart Mouth!"

Pandora, bound and wound, bolts for the door. By the time she hits the eastside of Oriental Avenue, her halo is dismantled. By the time she hits the end of Arlene's backyard, one braid is undone. By the time she hits the railway tracks, the other braid is undone.

Pandora Palomino gallops, mane streaming, alongside a Silver Flyer — *and almost wins!*

Pandora Daedalus dangles from the top of the rotten apple tree of life, golden kite spread to catch that one vagrant puff that will send her hurtling over the sun.

Pandora Medusa eye-blasts the Clays from the centre of her fire corona, AND TURNS THEM TO STONE!

Capricious acts of disobedience?

No, acts of survival.

It is Pandora's hair that Perfect Strangers fondle when they say, "What a pretty little girl. What's *your* name?" It is her hair, spun into rag chrysalises every Saturday night, that turns her into Shirley *butterfly* Temple every Sunday morning. It is her long golden hair — all the books agree — which is standard equipment for all princesses, all nymphs, all angels, all fairies.

Pandora's hair is the key to both her fantasy life and her identity.

Pandora Gothic, without her hair, is just a bad-tempered little girl, frustrated with the present and shorn of all future possibility.

Pandora slinks home. Her braids, replaited by Arlene, are a testament to determined amateurism. One of her elastics is broken. Pitch-forks stud the reinstated halo like a cockeyed crown of thorns.

Adelaide notices, whenever she has the strength.

* * *

Where's Charlie-puss?

"Here puss, puss, puss, puss, puss. . . ." Pandora looks under the backstoop by the pail of pollywogs she and Arlene are hatching for their Frog Circus. She looks into the centre of Mrs. Newton's lemon lilies where the foulest deeds involving Charlie-puss are said to unfold. She inspects, with terrible premonition, the burdock patch by Mrs. Dicey's poisoned garbage-pail.

She crosses Oriental. "Have you seen Charlie-puss today, Arlene?"

Arlene is batting her Bo-Lo ball. She shakes her head.

"Dicey probably poisoned him!" teases Sydney. "That lame old thing must be older than the adeetse man!"

"You shut up, Sydney Goodfellow, or you'll wish you had!"

Arlene collapses into her ricocheting Bo-Lo ball. "A hundred-sixteen! You wanna try Pandy?"

Sydney snatches the bat. "*I* can do better than *that*, even if it is a silly girl's game."

"One . . . two . . . three. . . ." Sydney bats and counts, in a lispy showoff's voice.

Pandora turns with scorn. "Why does Sydney hang around us? Why doesn't he play with the boys?"

"There aren't any boys, that's why!"

"What about the Clays?"

117

"They're bullies."

"What about Stinky Stinton?"

"He's a sis!"

"*Sydney's* a sis!"

"He is *not!*"

"*Ha!* Just *look* at him!"

Arlene bristles. "Who invited *you*, anyway? Why don't you go home?"

Pandora stalls. "Why should I, if I don't feel like it?"

Arlene advances, copper coxcomb blazing: "Because it's *my* property, and I'm telling you!"

Pandora spins on her heel. "*I* wouldn't stay here if you paid me in gumdrops!"

Sydney drops his Bo-Lo bat. "A hundred-twenty! I *said* I could beat." He turns up his hearing-aid to hear himself admired.

"Go suck eggs, Sydney!"

Arlene holds her nose: "Good riddance to bad rubbish!"

Pandora stamps up her front steps.

"*Don't* slam the door!" growls Lyle.

Adel-Ada are at the kitchen table, pasting in their Royal Family scrapbook.

"Wanna play?" growls Pandora, daring them to accept.

"How can we?" says Adel, tapping her broken right arm.

"We aren't allowed," says Ada, tapping her broken left arm.

"Peas-in-a-pod! Peas-in-a-pod!" taunts Pandora.

"Pandora!" rebukes Adelaide. "Stop that meanness!"

Pandora scoops a handful of peapods from a basket and thrusts the literal truth under her mother's nose. *See?* "Peas-in-a-pod!" *Why do you always misjudge me?!*

"Don't slam the door!" snaps Adelaide.

Pandora sits on the backstoop angrily tossing peapods at her mother's irreproachable lilies. The summer churns like curdled cream in her stomach. She starts to cry, then thinks better of it. *Cry like a baby? Hola! I will play GOD instead!*

Pandora saunters down her backyard. She stands, arms folded, above her father's Asparagus Patch. She watches, in-

118

tently, as a half-dozen ladybugs graze over the juicy spears. One feeds on the Asparagus Tree of Knowledge. Pandora tears off its copper coxcomb. "Go naked! Go eat dust!"

Pandora moves to her father's Tomato Patch. She stares fiercely at a tomato bug. It looks back at her. She sprinkles it with garden lime. "I *warned* you!" It writhes into a pillar of salt. "Next time, *turn up your ears!*"

Pandora Passes Over the Cabbage Patch where a half-dozen cabbage worms obediently bloat themselves on her father's detested cabbages. She settles, by a saturn-ringed anthill, busily attended by black ants. She sets a sacred clothespin by the door. An aunt puts her hands on it. *Splat!* Pandora squashes her. "Wash your dirty hands! Oh where, oh where, have you placed them?"

Pandora makes a great rain to rain out of the garden hose, for forty black seconds with her eyes closed, and forty white seconds with her eyes open, until — lo! — the whole wicked world is a tub of water. Pandora floats a rose leaf, of generous proportions, on the water. She drops ants and beetles and ladybugs and caterpillars into the tub. The first two of every kind that scramble onto the leaf she allows to live . . . occasionally breaking an arm. *Peas-in-a-pod! Peas-in-a-pod!*

Pandora lies on the grass, in the midst of her freshly cleansed world, admiring the rainbow in the hose spray. She feels lonely. She wishes she hadn't quarrelled with Arlene. She wishes Adel-Ada liked her better. She wishes everybody would stop screaming at her. She wishes she could find Charlie-puss. . . .

Pandora buries her face in the grass. The grass feels warm. She sees a caravan of ants struggling under loads three times their size. She moves sticks and stones from their route. *I can be merciful. . . .*

Pandora lifts one of the ants, with its load, to the door of its home. The whole line scatters. *"After I slave!"* Pandora gouges out their home with her thumb. *"Don't* slam the door!"

Pandora decides the ant population is too dumb to appreciate her. *I will choose a new bunch, a SMART bunch.* She remembers the pollywogs, even now turning to frogs under her backstoop. *Yes! I will teach them to walk on their hind-legs. I will teach them to jump through hoops of fire! Then I will have a Frog Circus without Arlene, and I will charge everyone seven cents.* Pandora thinks about that very seriously. *Arlene and Sydney will have to pay TWELVE cents.* That's the same price Cecil B. DeMille charges at the Ventnor! *Oh, I can be FIERCE!*

Pandora pulls her pollywog pail from under her backstoop. Oh!

She recoils: *OH!*

Her pollywog pail is a stinking swirl of maggots and rotting flesh. Pandora hastily empties it into the burdock patch by Mrs. Dicey's poisoned garbage-can. She sticks burs into the toes of her running shoes, and jumps up and down the alley, calling: "Puss, puss, puss, puss. Here puss, puss, puss. . . ." A terrible truth oppresses her:

Sometimes GOD likes to play God!

Adel-Ada have put away their Royal scrapbook, and are writing to a penpal in Mexico, sentences turnabouts. Pandora looks at their pretty mauve writing paper, twisted with violets. The violets remind her of grapes. Grapes remind her of . . .

"I guess *I* should do *my* correspondence, too," says Pandora with casual self-importance.

"Oh?" Adel is openly skeptical. "Who do *you* know?"

"A friend . . . A boy . . . He's sick. I promised to send him a Get-Well card."

"What's the matter with him?"

"He's in the Sand."

"With T.B.?" Adel is clearly impressed.

"Yeah. . . ." Pandora tries to remember, for authenticity's sake, what Dirty Danny looks like. She remembers the black hands. "He was a foreign friend. With purple skin. An Eskimo friend. We were insupportable."

"Oh, *that's* a whopper!" scoffs Adel. "Eskimos don't have purple skin." She has just finished reading every-other-sentence in Eskimo Twins, and so she knows. "An Eskimo's skin is brown."

120

"So was my friend's. Except for the elbows. They were purple. Miss Warner always thought they were dirty and gave his row a germ-hand."

Adel-Ada shudder: They remember Miss Warner's germ-hands.

"I'll give you an envelope if you want to write," says Ada.

"You can have this stamp," offers Adel.

Pandora looks through a half-dozen magazines for a picture of some grapes to paste on the letter page. She doesn't find any. She *does* find a picture of a soldier, shooting at some Nazis with a tommy-gun. He is wearing a hearing-aid.

DEAF CAN FIGHT TOO!
We place the deafened at the Service of the Nation.
Acousticon Goes to War!

Pandora scrawls on the bottom of the picture: "Sydney, why don't you go play with the *boys,* and leave Arlene and me alone??????"

She puts it in Ada's envelope.

She licks Adel's stamp.

She forgets all about Dirty Danny.

Pandora sits on her three-legged stool, made of patches of Grannie Cragg's dead children, and she contemplates the Universe through a lens ground out of bits and pieces of Catechism:

Q. Who made the World?

A. In the Beginning, God made the World.

Q. Who made God?

A. No one made God. He Always Was.

Pandora looks deeply into the thickest, creamiest part of the Milky Way. She tries to see the *last* star, beyond the one that is just after that. *If I see behind the very last star, would that be Always Was?*

Pandora stands, naked, in front of her vanity mirror, which

is triple-arched like a church window. Her body glistens with bathwater. She is illuminated by the streetlight outside her window, which she pretends is the full moon.

Mirror mirror mirror. . . .

Pandora folds in the right side of her mirror. She folds in the left side. She sees a line of naked Pandoras stretching endlessly, backwards and forwards, into the mirror . . . butterflies pressed in quicksilver. . . .

Pandora closes her eyes. She opens them quickly. She tries to catch the last Pandora when she isn't looking. *If I catch the LAST Pandora would that be Always Was?*

The bathwater trickles, like tears, down Pandora's flesh. She has a sudden, sickening vision of herself somersaulting backwards through space. She flings open the mirror *Fly! fly! butterfly!*

* * *

Adelaide ties Pandora's yellow sash. She fluffs her Shirley Temple curls. She inspects her ears, neck, elbows.

"Why do we have to go to Other Grandma's?" complains Pandora.

"We don't *have* to go," corrects Adelaide. "We *want* to go."

"We want to take Grandma Pearl a jar of lemon preserves," says Adel.

"And a nice bouquet of rhubarb."

Pandora, in sunshine-yellow, Adel-Ada in sky-blue, Adelaide in cinnamon-brown, Lyle in gloss-black, board the 9:11 a.m. Greyhound bus, north from Mill City.

Other Grandma lives in the country, in a place without a name. . . .

The air is explosive with undischarged thunder. Lyle Gothic twitches wetly in the front seat of the taxi. "I don't know why it always takes ten cents more to get to mother's than it does to return."

The taxi turns up Other Grandma's cinder drive, through an aisle of dead elms that meet overhead like the staves of a

122

burnt-out church. The house stands at the end of the arch —
dark, massive, Victorian; a witch's wedding cake, lavishly
trimmed with black iron and rows and rows of skinny windows
blowing with torn lace.

*That's real lace, handmade in Paris. Your grandmother was
educated. She knew the world. Your grandmother danced with
Neville Chamberlain.*

No one answers the door-clanger.

The Gothics huddle in the vestibule.

"Are you sure it was today?" asks Adelaide.

"Of course, I'm sure! Just because *you* never listen doesn't
mean *I* suffer the same affliction."

Lyle lifts the latch. He pushes open the door. "Estelle must
be upstairs." *She does it to spite me.*

The Gothics grope, in human chain, up black-marble stairs,
through mirrored halls, past grottos shrouded in night-purple,
ink-blue, and other colours that have died, past ebony tables
so high Pandora can't reach the top, pushing up, through the
dark, until . . .

WHITE!
An explosion of white!
We are in the Palace of the Snowqueen.

Other Grandmother lies under a vaulted ceiling, three steps
up, in an ivory bed, that floats like an iceberg, over the black
floor. White curtains drift across the top and sides of the bed,
scooped elegantly low like a cutter. Lace cascades over the
satin coverlet — a blizzard of lace, each piece as different as
a snowflake.

Other Grandmother is long and lean and white, like marble.
Her teeth are large, like tombstones. Her eyes are frosty, the
kind of ice you shouldn't suck. She is not old: Her skin is
lightly etched porcelain. Her white hair tumbles from a sharp
widow's peak.

Lyle approaches the bed, his good black hat in his good
flesh hand. "Good day, mother."

123

Mother Pearl is making lace. Her fingers twitch in mindless agitation, under the prismed light of her crystal chandelier, twisting the silken thread that winds down from a diminishing snowball. . . .

Lyle moves forward, on eggshell toes: "Good day, mother."

Other Grandma continues to make lace. She makes it for Uncle Damon, who ran away. She makes it for Damon's bride — yards and years of lace, enough for ten brides and the shrouds of as many corpses.

"She doesn't hear," whispers Adelaide.

"Do you *always* have to state the obvious?"

Lyle advances up the white steps, his suit oily in the crystal light, the stump of his amputated hand sweating against his jacket. He kisses his mother on the chalk cheek.

Mother Pearl drops her hook. "Upon my word! When did *you* get in?" She embraces Lyle with marble arms, suddenly supple. "You'll be the death of me yet, Damon. Couldn't you even spare your mother a postcard?"

Lyle reddens. He tries to free himself from the cat's cradle of arms and fingers that reach out to ensnare him. He hears a noise behind him. He turns. Pandora turns. It is Aunt Estelle. She is standing in the doorway. Her black-wire hair is parted down the middle and coiled over both ears. Her eyes are folded bat's wings. "Sorry . . . I didn't hear you. I was scrubbing mother's bedpan." She sets her lips in a line, not entirely of displeasure. *"Somebody* has to do it."

The Gothic women arrange themselves, in a dark crescent, around Grandmother Pearl's bed. Adelaide draws fancywork from an old pillowcase marked "Hers." She begins nervously cross-stitching "Tribulation is but the Upward Slope of Triumph."

Estelle plumps Mother Pearl's cushions. "Comfy, mother?" She sits on the bed. "I'll do your hair." Lyle draws away. Mother Pearl pulls him back. *"You* stay here, Damon. *Estelle* can move."

Pandora squirms. The chair carving scratches her back. The caning stripes her rump. She turns sideways, waiting her chance. She darts through the shadowy arch. . . .

It is cold in the hall. The floor bites through Pandora's

running shoes: *It is always winter in Other Grandmother's house.*

Pandora starts down a spiral staircase, setting her mind against fear of the dark, and holding the slippery rail with both hands. . . .

Other Grandmother's parlour is draped in dust. Skinny windows illumine a needlework tripod, a satinwood cabinet.

Pandora peeks inside the cabinet. She sees a crystal butterfly, a porcelain bird, a milkglass shepherdess. . . . Except, she doesn't *really* see them. She sees the spots in the dust where they used to be, in the same way as she sees the ghosts of paintings that used to hang on Other Grandma's walls. . . .

Pandora tries the cabinet door: It is locked, of course. Aunt Estelle keeps the keys on a chain around her waist, which is why Aunt Estelle *clinketty-clanks* when she *clinketty-clunk* walks.

Pandora starts back up the spiral stairs . . . up, and around, and . . .

Once upon a time, oh, so very long ago, Aunt Estelle let Pandora and Adel-Ada climb the ladder into the attic.

Ohhhhh. . . . The treasures they saw that day:

A steamer trunk stuck with labels — Paris! India! Japan! A silk fan! A monkey cape! A *photograph* album, thick with the secrets of time. Adel, Ada, Pandora, turn each page with a sense of sinful revelation.

Ho! Grandpa Gothic, *in a top hat!* staring fiercely into the camera, with Uncle Damon sprawled across his shoulder.

Grandma Pearl, *with red hair!* gaily frivolous under a parasol, with Uncle Damon bending over her hand.

Aunt Estelle, in old-fashioned bathing-suit, *laughing!* as Damon pushes her into the water.

Father! with two hands! with hair! squinting into the sun while Damon, five years older, makes bunny-ears over his head.

Uncle *oh, isn't he handsome* Damon in Norfolk jacket, smiling at *who? who?* scissored off. Two hands, *a man's? a woman's?* intertwined without benefit of caption.

"Where's Aunt Rosie?" asks Pandora.

"These are old pictures," says Adel. "She's a lot younger than the rest."

"Besides," says Ada, "Aunt Rosalind was adopted."

"Then how come she looks exactly like Other Grandmother and Aunt Estelle?"

"That's because they match you up at the adoption agency."

Pandora picks up a Chinese box, inlaid with a mother-of-pearl dragon. "Why did Uncle Damon go away?"

"I don't know," says Adel. She and Ada exchange sly looks. "We're not supposed to ask."

Ada adds eagerly, "We've heard things though."

Pandora examines the Chinese box, looking for a catch. "What things?"

"About father and Uncle Damon."

"They quarrelled!" exclaims Ada. "That's when Uncle Damon ran off with the money."

"No, he didn't," corrects Adel. "He'd already spent it. He was a gambler."

Pandora slides a mother-of-pearl inlay at the end of the dragon's tail: The box opens. "Is that why father and Uncle Damon quarrelled?" There is an identical box inside.

"Yes," says Ada.

"No," says Adel.

"Yes and no," ventures Ada.

"Both," affirms Adel.

Pandora slides the catch in the second segment of the dragon's tail: That box opens. "Did Other Grandma go funny because Uncle Damon went away?" There is a smaller lacquer box inside.

"It might have been because Grandpa Gothic died," says Adel. "It all happened together."

"He killed himself," blurts Ada.

"No," chides Adel. "He did *not!* He banged his head on a nail. It was an accident."

"He thought he'd committed the Sin against the Holy Ghost! The sin for which there is no forgiveness!"

126

Pandora looks up from the third Chinese box. "What sin is that?"

"Nobody knows," says Adel. "St. Paul just puts it that way in the Bible. Even Grandpa Gothic didn't know. He just thought he must have committed it."

"He used to bang his head on the wall at church, and one day there was a nail where they took down the Cradle Roll to add more names."

"Grandpa stuck his head right into it."

"It went through his brain."

Pandora presses the third segment in the dragon's tail. Nothing happens. She shakes the lacquer box.

"When did Aunt Estelle go funny?"

"Aunt Estelle? *She's* not funny."

Pandora presses the dragon's mouth, the dragon's snout, the dragon's eyes. . . . "She seems pretty funny to me."

"That's just 'her way'," says Adel in a grownup voice.

"But she hated Uncle Damon!" exclaims Ada.

"No, she did *not*!" Adel smiles at Ada: "How *could* she when they're *twins*?"

Pandora throws down the Chinese box. "I'm sick of puzzles! Let's play something else."

Pandora finds a carton covered with flowered wallpaper.

"It's Grandma Pearl's," says Adel. "See? Here's a book of poetry she's written. Mother says she's very accomplished."

They overturn the carton: a Spanish shawl, a china doll with the eyes scratched out. Adel, peering through a gold lorgnette, sits grandly on a potty chair. The three sisters burst out laughing.

"Let's put on some music!" exclaims Adel.

"I'll wind up the victrola," says Ada.

"I'll dust the records," says Pandora.

"When father papered the par-lour,
You couldn't see Pa for paste. . . ."

Pandora, Adel, Ada dance and sing, until Aunt Estelle — smiling for once — pokes up through the trap with three pieces of devilsfood cake on a silver plate. Adel-Ada fight over the smallest piece, Pandora snatches the biggest, and everyone remembers how much they dislike each other.

Why, asks Pandora, squashing her cake to make it look smaller, *can't anyone cut three pieces exactly alike?*

Estelle, glowering, yanks Pandora up the last three steps. "Snooping, eh?" She propels Pandora back into the Ice Palace.

Pandora squirms on her cane chair: Other Grandmother, her snowy hair tied with a pink ribbon, is turning coquettishly before an ivory mirror, frosted to protect her from too-harsh reality, and chatting animatedly. Lyle, sweating gall, leans tensely over the satin coverlet, trying to claim his birthright. "No, mother. It is *I*, Lyle. It is *not* Damon. Mother, I am *Lyle.*"

Other Grandmother laughs with the sound of tinkling cymbals. "Oh *Damon*! You are your mother's tease!" She reaches for Damon's hand. She clasps Lyle's hook. It pierces her palm. She stares, in stupefaction, at the tiny blood-bead. She stares at Lyle's hook. Reality seeps in through the prick in her skin. "*You're* not Damon."

"No, mother."

Lyle tenderly covers his mother's wounded palm with his good one. "I am *Lyle* . . . your youngest son, Lyle."

Mother Pearl's frosty eyes begin to clear: "Who?" Her voice falters. "Ohhh. . . . *Lyle*, dear." She says, in gentle reproach: "Why did you pretend to be Damon?"

"I didn't, mother. You were confused."

"That was *cruel* of you, Lyle. . . . Oh, dear!" Mother Pearl picks up her ostrich fan. "I feel . . . a little faint. Fetch me my smelling salts, please, Lyle, like a good boy. Fetch them for mummy, and make her feel better after you've made her so sad. . . ." Her voice sharpens. "Then I think, dear, you'd best go straight to bed. I can't have you creeping in here, at night, into mummy's bed. You're getting too big a little man for that. . . . Now, fetch mummy her smelling salts and — "

128

"Mother!" explodes Lyle. "I am not a child! I've brought *my family* to see you. I've brought my *wife*, and my daughters. We've come to pay our respects."

Mother Pearl drops her tattered fan. Her eyes are very blue. "Your *wife*?"

She stares past Lyle into the crescent of embarrassed females. "Ahhhh, yes. . . . Adelaide, the twins, and little Pandora. How very nice. . . ."

Lyle, too eager to please, yanks Adel from her chair. "Go see your grandmother!" He upturns Ada and Pandora. "Hurry! Can't you see? Your grandmother *knows* you!"

Adel-Ada climb the steps to Other Grandmother's bed, are lightly kissed, and stiffly embraced. Pandora climbs the steps, making herself rigid with courage.

"Well, well, well. . . ." Other Grandmother reaches out her sugar-tong arms. "Little Pandora. . . ." The crystal voice is jagged with pain. "Well, well, well. . . ."

Other Grandmother's white lips touch Pandora's cheek: *Like the time Jessie Christie touched me with dry ice, like the time I stuck my tongue on the frozen mailbox . . .* an icy kiss with a fiery centre.

Other Grandma holds Pandora at arm's length. "My, my, my, how you've grown." She cocks her head, on the same angle as Pandora's. She takes the pink ribbon from her own hair, and ties it around Pandora's hair as if she were looking in a mirror. She runs icicle fingers through Pandora's hair, spinning it into snowflakes. "How time flies!"

Tears scald Other Grandmother's cheeks. "Estelle, I want this child to have sweets. Fetch her a silver dollar from my silver chest. Little Pandora must have sweets."

Other Grandmother releases Pandora. She wipes her eyes with a lace handkerchief — a gesture that begins in pain, and then becomes merely pretty. She picks up her ostrich fan.

When Estelle returns *clanketty-clank* with the silver dollar, Other Grandmother is making lace . . . caught in the threads of her own silken web, spinning geometric complexities out of her own diminishing substance.

There is a dicey moment: Will Pandora get her silver dollar? Estelle grudgingly hands it over, and, of course, it leaves a puddle in Pandora's palm, for *what has King George been doing with his hands?* Estelle has washed it.

Estelle plumps Grandmother Pearl's pillow. "We mustn't tire her."

She escorts her guests down the spiral stairs, through dust and velvet, carrying candles past empty light-sockets, winding down and around, back and forth, weaving black snowflakes out of their own shadows.

The world is wet.

The sun is shining.

Pandora remembers, with surprise, that it is summer.

"Here, puss puss puss puss! Here puss!"

Pandora — still in her Sunday-best from the trip to Other Grandma's — looks for puss under the backstoop with the poison toadstools. She ransacks the centre of Mrs. Newton's bitter-lemon lilies. She combs, again, Mrs. Dicey's bur bushes, now spun with skeins of her own hair. She scouts every garbage-pail from the railway tracks clear through to the setting sun, crawling on all fours to get the proper perspective.

"Here puss puss puss!"

She catches a flash of crumpled silver from the Gothics' garbage-pail. She finds Charlie-puss' bed, stuffed with rotten cabbage leaves, and his red flea-collar lying on top in a bleeding smile.

Adelaide is in the living-room playing oughts and crosses. Lyle is playing Monopoly, and — incidentally — beating the pants off of J. P. Morgan, his guest opponent. Adel-Ada are playing Hear-No-Evil See-No-Evil, forfeits turnabouts.

Pandora, breath held tight, holds up the red collar. The elder Gothics exchange uneasy glances. Lyle reshuffles his Monopoly deeds. Adelaide sighs. She puts down her oughts and crosses. "Puss was getting old, Pandora. His eyes were bad. He couldn't see so very well. . . ."

"He smelt like a sewer!" snorts Lyle. "He had *fleas!*"

130

"It got so Mrs. Newton was calling up every day. . . . He's really much better off, Pandora. It was a *kindness*."

"He was diseased," grumbles Lyle. "If you hadn't mauled him so much. . . . If you'd kept your face away from him. . . . You really have only yourself to blame."

Pandora lets out a shriek: *"I thought it was Mrs. Dicey, but all the time it was YOU!"*

"Hush, Pandora," exclaims Adelaide. "The frontdoor's open. The whole neighbourhood will hear!" She conscientiously calms herself. "Your daddy and I did what we thought was best. It isn't fair for you to blame us for something we couldn't control."

"You should have *told* me! I had a *right* to know!"

"Now Pandora, be reasonable. How would you have reacted? No. . . . We did the only sensible thing. Mrs. Newton offered to take him and . . ." Adelaide realizes she is saying too much. She bites her lip: "Your daddy and I thought maybe you'd like a new little pet. Maybe one of those green turtles with the flags. They're awfully cute! You could put aside the silver dollar your grandmother gave you, and maybe if you don't make too much fuss, your daddy might give you . . ."

Lyle, on cue, jiggles the coins in his pocket. "Maybe we could start a fund right now." He palms a coin in awkward joviality.

"See, Pandora? Your father's got something for you. See? Your father understands."

Pandora, still sobbing, is propelled stiff-legged across the room. Lyle, flexible for a change, extends his good hand as far as it will go.

"Look. Your daddy's got a *quarter* for you. . . . Now, don't let your stubbornness ruin everything, Pandora. It's up to you to meet him halfway."

Pandora, under iron pressure, picks up King George by the scruff of the neck.

"Now, what do you say to your daddy?"

Pandora stares at the coin. She flings it to the floor: *"I don't want your bloody money! YOU KILLED PUSS!"*

Lyle, stabbed in the soft-centre of his good deed, rears out of his chair. "Apologize! Apologize *this instant*!"

Adelaide grabs Pandora by the shoulders. "*Please*, Pandora, *stop it*! You're only going to make yourself ill. Puss was old and sick. . . . We did what we thought was best. . . . Apologize to your father, *please*. Just apologize and . . ."

Lyle points imperiously to the floor. "Pick up that quarter. Pick it up, say 'Thank you,' and bring it here, to me."

Pandora kicks hysterically at the air between herself and her father. "*You killed puss! You gassed* him the way you always said! Why don't you send Grandma Pearl to the pound? *She's old and she stinks*!"

Pandora freezes in mid-convulsion: Her tongue turns to ashes.

Lyle recoils. His face turns to marble. "I will not have such words spoken in my house! Either get down, on your knees, and beg your grandmother's forgiveness, or *get out of my house*!"

Pandora is paralyzed by the awesomeness of the choice.

Lyle, his feet set on the road of melodrama, strides relentlessly forward: "Very well, if you refuse. . . . Adel! Ada! Say good-bye to your sister. You will never see her again. She is going to be sent to an orphanage."

Pandora gasps. She screams. She bolts for the door.

Lyle grabs her arm. He flings her to the ground. "Not so fast, Missy. If you leave this house, it will be the same way you came. I want everything that's mine. Take off those clothes, every stitch, and put them in a neat pile by the door as you leave."

Adelaide clutches her husband's good arm. "Lyle, I don't think . . ."

Lyle has been half-aware of his own absurdity. His wife's opposition is just the reassurance he needs.

"I don't care *what* you think. I've had enough sassing in my own home! I'm going to strip this girl of her brattishness, once and for all." He turns to Pandora. "Well? Didn't you hear? I said *strip*! Get those clothes off, and get them off fast, or —" He gestures with his hook.

Pandora yanks off her sunshine-yellow dress. She flings it at her father's feet. She yanks off her running shoes. She hurls them on top of the dress. She rips off her ankle socks. She kicks them on top of that. She reaches for her slip. She bursts into tears. "This is *my* slip! My mother made it for *me*!"

"Your mother may have made it, *but I paid for it*," thunders Lyle. "I pay for *everything* around here. . . . Every stitch you own. Every bite you eat. . . ." He is on familiar ground now, declaiming to the whole room: "I work, day-and-night, for what? To be defied in my own house! Well, we'll see about that." He turns to Pandora, grimly vindicated: "I want the rest of my property, Miss. Give it to me, this instant, and let's have no more fuss."

Pandora crouches on the floor in her slip. She squiggles her arms inside it. She lifts the white shell over her head, keeping her legs modestly jacknifed against her chest. She folds the slip very neatly. She folds the sunshine-yellow dress, hiding the place where she has torn it. She turns one white ankle sock into the other. She lines up the white running shoes. She plumbs the clothes pile. She looks, ingratiatingly, up at her father, a good camper waiting for bed inspection.

This should be the end of it: victorious father, repentant daughter; but Pandora has gone on too long. There has been something about her fluttery little tidy-up gestures, so clearly designed to charm, something so mocking about Grandma Pearl's pink ribbon bobbing in her white hair. Lyle is goaded into darker explorations.

"I said *everything*. I *meant* everything. Take off the rest of those clothes, and make it snappy."

Pandora sucks in her lower lip. She hooks her fingers into the band of her underpants.

"Do it!" urges Adelaide, giving the advice she has often taken. "Just do as your father demands, and get it over with. Your father's seen you naked before. Everybody has. It isn't worth fussing about."

Pandora, defiant, stretches her pants up over her chest. She crouches on the floor in a tight ball. Lyle strides toward her.

"No!" Adelaide pushes in front. She beckons to Adel-Ada. "Quick! Help!"

Adel pins Pandora's shoulders. Ada uncoils her legs. Adelaide, with a look of supreme distaste, pulls down her pants. Pandora tries to squeeze them between her thighs. The cloth peels away like adhesive from new skin.

Pandora, screaming, rolls over on the floor. She presses herself into the carpet. Lyle, with a deft swipe, yanks the pink ribbon from her hair. Pandora's head snaps back. She spits on her father's foot on the way down.

Lyle can't believe it.

He stares, stupefied, at the slime on his toe. Bellowing in a rage gone cockeyed, he scoops up Pandora with hand and hook, and drags her, knees *bump bump bumping* into the hall. He hangs her, full-length, in front of the mirror.

"There," he snarls. "That's all you are, and all you'll ever be. Everything *decent* you get from me. If you try to leave this house with one stitch of *my* property, I'll call the police, and they'll put the bloodhounds on you, and they'll track you down to whatever garbage patch you hide yourself in!"

Pandora gapes at herself in the mirror. She sees the mirror tremble, warp, then begin to melt. She feels herself tumble, backward, into the mirror . . . over and over and over and over into the liquid silver. . . . She tries to catch hold of the mirror. She catches her own flesh. She reaches down, gently, to cover her wounds.

Lyle slaps her. "Filthy brat! How dare you 'handle' yourself in front of me!"

Pandora collapses in shame. *I thought it was the breadman, but it was YOU!*

Lyle digs his fingers into Pandora's neck. He propels her — *hurry! hurry!* before the madness leaves and *he* is naked — through the kitchen, into the pantry, down the trapdoor, past her mother's fruit-crypts, past the Frankenstein furnace with its hot-tin arms and ash-bleeding mouth. . . . *The Kindergarten Rhythm Band is playing great tunes from The Great War, such as Pack Up Your Pussycat in Your Old Kit Bag and We'll*

Meet Again, Pussycat. Lyle opens the winter storage vault. *The sign overhead says BATHS.* He hurls Pandora inside. "You have two choices. Either leave my house, by the cellar door, exactly the way you are, or crawl upstairs, on your belly, and beg my forgiveness. Then *maybe* I'll let you stay. I'm not entirely sure I want such a filthy brat in my house!"

"I'm *not* filthy!" wails Pandora. *It isn't ME, it's Dirty Danny.*

The door is bolted, and sealed. Black Hands push Pandora's head toward the toilet bowl. It is full of . . . No! it is full of flowers — red, gold, blue — floating in sweet milk. Pandora sticks out her tongue. She dips it into the milk. It scalds. It shrivels. It falls off. It floats away on a heaving bosom of sour milk.

Pandora smells mothballs. Blue gas rises in a cloud from the flowers. Her green eyes bleed, then pop, first the right, then the left. Her lungs sear, expand, explode. She claws the gas chamber with the bloody stumps of her paws. The poison riddles her white fur. Her guts pour through her skin like tomatoes through a sieve. A cleat-boot stands beside her. "Strip! Go naked to the orphanage! Go eat dust!" Pandora tries to wriggle free of her white fur. She tears off her Elizabethan ruff, leaving a blood noose around her neck. She tears off her Dutchman's breeches: They stick, like adhesive. She is naked except for . . . The cleat-boot clasps the prideful plume with its Black Hand. It skins off all the hairs, in a single stroke, including the proud lonely hair at the tip.

Pandora lies naked, on the pound floor, scored like a butcher's block. ZZZzzzz. Thud. Splat. The cleat-boot slices her into serving-size pieces to be hung on silverhooks and sold to Mrs. Newton at a silver dollar a pound.

A warm marble falls from Pandora's throat. It rolls over and over, across the floor, crying, "I'm sorry! I'm sorry!" The cleat-boot stamps on it. It pops like a cabbage-worm. Twenty-three spots fall out: It was her polka-dot purr!

Pandora sits on her three-legged stool, made of patches of Grannie Cragg's dead children, and she contemplates the Universe through a lens ground from bits and pieces of her Revised Catechism.

Q. Who made the World?

A. Nobody made the World. It hatched from a rotten egg with a bloodspot in it. It exploded one day, with a slimy yellow bang, and everything went *pfft* — all over, and the sun is the gucky-yolk, and the moon is a piece of mouldy shell, and the stars are eggwhite dandruff, and the bloodspot — that's all the people, and they're all mad!

"*No, Pandora,*" cackles Aunt *diphtheria* Cora from Pandora's mattress. "*In the Beginning God made this lovely world. God who is Good, and who Always Was.*"

"No, it was my *father*, and he stinks, and he *Always Was WRONG!*"

"*It was God!*"

"It was my father. He laid the World, and he killed the Easter Bunny, and he *choked* Baby Victor!"

"*No, Pandora. It was God. God laid this great big egg. Give discredit where discredit is due.*"

The strange object is as large as a head — roundish, whitish, with a faintly ruttish odour.

"That's a puffball," says Davey Clay.

Sydney peels back the scalp with his Boy Scout knife. It is pulpy inside, and very vulnerable. The gang plays catch with it, then tosses it aside for a dented soccer ball.

Pandora takes the puffball home. She lays it on tissue-paper in the attic. She tapdances on it in old shoes to which she has nailed King Cola crowns. She dances it — *squish squish squish* — into a slimy pulp. She imagines it is a globe of the world. She imagines it is her father's *tap-tappetty squish-squash* head.

Pandora stands on her porch steps, in white shorts and blouse, her pyjamas rolled under her arm in a brown bag.

She is waiting for Aunt Rosie to pick her up on her way home from her 8-to-4 shift. She is going to Aunt Rosie's snazzy apartment, five stories up, on Marvin Gardens, to guzzle Cokes and play Rummoli, with *real* poker chips, not just buttons, because Ruby Fenwick, who is Rosie's roommate and wears too much rouge and round garters but is good-hearted and plays the "squeeze-box," is engaged to a real bartender who works at the Baltic Avenue Tavern.

After that, they are going to sit on Rosie's chrome chairs, with the legs that kneel on the floor that Pandora likes to bounce on, and they are going to eat hamburgs with the buns toasted in Ruby's pop-up toaster, and Pandora is going to drink milk with bananaflakes, and they are all going to have Baked Alaska.

After that, they will spin platters on Ruby's swell Admiral phonograph, with automatic changer, and read Rosie's Photoplay mags, and stay up till all incredible hours listening to John and Judy, and Fibber McGee and Molly on Ruby's portable radio with the police band.

After that, Pandora will sit in front of the round mirror, at Rosie's blonde-maple dresser, and she will douse herself with *eau de smells* and *oooo de colours*, and then she will have her choice of sides in the pink-satin bed with its shiny wood grains running every which way, and Rosie, in her shocking-pink nightgown, will blow noisy kisses to the soldiers/sailors/airmen, both living and dead, on her blonde-maple highboy, and she will say, "Well, toots, into the arms of Dreamland — and others!" and she will yank the chain on her organdy bed-lamp, and they will all go to sleep, with Ruby snoring good-heartedly on the pullout divan.

Pandora knows that's what will happen, because that is how she has asked for it, and that is how Rosie has promised it. Ordinarily, she would be in ecstasy, but . . . well . . . the price of everything has come very high this terrible terrible summer.

Ding-a-ling!

Rosie sweeps around the corner onto Oriental Avenue, jangling the bell on her carmine top-priority StreamLine bicycle, exuding Evening in Paris perfume, and wiggle-waggling, to great advantage, in all the potholes.

Mrs. Newton looks up from her flowering crab.

The Clay children pop out of their stinkweed suckers.

Mrs. Spittal drops a hot horseball.

Even old Mr. Grandby leaves off dying for a few minutes to bulge his rheumy eyes at the technicolour extravaganza fast-braking at the Gothic curb, and to mumble, without conviction, "Oh, it's a disgrace, not to mention . . . not to mention . . ."

Ding-a-ling!

Pandora can't help feeling a stir of pride: Her Aunt Rosie — purple double-bubble sweater, pink pants, gold bikeclips — is the chickest thing ever seen on Oriental Avenue.

"Hi, Pandy! Climb on the caboose, and let's vamoose!" *Oh, that Rosie, she is a card!*

They zoop down Oriental, with Pandora waving to the bemused populace, then turn into the traffic line on Pennsylvania Avenue: *Hubba-hubba. Zowie. Woo-woo. Honk-honk.* Rosie laughs in giddy self-appreciation. Pandora's spirits soar: *Oh, this is heady stuff!*

They sharp-left onto Marvin Gardens, and accelerate down the long hill with Rosie's paddy-green snood flapping like Superman's cape in Pandora's face. Pandora can feel her own hair stream out the back, except, of course, for the tumour behind her left ear, which — she is sobered to recall — is what this whole excursion is about.

Rosie brakes at the side of her apartment.

"Hop off, Pandy! End of the line."

The shop is black and white with a candystriped awning and a candystriped . . . "Ahh, Rosie, *please* don't make me."

Rosie groans. "You can't back out now, Pandy. I promised your ma. It'll look swell, you'll see! Besides . . . you can't go back to school with one ear stuck to your pointed head!" Pandora allows herself to be led forward, on the strength of Rosie's prestige and reassurances.

There are two white-smocked barbers — an old one with a face like cold porridge, and a young Italian with toasted-chestnut eyes. Rosie grins at the Italian. Porridge-face beckons Pandora into his black chair. He clips a sheet around her neck.

Rosie makes snip-snip motions behind Pandora's head, especially around the wad of Fleers Double Bubble gum matted behind her left ear.

The barber nods, unsmiling. He selects a long-handled razor.

"See? He's going to give you a razor-cut. They really know their beans in this place. It's as good as a beauty shop."

Porridge-face flexes his hands. Rosie is, of course, talking to the young Italian.

Cold fingers slip into the hollow of Pandora's neck. She closes her eyes. The barber's breath is tainted with tobacco and lozenges. He tongue-clicks the William Tell Overture in a brisk monotone.

The barber clasps a handful of Pandora's hair. Pandora stiffens. *ZZZZZzzzzzzt.* The blade tears through a dozen strands below her ear. Pandora yanks her head away. The razor gashes her ear. Blood spurts.

"Damn!" The barber drops his tongue-castinets. He grabs for a towel.

Blood runs down Pandora's cheek. It spatters the white sheet. Pandora thinks her hair is bleeding. She tries to pull away from the black chair.

"Pan-deee!" wails Rosie. "Sit still, you *goose*! You can't go out with your head *half-shaved*!"

It is a poor choice of words. Now the Italian is needed to clamp Pandora's wrists to the black arms of the chair. Rosie holds Pandora's head: Her sweetish perfume is as heavy as chloroform. Pandora feels herself pitching forward, through the thin crust of Time and Place that other people call reality. The arms of the chair coil three times around her. They encircle her throat with their Black Hands. . . .

The porridge-faced barber slides his clippers across Pandora's almost-naked neck, clicking his tongue, at a full gallop, through almost-open country, *on a fiery horse, with the speed of light, in a cloud of dust, with a hearty "Hi Ho . . ."*

Pandora's head lolls like a snapped dandelion on her chest. She can hear Rosie flirting with the *kemosavi* Italian. The

William Tell Overture builds to a flashy climax, then comes to a self-satisfied end. The porridge-faced barber flicks a whisk across Pandora's neck.

"Hey, you look swell!" exclaims Rosie, dubiously. "Doesn't she look *great*, eh Joe? A real Glamor Girl! The kids at school are gonna swallow their bubble gum when they get a load of you!" Another poor choice of words.

Pandora looks in the mirror. She sees a bobbed head stuck on a pyramid splashed in blood. A blood clot, on her left ear, gives her a comically lopsided look, like Mrs. Newton, when she has been listening on the party-line and forgotten to put back her earring.

Pandora sees nothing in the mirror that she recognizes. She sees more of herself on the floor.

The barber removes the stained bedsheet.

Pandora unglues herself from the barber's chair and, falling on one knee, wordlessly scoops her hair-clippings into her pyjama bag.

Rosie arches her eyebrow, then shrugs. She follows the young Italian to the cash-register. Porridge-face starts in on another customer.

Pandora waits outside the barber shop, under the candy-striped awning, clutching her brown bag. She hears Rosie laugh, *flutey-flute*, at the top of her voice, then walk towards her, *akkity-akk-akk*, on her staccato heels.

"Well, Pandy, that didn't take long, and I even got a date out of it for Saturday night. Isn't Joe a cutey, eh? He reminds me of Lon McAllister — just when he grins, I mean."

She kicks up her bikestand. "Let's wheel around the back, and then we can go up and see what's cooking with Ruby."

"Ahhhh. . . ." Pandora hangs back. "I don't think I better. . . ."

"Hey, what's wrong?" Pandora is examining her shoe. "You're staying tonight, aren't you?"

Pandora shakes her head. "I don't feel so good."

"Say, you aren't *sore*, are you?"

"I don't feel so good. . . ."

" 'Cause you haven't the right to be sore, Pandy. I only did it as a favour to your ma because I knew the guys here were good, and lotsa fun. *I* didn't stick the gum in your hair."

Pandora holds her stomach: "I don't feel so good."

"Wanna lie down?"

Pandora shakes her head. "No, I just want to go home. I think I got uh . . . collywobbles."

Rosie frowns. "Suit yourself." She throws her leg over her carmine StreamLiner. "Here. Jump on. I'll zip you back."

"No thanks. . . . I . . . uh . . . I'll feel better if I walk."

Rosie shrugs. "If you're sure."

"Yeah, I'm sure."

Pandora starts up Marvin Gardens.

Rosie wheels her bike down the alley past a stalled delivery truck: *Hubba-hubba. Zowie. Woo-woo. Honk-honk.* Rosie laughs in giddy self-appreciation.

Pandora rummages through her vanity drawer — under the pink seashell and the "Hi Sweetheart" pillowcase, under the bunny-puffs cut, for meanness' sake, from Adel-Ada's slippers. She pulls out the RCAF compact, given to her by Aunt Rosie, the one she has seen her use a hundred times to catch her mouth as she outlines it in Fatal Apple, then kisses it on a kleenex . . . leaving a scarlet valentine.

Pandora smashes the mirror. She smashes it with a hammer, over and over, until there is no sliver as large as a tealeaf. Pandora puts the ashes in an Evening in Paris perfume bottle. She buries them in an unmarked grave at the bottom of her God Garden.

"Stop that!" scolds Adelaide. "Now that just looks silly. Go look at yourself in the mirror, and see how silly that is. You can't glue hair on once it's come off. You're only going to ruin the rest. Honestly, Pandora, I never knew a child who has as many woes as you. I'm beginning to think it's all an act. I'm beginning to think you don't have any *real* feelings."

Pandora screams.

She screams without sound.

She screams and screams and screams and . . .

Pandora stands, naked, in front of her *mirror mirror mirror.* . . .

She looks at her cropped head. She looks at her spindly body.

Pandora opens a bottle. It is no ordinary bottle. It is a skull-and-crossbones bottle, stolen from the medicine chest.

Pandora withdraws the glass wand. She outlines her lips in Fatal Iodine. She kisses a kleenex, leaving a poisoned valentine.

Pandora's lips burn. She tips the bottle: There isn't enough to drink. She *imagines* it burns her throat.

Pandora turns out the light and climbs into bed, which she has puckered and pleated to look like Grannie Cragg's coffin. She sucks in her cheeks, and folds her arms in a crossbones over her chest: That's to make the poison work faster. She imagines it will take about three minutes.

Pandora says her prayers, revising them, as she always does, to cover the present situation: *"If I should wake before I die. . . ."*

142

School: Us

Fall, 1944

Miss Donnegan chews gum. Miss Bell scratches her bum. Pandora is in Miss Macintosh's room. Miss Macintosh has a ruddy face, like a jolly apple that has passed its prime: *Miss Macintosh's slip shows.*

Pandora saunters into Room 6, hangs up her coat, and falls into animated chatter with Ruth-Anne Baltimore and Georgia Brooks, her good friends from Room 3. She does not bother to eye the real-estate, for this year all is known: *If you sit by the windows you get to pull the green blinds up and down, but you can't see out so good and the radiators spit over you in winter. If you sit by the blackboard you can snitch chalk, but you have to put your answers on the board. If you sit by the pencil-sharpener you get lots of visitors, but you can't get up with a busted lead and take a stroll yourself.*

Pandora long ago dismissed these things for what they are: false lures. Her primary goal this year is a prestige seat in the smartness hierarchy, surrounded by as many as possible of her bestfriends. Classroom legitimacy + stable bonding = female power. Her total Grade 1 experience verifies this.

Miss Macintosh closes the door (at the front of the room, establishing Seat 1, Row 1 as the cardinal seat). She strolls to her desk, her raspberry slip lapping against her legs. "Hi, kids! Have a good summer?"

Bleats of "yes!" mingle with surprised laughter: *Imagine being called "kids" by a teacher!*

"I *had* a seating plan here. . . . Ah, yes. Starting at the door . . . Pandora Gothic, Ruth-Anne Baltimore, Cecily Battersea, Roger Parker. . . ." She scrunches the paper. "Oh, heck! Just sit where you like."

A gasp. A scramble. Pandora and Ruth-Anne, who have already seated themselves with dignity, watch the others cope with the joys and terrors of freedom.

Hola!

When the aisles are cleared, the social devastation around them is worse than they could imagine. Magda Lunt, a failure from last year, grins at Pandora, with bad teeth, from the seat beside her. Jessie Christie, last year's bully-showoff, with glasses as thick as Coke bottles, rattles his inkwells one seat over. Fat Flora Thwaite, the minister's frog-eyed daughter, fills-to-bursting the seat beside Ruth-Anne. "Blimpy" Bert Brown overflows the seat behind that.

These, then, are the persons *to* whom Pandora must entrust the passing of confidential notes; *with* whom she is expected to trade witticisms; *from* whom she must borrow coloured pencils and other luxuries not supplied by the school. What's more — *oh, this is too much!* — out of this crude assemblage Pandora will be expected to draw her boyfriend, since seats are equivalent to houses in the miniaturist world of the classroom, and there is a limit to how far romantic influence can travel.

Pandora and Ruth-Anne roll their eyes in sympathy. They are too well-bred to say what *could* be said, but . . .

Wait!

Miss Macintosh notices Blimpy Brown struggling in the little front seat he has chosen in defiance of his own realities. "Perhaps I might move a couple of you around after all. . . . Lucy Ford, why don't you exchange with John Johnson? And Jason Green . . . yes . . . would you please change with Bert Brown?"

Blimpy gratefully accepts the outsized seat at the back. Jason good-naturedly takes up residence beside Ruth-Anne and catercorner to Pandora. Jason has a glossy cowlick, nose-freckles, and an engaging grin. "He's a *whiz* at arithmetic," whispers Ruth-Anne. "He lives on my street."

"Now we'll need monitors." Miss Macintosh passes over the traditional paper-handlers, at either end of the rows, to name: "Flora Thwaite, John Johnson, Lillian Brill. . . . Come to the front for supplies, please."

Cecily Battersea denounces this new unorthodoxy in a scribbled note: "Wipe off everything you get from Silly Lily — *Nose snot!*" Ruth-Anne, finding this a bit raw for her tastes, passes it, without comment, to Pandora. Pandora opens it, but doesn't read it: She is too busy clinging to her desk and fighting for equilibrium. . . . *It has truly been a terrible terrible summer.*

Miss Macintosh hitches at her raspberry slip. "O.K., kids. Let's see what you remember from last year. . . . John Johnson — what's eight minus three?"

John scratches his groggy red head. "I . . . I don't remember, Miss Macintosh."

"Think of it as apples. If you had eight, and someone took away three, how many would you have?"

John squints one lemony eye, as if peering down a long time-telescope. He can picture ⋇, and, with difficulty, 88 88, but when he tries to take the one from the other, the spots won't stay still long enough for him to get them counted. "I don't remember," he says, with convincing finality.

"Phyllis Grove? . . . Marjorie Maitland? . . . How about five minus three?"

The mood in the class changes from bewilderment to indignation.

"*We didn't take those things,*" blurts Danny Ilson.

"You mean you didn't take *subtraction?*"

"Yes . . . but . . . We didn't take those numbers."

"What numbers *did* you take?"

"Uuuuhhhh. . . ." Danny, too, finds himself at the vanishing point of memory. "I forget."

Miss Macintosh writes a name on the board, in *yellow* chalk, confirming her reputation for galloping non-conformity.

"Georgia Brooks. . . . Who was FRANCIS DRAKE?"

"Um. . . ."

"Lucy Ford?"

"Ahhh. . . ."

"Yes Bert?"

"She's a friend of my sister's. She's in Room 11."

Miss Macintosh suppresses a chuckle. "Not *our* Francis Drake, Bert. Our Francis Drake was an explorer."

The recess bell rings.

"Ruth-Anne Baltimore. . . . How do you spell 'concert'?"

The class squirms.

"That was the *bell*, Miss Macintosh."

"What bell?"

"The *recess* bell."

"Recess? What's that?"

Room 6 is flabbergasted: "The *playing* bell. For the playground!"

"Recess?" Miss Macintosh's face brightens. "Oh, so that's what that clanging sound means. It's a good thing *you* remembered because *I* forgot."

Room 6 gasps, then explodes. *So that's it! It's been a GAME! Of course. Miss Macintosh is teasing them. Of course! Not even a teacher could be so unreasonable as to expect them to remember back to last June!*

Pandora and Ruth-Anne march out of Room 6, arm-in-arm. "Isn't Miss Macintosh funny?" burbles Ruth-Anne.

"Oh, she's O.K.," nods Pandora, too grudging to reveal the beginnings of a crush.

"Do you know what she reminds me of? A Macintosh apple!"

"She reminds *me* of a banana peel."

"Why a banana peel?"

"Because her *slip* is always showing!"

Pandora and Ruth-Anne, understandably collapsed by this repartee, find it difficult to walk upright, at a medium pace, inner hands joined, outer arms swinging, at fingertip distance front and aft, as required by Recess Drill Section III, Subsection A, Clause i of the Laura Secord Public School Criminal

Code. They are still laughing as they take up their stance on the Downstairs Girls' playground — not precisely where they held court last year, but close enough to suggest continuity. This easy confidence, amidst the raw nervousness of a first day of school, is irresistible. The other girls of Room 6 — twenty of them — cluster around.

It is a chattery group, but not a casual one: Georgia Brooks, Lucy Ford, Marjorie Maitland, Flora Thwaite — they are all under pressure to find a "bestfriend," and to find her quickly. The mechanics of classroom and playground life, as painfully learned last year, demand it. Ideally, a girl's bestfriend will reflect her status or improve it. *At least,* she must provide security — someone whose warm, preferably unpimpled, hand can be counted on when partners are called for gym or class projects. Someone to spare a girl the humiliation of being paired, forcibly, by the teacher with another "leftover."

Now there are just twenty minutes for pairing. Then the whistle will blow. Rule III A iii will come into effect: "All pupils shall return to class, in double-file . . ." Room 6 is an involuted, insecure society: Its structures will harden quickly. The couples who walk the fifty yards back to class, hand-in-hand, today and tomorrow, are as good as engaged. The girls who are rejected today and tomorrow face high risk of being leftovers, twice daily, five days a week, till the end of school: There will be divorces, there will be separations, there will be partner swaps, but these will be handled within the group, in an orderly fashion. No girl who is "in" will dare risk a general reshuffling that may leave her "out."

Pandora nudges Ruth-Anne. "There's Jill Peters."

The two girls call in unison: "Jiiii-il!"

Jill looks up, smiles, waves: Though she was their second-bestfriend last year, she makes no move to cover the ten yards of asphalt between them. Nor do Pandora and Ruth-Anne. They have been arbitrarily reassigned to new classroom societies. Though they have enough sense of social order to possess and structure these societies from within, they do not yet have enough sense of themselves as individuals to triumph over

149

such accidents of time and space. They know this instinctively. They knew it last June when, on the last day of school, they fell on Jill's neck, shed real tears over the announced separation, and exchanged Cracker Jack rings with intertwined hearts. Jill is lost to Pandora and Ruth-Anne over the gulf between village-classrooms. She is, at this moment, if she has a healthy sense of her own survival, deep in the urgency of another room's politics.

"I wish Jill were in our room," sighs Ruth-Anne. It is Jill's epitaph.

The whistle blows. *So soon? So soon?* Pandora and Ruth-Anne emerge, hand-in-hand, from the frantic Paul Jones, followed by four courting couples. The leftovers — some markedly inferior, others potential good citizens still too shy/confused to have chosen or been chosen — fall back, in a fluster, to the end of the long double-line. With one notable exception: Cecily Battersea, a smile like a leopard's spots spread under her brown bangs, jams up against Pandora and Ruth-Anne's clasped hands, crouching so Miss Warner, on playground duty, won't see she doesn't have a partner. Pandora and Ruth-Anne exchange a look: *Is Cecily trying to take Jill's place?* Neither one likes Cecily, but — they shrug philosophically — No. 3 is a difficult position to fill, requiring, as it does, a sort of imposed celibacy as the price of acting as a power reserve behind, and, on occasion, between the Big Two.

Last year Pandora and Ruth-Anne protected Jill (and the social order) by seeing she got first call on singles widowed by the 'flu bug or separated by a lovers' quarrel, and by rotating her around the group as a guest partner. Now they see — with grudging admiration — how boldly Cecily the Carpetbagger proposes to deal with this problem.

Miss Warner blows her whistle. She points imperiously to Magda Lunt, who is tucked behind the Room 6 couples, trying to creep up on Cecily in the mistaken belief she'll be thrilled to see her. Miss Warner gestures with her thumb, to the end of the line. Magda Lunt slinks back, past some fifty couples in diminishing stages of personal commitment, to Fat Flora, and Silly Lily, and Tokyo Phyllis, and the absolute rejects of other rooms, one slightly behind the other, stubbornly refusing to join hands until Miss Warner once more blasts her whistle, rebuking each in turn, forcing them to link up under the authority vested in her by Rule III A iii of the Laura Secord Criminal Code. Magda Lunt treads her shadow at the raggle-taggle end.

Pandora often wonders: *Why don't leftovers mate with other leftovers?* They seldom do: Fat Flora won't pair with Silly Lily because, after all, Lily is Silly. Silly Lily won't pair with Fat Flora, because, after all, Flora is Fat. They are still naive enough to hope for someone who will deny their outcaste state rather than confirm it. And, occasionally — just often enough — they flukishly snare a Georgia Brooks or a Marjorie Maitland. Never a Pandora Gothic or a Ruth-Anne Baltimore. As group leaders, these two possess the right of "bumping."

Magda Lunt is last into the classroom.

"Close the door, please," says Miss Macintosh. Magda does, but not without shooting a forgive-me look at Pandora: The door, after all, belongs to Pandora.

Miss Macintosh dabs at her rabbity nose. She tugs at her raspberry slip. "Since nobody knew who Francis Drake is, I guess we'd better start at the beginning."

She prints CHRISTOPHER COLUMBUS on the board. "Who is he?"

A dozen hands shoot up.

"Ahhh . . . that's better."

Miss Macintosh begins a patient review of the exploits of Christopher Columbus. Jessie Christie draws on a paper on his knee. He launches his drawing, simultaneously, with the launching of the Santa Maria. Pandora picks it up, as Columbus claims the Bahamas for Spain.

Jessie's drawing is a clever caricature of Miss Macintosh as a rabbit. Her cinnamon hair is labelled MOPSY. Her sagging bosom is labelled FLOPSY. Her trailing slip is labelled COTTON-TAIL. A stream of water gushing from between her legs is labelled PEE-TER PANTS HA! HA!

Pandora, shocked, rips up the picture as the Santa Maria

piles up on the rocks of Hispaniola. Jessie Christie — amply rewarded — chortles the lascivious, phlegm-scraping chortle of a man who gets his jollies by whispering obscenities to white-gloved ladies at bus-stops.

Miss Macintosh drops her yellow chalk. "Jessie! Pandora! That's enough. Any more nonsensery from you two, and you'll both stay after four."

Jessie smirks.

The class titters.

Pandora gags: *To be publicly linked with Jessie Christie on the first day of school! Can anything good come of the year after that?*

Ruth-Anne Baltimore moves in, in earnest, after lunch. There it is, spread across her desk for all the world to see, with Ruth-Anne presiding, at centre, like a princess over her dowry:

Construction paper of every hue.

A silver stapler with 150 staples.

A red ruler with a *thermometer* on the end.

A robin's egg pencil-holder with matching sharpener.

A *four*-drawer pencilbox overflowing with Aphrodite pencils: *emerald, topaz, jade, ruby, turquoise, sapphire.*

Then, of course, there are the leisure-time items: a white skipping-rope, long enough for double-dutch. A gold yoyo. A silver Bo-Lo bat. And, for after school: her god-damned patent-leather tapdance shoes!

It makes Pandora a little sick to see it all littered there: *Sometimes I hate you Ruth-Anne Baltimore!*

Ruth-Anne prods Pandora with an Aphrodite wand: "If you want to borrow anything, Pandora, just ask."

Pandora buries her green eyes in her fists: *Eat dirt, Ruth-Anne. Eat dirt!*

* * *

Pandora hides around the corner of Laura Secord Public School. She sees Miss Macintosh emerge — 4:26 — through the brass-ringed oak door. She sees her pause at the chrysanthemum bed where Janitor Frank Foukes, twisted by shrapnel from the *Pack-Up-Your-Troubles* Great War, sprinkles fertilizer. Janitor Foukes offers her a chrysanthemum. Miss Macintosh, blushing, accepts it. She secures her pancake hat against windgust and hurries, raspberry slip swishing, onto Lower Boardwalk.

Pandora pursues — at a discreet distance — darting behind mailboxes, verticalizing herself behind telephone poles.

Miss Macintosh stops at a drugstore on St. Charles Place. She buys a Mill City Clarion and a package of Pep-O-Mint Lifesavers. She discards a wrapper. Pandora scoops it up.

Miss Macintosh turns onto States Avenue. She climbs the side of an aging white triplex, and enters at the third floor. Pandora mounts the same fire-escape. She pauses between milkbox and garbage-can. She lays one green eye against a gap in the grey-white curtains. She sees Miss Macintosh with her feet in a tub of water and — *hola!* — puffing a cigarette. She is wearing a plaid bathrobe parted to reveal a slinky nightgown of the same raspberry hue as her wayward slip, and — *hola!* — white breast. Occasionally she reaches down her neck and *scratches* herself.

Pandora adds all this richness of detail to her growing cache of secret knowledge. Secret knowledge is, of course, secret power.

Pandora slides her black notebook into her trenchcoat pocket and slips, with Bulldog Drummond, back into the fog.

Scarlet! vermillion! gold!
The leaves turn colour, almost as you watch them.

Arlene and Pandora rake them into a waxy pyramid, and cannonball into the centre. They stuff handfuls down each other's giggling sweaters, and bell them around their legs in gaudy dancing skirts. They disguise themselves as blowing branches, and sneak up on Mrs. Dicey's chestnuts as an Act of God. They sew ten scarlet maples into a fan, luminous with its own mortality, and they present it to Old Mr. Grandby, who sweats in a time-warp of summer heat, and is dying. . . .

Yesterday's leaves turn to khaki in the gutters, and then to black mush. Lyle Gothic gathers them in sacks for next year's cabbages. Mrs. Niobe turns them to smoke that hangs about her head in an acrid yellow shroud.

Pandora peels an onion, the way Grannie Cragg taught her:
"If the skin is very tough,
The coming winter will be rough."

Pandora has a new subject. It is called Current Events. On the first school day of every month she is supposed to select the news story that seems most important to her.

Pandora spreads the Mill City Clarion, October 2, 1944, across the living-room rug. She reads, with the help of Adel-Ada:

1,000 Bombers Hit Siegfried. . . .

Beautiful Gams Insured. . . . Mme. Mistinguette, famed singing star, displays the legs she insured for $3 million owing to the danger of bicycling in wartime Paris.

Allied Planes Shoot Allied Prisoners. . . . "Our lads up in the air had no way of knowing we were their own chaps. It was marvellous work!"

Nazi Whip of Human Hair Sent Son by Soldier. . . .

Pandora thinks for quite some time before cutting out of the paper:

Newly Released 630th Casualty List Contains 153 Names. . . . Whitesides, Joseph, Pte; Kenny, Ronald, Cpl; Reginald, William, Pte. . . .

If the skin is very tough,
The coming winter will be rough.

The girls of Room 6 congregate in a pinwheel of popularity with Pandora and Ruth-Anne at the centre.

"Let's play Spanish tag."

"We played that yesterday."

"What about Red Rover?"

"O.K. Who's going to pick?"

"It's Lucy's turn."

"Yeah, Lucy and Georgia."

"First call!" shouts Lucy.

The two captains stand on either side of the group.

"Ann Billings," says Lucy, choosing her bestfriend.

"Marjorie Maitland," says Georgia, doing the same.

"Pandora Gothic," says Lucy, with little hesitation.

"Ruth-Anne Baltimore," says Georgia, with even less.

As the pool of talent shrinks, the time required to choose expands. This, of course, has nothing to do with assessing anyone's ability to play Red Rover: Such minor competence is assumed. What Lucy and Georgia are, quite unabashedly, telling the group is whom they like today, and in what order. It is their right/duty as captains.

"Hannah Gibbs," says Lucy.

"Myrtle Levers," replies Georgia.

Now Lucy must knit her brow with the sheer challenge of finding merit in the remaining mediocrity. The unchosen ones shift and simper: They do not consider leaving. The girls of Room 6 — from the top of the hierarchy to the bottom — are already prisoners of society, programmed to seek a sense of identity through something called "niceness." Niceness is a social quality measurable only in relation to others. In a society as naive as Room 6, this means the relentless taking of popularity polls. That is why the office of captain is more-or-less rotated around the group: It is more important for the girls of Room 6 to be conspicuously chosen than to exercise the power of choice. Popularity *is* power.

"We've got seven each," says Lucy, pushed to the limit of tolerable choice. "I guess that's enough, eh?"

"Yeah, that's enough."

Of the seven "castoffs," four scamper away to form a second playgroup. This leaves Silly Lily, Fat Flora and Magda Lunt as hardcore rejects. They doggedly take up a position around the main group, not as part of it, but available should the call go out. They are, in the official glossary of Room 6, "bystanders" — the same girls who will be transformed, by the blowing of the end-of-recess whistle, into leftovers. Primary school is rich in the argot of rejection.

There are five minutes left to play. The teams join hands in facing lines. Lucy and Georgia remember at exactly the same time: "First call!" With little at stake, it is time for democratic illusion: "One potato, two potato . . ."

Georgia's team gets first call. Her line advances, singing: "Red Rover, Red Rover, let *Pan-dee* come over!"

If Georgia's team were seriously playing to win, it would have called over the weakest member of the other side to attempt to break through its locked hands instead of the most popular, but there is something *mystical* about the chanting of a name that requires it to be done on the basis of who's who and what's what: Room 6 is exercising its real priorities.

Pandora easily crashes the line. If she had failed, she would have had to join up with Georgia's side. By the end of recess, so many players will have changed teams that nobody will know who won, or what side she's on. Nobody cares. The real game ended with the choosing up of sides.

Cecily Battersea lets go her hand as Marjorie Maitland barrels through. Marjorie cuts her knee, and is sent to the nurse's room.

"By-stander!" calls Lucy.

Magda, Silly Lily, Fat Flora look at once resentful and eager. Now there is no question of Lucy's choosing for popularity: *What Solomon could?* Lucy sizes up the physical potential of each bystander as if she were a coach in championship play.

"Pick Fat Flora," whispers Cecily. "She'll be like a tub of lard."

"Floo-rah!" calls Lucy. She does not say *Fat* Flora. Only the boys are mean enough to say that to her face.

Flora makes a dignified attempt at reluctance. "Oh, all right."

The whistle blows.

"Whoops! Sorry! Guess we gotta go."

The Red Rover girls line up in two's, in accordance with Rule III A iii. Georgia pairs with Cecily, despite her resentment over Marjorie's accident: Nobody likes Cecily, but Cecily is stuck on herself, and that has a potency all its own in a society as insecure as Room 6.

Miss Macintosh is putting arithmetic problems on the board: The girls enter the class in a tidy block. The boys straggle in, in one's, two's, three's.

The boys did not play together as a classroom clique: Roger Parker "subbed" as shortstop in a baseball game on the Big Diamond. Danny Ilson played scrub on the Little Diamond. John Johnson and Bob Worth watched the Big Diamond game: They were spectators, not bystanders. Jessie Christie, who is brawny for his age but a poor athlete because of his glasses, bloodied the nose of a boy who called him Four Eyes. Jason Green played chestnuts and lost. Bertie Brown played marbles and won.

The boys — unlike the girls — are learning to define themselves, as individuals, by what they can do, rather than as group members, by how others react to them. Their teams are, to a considerable extent, chosen across grade and classroom lines on the basis of skill and dominance. Most of them are more concerned with what they play, than with whom they play. Rules and rituals are used to define the game, not who plays it. When material wealth changes hands, it does so as the spoils of victory, not as tokens of friendship.

Now Bert Brown rattles his hard-won marbles in his inkwell. Buoyed up by the confidence this gives him, he whispers a dirty joke to Roger Parker. Roger, high on adrenalin from his baseball game, guffaws louder than is wise.

"Less noise, boys," says Miss Macintosh, over her shoulder.

Roger passes the joke on to Danny Ilson: Danny snickers aloud. Jessie Christie, resentful at being left out, throws a paper airplane at Danny Ilson.

Miss Macintosh spins around: "Boys, *please!*"

Danny Ilson tosses back the airplane. It crashdives on Jason's head. Jason giggles.

"This is the *last time!*" snaps Miss Macintosh, switching to red chalk. "*Next* time there'll be extra arithmetic problems."

Most of the girls already have their scribblers on their desks, with margins drawn: Since they carry their social structure to and from the playground, on their backs, they have little trouble settling down now or in identifying with the efforts of their teachers (all female, more because of the poor pay than The War) to maintain discipline. Several of the more "ladylike" girls, already deep in their roles as preservers of the petit bourgeoisie, shoot the noisier boys reproving glances.

The boys' playground society is a *symbolic* representation of adult male society. On maturity, the boys will be expected to transfer the same sportsman-like qualities of competition and teamanship to the business, scientific, academic and professional worlds. (Though the athletic arena, where they were blooded, will remain a place of high romance, and some will lose their souls there.)

The girls' playground society is a *true,* rather than a symbolic, representation of adult female society.

During the adolescent years, many girls will fight for a sense of identity apart from their popularity rating, but, during high school, social pressure, exerted through the dating system, will push them back to the passive position of waiting to be chosen rather than of choosing. Now, however, they will be doubly passive, since their popularity rating will come from outside their own group: from the male group. This induces them to disband their own groups, as irrelevant, or at least to make them subservient to the male groups. Female identity, as defined by doing rather than being, will become a maverick quality largely unsupported by group structure.

Even where independent female groups exist, they will be microcosms for which there is no macrocosm. It is implicit in all male groups that they refer back to the political system from which they derive a strong mystique.

So it is on Laura Secord playground: The girls form highly structured city states, which co-exist: They are provincial. The boys participate in shifting groups within a single power pyramid: They are universal. At Laura Secord, politics = baseball. The Big Boys who play the Big Diamond hold the cabinet posts.

"O.K.," says Miss Macintosh, putting down her chalk. "Start on these problems, and no more fuss. Those that aren't completed will have to be done as homework."

There is a collective boy/girl groan — at least this much is in agreement here and now.

* * *

Pandora strides out into the continuing panorama of autumn with a heavy sense of purpose.

She collects a sampling of leaves from the Goodfellows' casual orchard — rotten apple, wormy plum, blighted peach, buggy pear. She adds a floppy elephant ear from Mrs. Newton's nosy catalpa, a shiny tongue from Mrs. Lawrence's jolly holly, a crabby brown hand from Mrs. Dicey's horsey chestnut, an elegant golden finger from the Stintons' snooty laurel, a teardrop from Mrs. Niobe's sad black ash, a greenback from the Barkers' parsimonious persimmon, a flaming tongue from St. Cecilia's burning bush, an irregularity from Mrs. Spittal's queer chokecherry and a bad smell from the Clays' socially unacceptable stinkweed.

Pandora presses, waxes and mounts her leaves. It is a considerable collection, but there is one leaf missing: a leaf from the flowering dogwood behind the highboard fence at St. Cecilia's Home for Cripples and Incurables.

"It's the crucifixion tree," Pandora's mother once told her. "The petals form the cross. In autumn, the berries are like drops of blood."

Pandora peeps through the overwrought iron-gate.

It is Sunday: The Cripples and Incurables are planted about the lawn in their wheelchairs. Ladies in white robes take their temperatures. Ladies in black robes promenade, in pairs, among the verandahs, and balconies, and cupolas, and arches, and pilasters of the white-washed building that rambles, in disciplined incoherence, through many architectural styles, over three green hillocks.

It is noon: The shadows of the nuns are smothered in their robes. They look like tapestry figures pulled into Ascension by the drawing rays of the sun.

Beep! beep! beep!

Pandora leaps back from the gate. A Cadillac swoops past. It disgorges men in black robes. One slams the door. Another laughs. A third makes choppy hand motions. The nuns hold out for awhile, then they, too, become brisk, practical, a little fussy, jarred out of archaic serenity into the present tense.

The group moves inside, past a doorpost carving of the crucifixion that Shelly Clay says sheds real blood every Easter.

Pandora studies her dogwood tree.

She is afraid of the Catholics. She is afraid of the Cripples, but. . . . Miss Macintosh has promised that the person who has the best leaf collection can wash blackboards *for a month*! It is not just the honour. Pandora is used to winning, but . . . she imagines . . . she *hopes* that . . . in the mellow sunlight, after the others have gone home . . . maybe . . . she will get to know Miss Macintosh — Tillie — better, and she will be able to tell her things . . . things that have accumulated inside of her . . . things that are becoming too heavy to shift. . . .

Pandora sprints ten yards through St. Cecilia's Cripples' gate. She dives under a juniper bush. She plunges into a hemlock hedge. A branch of dogwood protrudes into the hemlocks. She picks a ketchup-splotched leaf.

Crack! A twig snaps. Pandora spins. She sees . . . *hola!* A drooling mouth! four brown teeth! eyes like broken eggs! hands like tangled fishhooks! . . . He is holding a book on his wheelchair-lap. He points to his name in block letters: JOB, MY BOOK.

He smiles. He beckons with a hand possessing — Pandora curses the day she learned to count — *two thumbs!*

He opens his book at a glossy picture of an orange butterfly. "Mmmmmahmmm," he says, running his multiple thumbs over the name.

"Mon-arch?" asks Pandora, understanding him grudgingly.

Job nods with delight. He points to an iridescent blue-green butterfly.

"Great Pur-ple Hair-streak?"

Pandora reluctantly accepts the book. Bottling her repugnance, she concentrates on a vainglorious display of reading skill, sounding out each butterfly name with the stylish mummery of a talented reader adventuring through the Printed Unfamiliar. "Haaar-vest-errr . . . Black Swall-ooowww . . . OHH!"

Pandora saw the hand move, but not soon enough. The cancerous lump passes her lips and lodges in her throat. She gags: It scrape-burns her gullet.

Job extends his mangled hand containing two more humbugs matted with grey hair: *Another?* Pandora's stomach churns around the first. She bolts from the Cripples' Home. She spits outside the gate, *inside* the burning bush. She spits with all the fruity grandeur of the Clays in influenza season. She scours her mouth with Lifebuoy.

It is three days before Pandora admits these precautions have not been enough: There is a bud, the size of a B-B on her left thumb.

Pandora thinks about Job's hooked thumbs. She thinks about her father's steel hook.

Pandora shudders.

"Ugh!" says Ruth-Anne, dropping Pandora's hand on the way out to recess. "What's *that?*"

Pandora stuffs the thumb with the wart she has tried to saw off with a breadknife into her pocket.

"Gee, that's *awful*. What is it?"

Pandora blurts out her fears. . . . About Job. About his two hooked thumbs. About the humbug. . . .

Spoken aloud, on a bright Monday morning, none of it sounds so bad. Ruth-Anne is skeptical. Pandora, not wishing to appear the complete fool, tells her the rest: About Job's evil eye, set like a fried egg in the centre of his forehead. About the curse hung on the Cripples' post, with the bleeding Jesus. About the infectious diseases that waft, with the eastwind, through the Lepers and Cripples behind St. Cecilia's highboard quarantine fence.

Now that Ruth-Anne has the full story, the possibilities are too intriguing to dismiss: "I guess it *could* be another thumb.

Or a hook. It's in the right place, if you were going to have one."

"*Another thumb? Another thumb?*" Room 6 gathers excitedly around. Cecily Battersea snatches Pandora's hand from her pocket. "Say! Doesn't your father? . . ."

Pandora's Cripple's Curse becomes the sensation of Room 6:

"If I were you, I'd use toad juice."

"If I were you, I'd tie a string around it and choke its blood."

"If I were you, I'd wrap it with raisin bread and warm milk. My mother says the warts go into the raisins."

At first Pandora is gratified; then bored; then annoyed; then she panics. "It's just a wart! It'll fall off if I don't fiddle it!"

Room 6 is not to be cheated of its marvels so easily:

"If I were you, I'd rub it with spit on a white stone."

"If I were you — "

"If I were *me*," snaps Pandora, "I'd use a Magical Magnet! Whenever I had pins and needles, my grannie always held it over my foot, and they all came out, as if they were real pins and needles!" Now that Pandora has thought of it, the Magical Magnet is a good idea. "I'll bring it this aft and show you!"

Pandora returns to Room 6, after lunch, without her Magical Magnet: It was one of the pieces of metal Adel-Ada hauled off for their COG buttons.

Jessie Christie returns to Room 6, after lunch, with a bulge in his breeks' pocket: Whistling, he turns out a heavy metallic object. He holds it, casually, so Pandora can read the white letters painted on its side: REMARKABLE MAGICAL MAGNET. He amuses himself by making paperclips dance over a white paper.

Pandora has no choice.

"Can I see it Jessie?"

"You're *looking*, aren't you?"

Gently, reasonably: "In my hands."

"Nuts! You see with your *eyes,* not your *hands!*"

Morosely: "How do I know it'll work?"

"It'll work all right — you said so yourself. Besides . . ." Jessie underplays it coolly, "my father got it from an Indian."

"Oh." Pause. Pause. Pause. Humbly: "What do you want for it?"

"Not for sale."

"What for *use?*"

"Not for use!" Jessie chortles. "I'd sooner see you *with two thumbs!*"

A half-dozen girls skip "Rosie Apple" in the shadow and sunlight under Miss Macintosh's geranium boxes. Pandora hears them as she scrubs blackboards. She thinks, with a pang: *I'll probably never be able to skip again. My hooks'll get caught in the ropes. I won't even be able to be an ever-ender.*

Pandora drops her red blackboard rag into the scalding water. She watches it inflate, like a misshapen valentine. *And all for what? Miss Macintosh doesn't even stay in the room when I scrub. She talks in the hall with dwarfy Foukes, or else she goes home and leaves me.*

Pandora wrings her red rag. *It isn't even a decent rag! It doesn't even hold water.* She swipes at the blackboard. *It's too silky.* She shakes out the rag. In spite of herself, she giggles.

Pandora's wart is now the size of a pea.

"Poor Pandora. Another thumb. Another thumb," moues Room 6, keeping the horrendous fantasy alive with its sympathy.

At gym, Miss Macintosh capriciously pairs Ruth-Anne with Fat Flora, and Pandora with Maggoty Magda. What Pandora can't help seeing is this: Ruth-Anne doesn't seem to mind. What's more: Magda Lunt is not noticeably in ecstasy.

Pandora fixes Miss Macintosh with a shaft of ulcerated love. *Miss Warner wasn't Nice, but she was Fair. Miss Warner was Crabby, but you could count on her.*

Pandora eyes her blasted thumb: Whether or not she has the disease, it is clear she must take the cure. She confronts Jessie on the Boys' side of the cloakroom: "Jessie, I will trade you a *secret* for the Remarkable Magical Magnet. . . ."

Pandora sets her scrubpail behind the desk where Miss Macintosh is marking papers. She squeezes out her red rag, in a hot, gushy stream.

Miss Macintosh looks up. "I'd like to thank you, Pandora, for the conscientious job you've been doing on the boards." She smiles, with bruised eyes. "I do think, though, dear, it's a bigger job than either of us thought. I hate to see you working so hard when the weather's so nice."

Miss Macintosh wanders over to the window. Pandora tags her with uneasy eyes. "I think there must be more kids playing out there this evening than at recess." She plucks a spent geranium from her windowbox. "These lovely fall days don't last long, do they?"

Miss Macintosh wanders back to her desk.

Pandora hastily mounts her dunce's stool. She attacks the board in broad, determinedly hostile sweeps.

Miss Macintosh sits on the edge of her desk. Pandora feels a tight coil of panic stir inside her chest.

"Pandora . . . tell me, dear, has anything been troubling you lately?" Pandora feels the coil of panic start to unwind. She seizes her red rag, and starts jabbing at the board. "You don't seem very happy a lot of the time. If something's bothering you, it might be good to talk about it."

Too late, too late, too late!

Pandora frantically works on a stain she knows is permanent: *round and round and round,* with her slippery red rag. *Round and round and round . . .* trying to wind up the panic as fast as it unwinds. . . .

"Pandora, look this way a minute." Pandora turns, without looking.

"Look at your desk." Pandora looks.

"Look what's on the floor: bits of blotting paper. Chewed

pencil. The crumbs of a sponge rubber I saw you eat! Oh dear! Don't think for a moment I care about the mess. It's just that you seem so . . . so . . . nervous all the time."

Pandora stumbles from her dunce's stool. She rinses her rag.

"It isn't just the paper, dear. It's your hands. . . . You've chewed your nails past the quick. And look at your thumb! You've eaten it raw!"

Pandora works on her stain: round and round and . . . *It isn't even a decent rag! If only I had a decent rag so the water wouldn't slip out!*

"Another thing. . . ." Miss Macintosh bites her lip: "You mustn't mind if I split up you and Ruth-Anne sometimes. I think it's nice when the shyer girls get a chance to work with you. It might help you, too, if you'd make an effort to . . ." Miss Macintosh studies the resolute shoulders, the matchstick spine. She picks up her coat. She picks up her hat. She pauses, hand on the doorknob. "Don't stay too late, dear. Mr. Foukes will do the high spots."

The clicking of the lock snaps Pandora's spine. She tumbles from her dunce's stool. She sobs into her wet rag: *If only she'd given me a decent rag. How can you do a job if you don't have the right rag?*

Jessie Christie raps on the fire-escape door: *Ra-tat-tat.*

"Go *away!*" howls Pandora. "I changed my mind!"

"Oh no, you don't." Jessie has taken the precaution of jamming the door with a blackboard brush. Pandora hurls herself against the other side. He easily shoves past her. "O.K. here's the magnet. Where's the secret?"

"No secret." Pandora tries to look smug: "It was a *trick!*"

"No trick!" Jessie knows desperation when he sees it. "There's a secret, all right. Give it, or I'll break your warty arm."

Pandora hides her arm behind her back: Jessie sees a flash of red, of a distinctive hue.

"What's that?"

"What?"

"In your hand."

Jessie twists Pandora's arm. He wrenches the red rag from her fingers. "Ohhh *hee hee hee hee!*" His eyes rattle like marbles at the bottom of two Coke bottles. "I've got Macky's *silk pants!*" He twirls them around his finger. "I've got Macky's *dirty pants!*"

Pandora panics. "They're *not* dirty! That's just a scorch mark! Give them back!"

Jessie has been speaking figuratively. Now he examines the raspberry confection with reckless hope. He sees a brown stain at the crotch. "That's *shit!*" he whinnies in boundless joy. "Silly-Tillie has crapped her drawers!"

Pandora is aghast: "It's *not!* It's a *scorch* mark! My mother does it all the time. That's probably why she threw them out!"

"It's *shit!*" insists Jessie Christie, making the pants dance obscenely over his head. "Shit shit *shit!*"

Pandora snatches at the pants. "*Please,* Jessie! *Pleeeeeeease!* I don't care about the warts. *Pleeeeeeeeeease!*"

Jessie hesitates: *A woman's tears!* He suffers a spasm of gallantry: *Maybe I should just throw them in her face?!*

"Jes-seeeee!"

It is Godfrey Trumps, reminding him of his greater responsibilities. "A bargain's a bargain!" shouts Jessie, lunging for the door.

Godfrey Trumps and Horace Ghostie are waiting on the fire-escape. They snigger. They whoop. They rampage across the schoolground, snatching skip-ropes, confiscating tennisballs, annihilating hopscotches, taking female hostages, washing their faces in the silky pants and screeching:

"We've got Macky's shitty drawers!
Kiss her ass or we'll take yours!"

They burn Miss Macintosh's gallant red drawers under Room 6's window, with the smoke curling up through the geranium plants.

"Hot pants! Hot pants!" bawls Godfrey. "Come and get your Hot Cross pants!"

Jessie tortures the smouldering remains onto a stick. He prances back and forth in front of the windowboxes, mocking Miss Macintosh with effeminate gestures and an idiot's grin. Jessie's eyes, magnified on the ends of their glass stalks, look very very miserable, the way they always do just before he does something particularly nasty: Jessie Christie lights a cigarette in Miss Macintosh's burning crotch.

Pandora sits down on her dunce's stool. She sobs into her pail of dirty water. She cries for broken faith and the spilt milk of human kindness, and every guilty tear turns into a white maggot.

Pandora rips the bottom from her cotton slip. She scours the boards, most effectively, except, of course, for the permanent stain. *See? see? I could have done it, if only she'd given me a decent rag!*

Pandora's wart falls off.

"I told you it would," scoffs Arlene. "You don't get thumbs from humbugs, even if they *are* covered with Cripples' hair."

Pandora turns on Arlene: "Liar!"

* * *

Ruth-Anne Baltimore loves Jason Green.

Pandora Gothic loves Jason Green.

"That's not fair!" exclaims Ruth-Anne. "That means *you'll* get him."

Pandora nods: *That's true.* Most of the boys in Room 6 like her best. Ruth-Anne is pretty, poised, charming — all the things little girls are taught to be. Pandora is aggressive, dynamic, fearless — all the things little boys are taught to be. When it comes to a showdown between love and self-love in Grade 2, narcissism always wins.

Jason makes it official, that very morning, with an initialed heart carved on his pink eraser. He passes it to Pandora during social studies. Pandora breaks the news to Ruth-Anne at recess, after Ruth-Anne has stumped her with "Sabu Dastagir" in the Movie Star Game: No point in letting Ruthie hear it from someone less tactful. No point in letting Ruth-Anne break her heart.

Things move quickly after that.

Jason invites Pandora to play at his house after school. Pandora accepts.

Jason and Pandora stroll, hand-in-hand, across the playground. Ruth-Anne trudges behind, carrying their Garden of Stories readers. Jessie Christie trots beside, dishonouring them: "Shame! shame! double-shame!" Pandora plucks her hand from the hand of Jason, her lover. She retrieves her reader from Ruth-Anne, her friend. She brings it down on the head of Jessie Christie, her tormentor. Jessie crumples. His glass eyes slide down his nose. He gropes for them in the dead leaves.

Pandora is blasted by a terrible insight: *I shouldn't have hit him so hard. Now Jessie Christie will have no choice but to love me.*

Jason's house is a Boardwalk greystone three doors down from the Baltimores'. Ruth-Anne follows Jason and Pandora to the side-door. She pauses, expectantly.

"Oh, all right," says Pandora, secretly relieved. "But you have to leave if *I* say so, since I'm the Invited Guest."

Jason's basement is dark, low-ceilinged, walnut-panelled, with leather chairs, an artificial fireplace, a forest-fire lamp, and a brass-studded bar with four chrome stools.

Pandora is bedazzled.

It is the first recreation-room she has ever seen: *Where does Jason's mother do her washing? Where does she sift her ashes?*

Jason strikes a pose before the intimidating bar-panel. Ruth-Anne slides up onto a stool with the insouciance of a young Lauren Bacall. Pandora clambers up beside her.

"What'ull you have?"

" 'Scotch," says Ruth-Anne. "A double."

Jason nods. "One 'scotch-on-the-rocks, coming up." He scoops two dips of icecream. He squirts butterscotch sauce. He slides the tulip dish down the counter. "One double, on-the-double!"

Pandora is impressed. She is also aggrieved. She doesn't like Ruth-Anne's easy familiarity here. She doesn't understand the language.

Jason leans across the counter. "What'ull you have?"

" 'Berry!" Pandora adds boldly: "On the double rocks!"

Jason frowns. "We don't have 'berry."

"Pineapple?"

Jason is polite but firm: "All out."

"Banana?"

Jason drops his bartender's pose: "We only have butterscotch. The rest of the taps are my father's."

Butterscotch is Pandora's favourite (now that she has renounced chocolate) but not at the price of copying Ruth-Anne; not at the price of shattering her illusion that this is a magic world where everything is possible. "Just give me the icecream," she says more sharply than she intends. "We'll pretend it's got marshmallow."

Jason's aplomb is gone: He slops over the dish. Unforgivably, he gives Pandora less than Ruth-Anne.

"You should have asked for a *double*," whispers Ruth-Anne.

"I didn't *want* a double!" snaps Pandora. *Oh, she is getting fed up with this den of sophisticates!*

Ruth-Anne dabs her mouth with a Happy New Year serviette. She swivels from her stool. "Now *I'll* serve *you*!" She joins Jason behind the bar. They whisper. They giggle.

"What's so funny?" demands Pandora.

"Nothing," chirrups Ruth-Anne.

"Nothing," chuckles Jason.

Now Pandora is truly vexed. She wipes her mouth on a Bon Voyage serviette, jumps haughtily down from her stool, and ... "EEEEEeeeeek!" Jason's dog has pooped on the floor, and she has practically stepped in it!

Ruth-Anne and Jason whoop with laughter. Pandora snatches her Garden of Stories from the counter, and strides to the basement door.

"Wait!" calls Jason. "It's not *real* poop! It's *joke* poop!"

Joke poop? Joke poop?

Jason holds the disgusting blob *on his hand*! "Touch it."

Pandora does: It is hard, like plastic. It stinketh not.

"It's called Dog-Gone-It."

Pandora allows Jason to place it on her palm. She turns it over and over, marvelling: *Joke poop!*

Pandora giggles.

Jason giggles.

Ruth-Anne giggles.

Ruth-Anne whispers to Jason.

Pandora remembers, suddenly, the situation here. "I think we've had enough 'nonsensery' from you two for today. I think you had better go, Ruth-Anne. The rest of the planned activities are for Invited Guests, only."

Ruth-Anne is a lady: She leaves quickly, quietly. The sunlight flashes, briefly, through the basement door. Pandora and Jason are left, facing each other, in the gloom.

"Do you . . . uh . . . have any games?"

Jason brightens. "Sure." He opens a brass woodbox. "I got Sorry, Snakes'n'Ladders, Blitzkrieg, Chinese Checkers."

"Sorry will be fine."

"It's no fun with just two."

"Chinese Checkers?"

"I lost all the marbles to Bert Brown."

"I think I better go," says Pandora.

"O.K.," says Jason.

Pandora picks up her reader.

Jason screws up his face as if to suck a lemon.

"Well . . ."

Jason plants a noisy kiss on Pandora's cheek.

"*Well!*" Pandora's right hand tightens on her reader.

Jason, no fool, shoves the joke poop into her other hand: "Here."

Pandora is confounded: "For *keepers?*"

Jason nods.

This, then, is no fly-by-night affair. *This is,* as Rosie would call it, *a Candy-Box Affair.* "Thank you, Jason," says Pandora, very sincerely. "I admire it greatly."

Jason grins.

"Will you gift-wrap it, please?"

Jason fishes a Bar Mitzvah serviette from behind the

counter. Pandora frowns: "I don't think you'd better give me that. My mother is *death* on saloons."

Jason is puzzled, but obliging: He substitutes To the Bride, in gold script.

Pandora promenades down Boardwalk Ave. with her gift-wrapped joke poop held flat on her palm.

She hears footsteps in the leaves behind her: It is Ruth-Anne, of course.

"Hi!" Pandora flaunts her benefaction.

Ruth-Anne, ignoring it, falls into step. She asks simply, earnestly: "Are you in love with Jason?"

Pandora thinks about the joke poop: "Yes, I guess I am."

"Are you going to marry him?"

Pandora thinks about the icecream bar: "Yes.... Probably."

"That's good." Ruth-Anne sighs in what sounds suspiciously like relief. "*You* may as well, because *I* can't. My mother won't let me." She cocks an adult eyebrow. "He's *Jewish*."

Jewish? Jewish? "That doesn't matter! My mother will let me if *I* say."

"I bet she won't."

"She will, too!"

"She's a Christian, isn't she?"

"Of course!"

"Then she *won't*! My *aunt's* a Christian, and she won't let my cousin marry Jason's brother!"

This is too much specialized information for Pandora to absorb. "Why don't you go home, Ruth-Anne! I can hear your mother calling!"

"*Oh!*" Ruth-Anne turns on her heel. "My mother has never called me *on the street* in my life!" *The very idea.*

Adel washes the last Tranquillity Rose plate; Ada dries it; Pandora puts it away. The twins retire to their corkwork, nails turnabouts.

Adelaide is in the kitchen, ironing butcher's aprons, sprinkling them with water from a vinegar bottle, and burning herself quite frequently.

"Mother. . . ." Pandora goes straight to the point: "Can I marry Jason Green?"

Adelaide smiles indulgently. "Is Jason one of the little boys you know?"

"He's in my class. He's a Jew."

Adelaide winces: *Darn!* She sucks her burned hand. "Don't say 'Jew,' Pandora. Say 'Hebrew.' "

"Well. . . . Can I marry him?"

Oh dear! Adelaide strives to be fair, but the crucifixion is the heart and soul of life to her. She sprinkles vinegar water.

"*Can* I mother?" Pandora shifts ground impatiently: "What's a J- - a what-you-said?"

Adelaide relaxes. *Ahhh, that's better.* "An Hebrew," she replies in the same confident tone she would use for her Sunday School class, "is one who does not accept Jesus Christ as his, or her, personal Saviour. An Hebrew does not believe that Jesus Christ is the Son of God. An Hebrew does not believe in the crucifixion or the holy birth."

Pandora is startled. "Not Easter, or Christmas?"

"No. Not anything in the New Testament. An Hebrew believes Jesus Christ was an imposter, and that's why they put Him to death on the cross."

Pandora is amazed: "Is that why the Nazis burn them up?"

Adelaide leans heavily on her iron. "I don't know *why* the Nazis kill the Hebrews, Pandora, but I do know it is *wrong*. In a Christian country we don't kill people who are not Christians. We leave it to God to punish as He sees fit."

"Are Japs, Jews, or are they Christians?"

"Don't say 'Japs,' Pandora. Say 'Japanese.' " Adelaide moves into well-tilled church ground: "There are good Japanese, and there are bad Japanese, Pandora, just the same as there are good and bad Canadians. Remember the picture on your World Friends magazine? There's a little Japanese girl, in a kimono, holding hands with a poor little African in a loincloth, and an Indian in a featherhat. Christians don't look down on people because they have a different coloured skin, Pandora. Christians think about the heart, and the soul, under the skin."

"Can I marry Jason Green?"

Oh dear. Commonsense tempts Adelaide to try a gentle waffle — after all, she won't have to face this problem for years yet — but she has just come from a Home & School lecture in which a psychologist told the ladies they must always answer their children's questions honestly, directly, specifically.

"No, Pandora, you may not marry Jason Green if he is an Hebrew," says Adelaide, honestly, directly, specifically. "How would you feel, day by day, living with a man who doesn't accept Jesus Christ? How would you feel, knowing you could never enter the Kingdom of Heaven together? No, Pandora, I'm sorry, but it states very clearly in the Bible: 'Be ye not yoked to a non-believer.' "

Pandora turns thoughtfully from the ironing-board. Adelaide allows herself a tiny nibble at the Sin of Pride. *Well, that went rather well, if I do say so myself. . . .*

Pandora puts Jason's joke poop in her treasure-drawer, under Sydney's "Hi Sweetheart" pillowcase from Bala. She conjures up Jason Green, the giver: glossy black bangs, crinkly nose, pleasing grin. *Who would have guessed it? An heathen!* Pandora always knew heathens existed in foreign lands — that's why they send the Missionaries — but Jason Green is the only person she has ever known, in her entire life, who lives *in this country* and doesn't believe in Jesus Christ!

Hola! I almost married him.

Pandora breaks it off, formally, with Jason in a note inspired by the fusion of her ironing-board conversation with a note of romantic dissolution she once found in Aunt Rosie's lunch-pail.

Dear Jason,

Farewell, Lover! This can never be. My mother says Jesus says I can't be yolked to a non-beaver. I love another (not heathen). Farewell! I can't marry you! It was dee-vine on Cloud 9.

Your friend,
Pandora (age 7).

P.S. I shall keep the gifts.

Jason stuffs the note in his inkwell. Jessie Christie fishes it out with a compass point.

The girls of Room 6 have to break arms to walk around the unfortunate incident on the sidewalk: Jason Green is kneeling on marbles. Jessie Christie, Horace Ghostie and Godfrey Trumps stand over him, faces jutting from gold-felt crowns studded with bottlecaps. Godfrey flicks dirty water at Jason with his pen-nib. "I baptise, I baptise." Jason Green is praying — on request — to Jesus Christ to save his soul.

Pandora, feeling a certain nagging guilt (although she has broken it off cleanly) kicks Jessie Christie in the shins: "You're so *mean!*"

"*All* boys are mean!" chides Lucy Ford. "They're bullies!"

The girls pause, in a group. Jason, reinforced, stops moving his lips. Godfrey jabs him with his pen-nib. The girls of Room 6, their moral instincts offended, encircle the Inquisitors. They chant, *"Bull-eees! Bull-eees! Bull-eees!"* their faces twisted with scorn. *"Bull-eees! Bull-eees! Bull-eees!"* They stamp their feet, adding tambourine-gestures with their hands.

"Shit on you!" shouts Jessie Christie, making a dirty sign. Godfrey and Horace chime in: "SHIT! BUGGER! SHIT!" They ram the girls' circle with their crowned heads. They thrust their fists up the girls' skirts.

The girls run screaming, hands over ears, to their own side of the playground.

"I'm going to tell your *father,*" calls Ruth-Anne. "He'll fix *you!*"

"*Shit* on the old man!" bawls Jessie, but he looks a little sick: Jessie's father beats him with a razor-strap. Jessie's father is a judge.

The girls regroup, at a safe distance. They watch the three spiders recapture their fly.

"I'm glad *I'm* not a boy," scoffs Georgia Brooks.

"They pick on each other."

"They talk dirty."

"They're noisy."

"They're not clean."

Ruth-Anne spots Roger Parker, on whom she and Pandora have recently levied their affection, whistling towards them, hair rippling in the wind. Dimpling, she reassesses: "My mother says boys are rough, but if they like you they'll do what you want, but you have to tell them without them knowing, because girls are more ci-vil-ized."

"Phaw!" snorts Pandora. "Why shouldn't you tell them they stink if they stink? There's three I'm looking at right now that I'd like to punch in the kisser!"

"Pandora!" reprimands Ruth-Anne, as she always does when Pandora talks street talk. "That's not nice."

Cecily Battersea nudges the group. "Bad news!" She points to Magda Lunt, loping towards them with a half-dozen sticks of licorice open in her hand. "Magda doesn't wash after she pees," whispers Cecily. "I've been watching her!"

The group dissolves.

*　　*　　*

Knuckles crack in anticipation. Eyes rake the space between east doorframe and west. *This is Invitation Day: Where is Ruth-Anne Baltimore?*

Georgia Brooks has had her birthday party. So has Marjorie Maitland. The pattern for this auspicious Room 6 ceremonial has been set. *What can be keeping Ruth-Anne Baltimore?*

No one knows exactly who is on Ruth-Anne's list. Every hostess reserves the right to add or subtract names right up to the last minute: It is so important to get the thing right! A girl's party provides her with an opportunity to impose her taste in friends on the group for a week; it also saddles her with the responsibility of fast-freezing her list of favourites for the year. Thus, unless a girl wishes to leave herself open to the charge of fickleness, she must reach beyond present whim to some kind of universality. She must remember the girl with whom she shared the richness of friendship in October as well as anticipate the girl with whom she might wish to be intimate in May. There are also outside pressures: Marjorie Maitland's mother made her invite Fat Flora, because she is their minister's daughter. With Ruth-Anne, it's cousins: Of twenty invitations, only twelve are to be delivered among the twenty-one girls of Room 6 — just enough to cause the maximum in conspicuous heartbreak. *Has anyone seen Ruth-Anne Baltimore?*

Invitations go out on Friday, for a week from Saturday. Even now, Ruth-Anne should be roving the aisles, dealing out white envelopes in exact order of preference, and taking everyone by surprise: "What's this? For *me*?" Even now, recipients should be ostentatiously swivelling in their seats, mouthing to other possessors of white envelopes: "Did you get one?" "Yes." And then, as a courtesy: "Did you?"

Even now, Ruth-Anne should be taking her seat with two undelivered envelopes. Still-hopefuls should be straining to read the names through the scrollwork of her desk: *Is it me? Am I a "standby"?* (In Room 3, hostesses told the second-stringers who they were, but too many of them got sick from the tension. This year's hostesses are cannier.)

The first bell rings. An audible groan: *Where, oh where, is Ruth-Anne Baltimore?*

Ruth-Anne's party is, of course, no ordinary pop-and-peanut affair. For weeks the lusts of Room 6 have been keened by rumour: Pink hats! Pink balloons! A pink carousel! Pink-sugar angels! A real *magician* to pull — no one can quite believe this — a *pink* rabbit from a pink tophat!

A sliver of rubber pings Pandora. She ignores it.

The whole rubber clouts her. She turns.

What gives? mouths Cecily Battersea. *Where is Ruth-Anne?*

Pandora shrugs: *How should I know?* Her hauteur clearly states: *I am not at liberty to divulge that information.*

Now searching glances are openly exchanged. Wet palms are wiped on hankies pinned in pockets.

John Johnson *pssssts* Cecily Battersea. "What's the matter?" Cecily lays on the party, sparing no allurement. John Johnson reports to Bob Worth. They exchange wistful glances: Like many Room 6 boys, they spend their recesses under the spell-bindery of the Big Boys, who are aggressive, and their classes under the bossy patronage of the Little Girls, who are organized. It all looks so heroic, on the one hand, so warm and chummy, on the other: *But where, pray tell, is Ruth-Anne Baltimore?*

The second bell rings.

Pandora stalls-off closing the door.

Miss Macintosh cocks a questioning brow.

Pandora stands up as — *oops!* — Ruth-Anne darts by.

"Readers," says Miss Macintosh.

Ruth-Anne slides into her seat. Pandora waits for a white envelope to be mailed to her through her seat-slot: Nothing.

The recess bell rings. Pandora and Ruth-Anne file down the hall: Still nothing.

The recess line splits at the washroom stairs. Ruth-Anne nudges Pandora downward. "Will you help me pin my garters?" . . . *Aha!* It is a popular Room 6 ruse.

Ruth-Anne pushes Pandora into a toilet cubicle. They wait till the brown-laces have disappeared from the left side and the black-buttons from the right. Ruth-Anne lifts her pink sweater to reveal . . . *a manilla bulge!* "Will you help me deliver these, *please!*"

Ruth-Anne synopsizes for Pandora the following scene:

Ruth-Anne and her mother sit at a glass table in Mrs. Baltimore's bedroom nook. Dark curls frame Roxanne Baltimore's cameo face, so like her daughter's. She is wearing a Joan Crawford beige-satin dressing-gown and just-a-dash of lipstick. Ruth-Anne is prettily dressed for school.

Ruth-Anne and her mother breakfast together every Friday: It is a civilized affair, with linen, crystal, silver, tasteful conversation and yellow roses, but today Ruth-Anne is inattentive and fidgetty.

Mrs. Baltimore, nibbling dry toast, delivers a graceful reprimand: "Please, Ruth-Anne, do try to sit more quietly. You're such a pretty girl, I enjoy watching you, but not when you're working yourself up into a pink flush."

Ruth-Anne stops squirming. "I'm sorry, mummy. I guess I was just worrying about my party invitations. About getting them delivered."

Mrs. Baltimore considers the brown party packet. "Don't you think, dear, it would be ever so much politer to mail them?"

"Oh no, mummy! You're supposed to *deliver* them. *Everyone* does. You *have* to!"

"Well, if that's the way *everyone* does it, then I guess that's the way it should be done," says Mrs. Baltimore, teasing her daughter's earnestness, but endorsing the principle, too.

"Oh yes!" continues Ruth-Anne deadpan. "You have to deal them out before the bell!"

Mrs. Baltimore asks a few more idle questions about Room 6 party form. She receives the answers with deepening indignation. "Do you mean to tell me, Ruth-Anne Baltimore, that you march up and down the aisles, dropping invitations on your *friends'* desks with all the other children just looking on? Ruth-Anne, that's *awful*! I've never heard anything so tactless! I'm very very disappointed in you!"

Ruth-Anne flushes in terrible embarrassment. "*Every*body does it, mother!"

"There are *times*, Ruth-Anne, when that isn't good enough. It may take more effort to do the diplomatic thing, but you'll find it pays rich dividends in happiness and friendship. It's *graciousness*, at all times, that distinguishes the true lady."

Ruth-Anne's sooty lashes tremble. "I didn't *mean* to be mean."

"I know, darling, but thoughtlessness is sometimes crueler than deliberate meanness. A birthday party should be a time of specialness and joy. If people are hurt by it, then it isn't worth having."

Ruth-Anne blurts: "Then I won't have a party! I'll just rip up all the invitations!"

"Now, Ruthie. . . ." Mrs. Baltimore draws a lacy hanky from her sleeve. "*Of course* you'll have your party. We'll just see that you aren't unkind to anyone in the process."

Ruth-Anne brightens. "Oh, mummy! Can I invite *every-one*?"

Mrs. Baltimore frowns: "How many would that be?"

"Twenty-one."

Mrs. Baltimore blenches. "Oh dear! Enid wouldn't stand for it. No, Ruth-Anne. We'll have to find another solution. Besides, that wouldn't be realistic. You can't go through life always inviting everyone to everything."

Ruth-Anne is quiet for some time. "Mother. . . ." She chews her lip under the stress of revolutionary impulse. "I'd like to invite all the kids that never get invited anywhere — I'll bet Magda Lunt's never been to a party in her life! I'll invite all those I was going to leave off, and I'll just take the rest birthday cake to eat at recess."

Mrs. Baltimore smiles indulgently: She has intended to teach her daughter the benefits of social charm, not to handicap her with moral sainthood. She twists a tendril of Ruth-Anne's hair around her wedding finger. "No, darling. That would just cause bad feelings of a worse sort. Invite whom you want, but go about it discreetly. So often it's not *what* you do, but *how* you do it that people notice. That would be the adult way of handling it, dear."

Ruth-Anne dries her eyes.

Kisses are exchanged.

It isn't until Ruth-Anne hits the playground — running, now, because the line has gone in — that she appreciates the impossibility of her situation: Keeping her party secret, after all the advance publicity, will be like trying to hide Christmas.

"Oh, you got a mess, all right," agrees Pandora. "I don't see how you can do it."

Still, Pandora is inclined to help her try. Ruth-Anne has not been stingy of dialogue. Around Mrs. Baltimore's graceful homily Pandora has woven a glowing tapestry of mother-daughter detail: perfumed hankies, trembling eyelashes, crystal tears. Against this, she has been forced to replay the mother-daughter scene in which she herself participated at approximately the same time:

"I *hate* garters! Why can't I wear knee socks?"

"Your legs will *freeze*, Pandora. They'll grow hairy, like an ape's."

"I *hate* brown stockings."

"You're just going to have to wear them."

"I *hate* them. *They make my legs look like poop!*"

The memory of that stinging one-liner, flung recklessly over her shoulder, now causes Pandora to burn with shame. She feels the need to sweeten her soul with niceness of an accredited sort. "I'll help you deliver your invitations, Ruth-Anne. We'll do it in secret, just like your mother says." She adds, with only a touch of guile: "Why don't you invite Magda Lunt instead of Cecily Battersea? That'll be a sure sign this party is *different*."

"That's a wonderful idea!" beams Ruth-Anne. "Magda will be thrilled!"

The girls of Room 6 are playing an edgy game of frozen statues when Ruth-Anne and Pandora join them. Eyes track, interrogate, beseech Ruth-Anne at all times. It is the same in class. By 4 o'clock, Ruth-Anne, aided by Pandora, has delivered only two invitations: The girls of Room 6 are doomed to a jittery weekend.

Ruth-Anne and Pandora are back at it first thing Monday at recess. Pandora decoys Ann Billings away from Lucy Ford. Ruth-Anne lays upon Lucy the white invitation and her mother's sacred trust: "A birthday party should be a time of specialness and joy. If people are hurt by it, it isn't worth having." She adds, so there will be no mistake: "You *blab*, Lucy Ford, and you can't come!"

Now Pandora decoys Lucy Ford away from Ann Billings. Ruthie repeats the procedure.

The whistle blows.

By Tuesday afternoon, the girls of Room 6 have caught on that if they want an invitation, they'd better be ready to receive in private. Bestfriend shuns bestfriend. Room 6 society

— once so inviolate — is flung to the four corners of the playground.

A funny thing happens: Ruth-Anne and Pandora begin to foul up each other with as much ingenuity as they used to abet each other. They have, quite unconsciously, exchanged personalities: Ruth-Anne is intoxicated by the raw exercise of power. Pandora is enchanted by the sweet smell of her own niceness. It is all so new, they don't want it to end.

By Wednesday, Room 6 is in stunning disarray. Normally, this would be a high point of togetherness for all party personnel. Normally, they would find more and more reason to knot in the cloakroom and to chatter at the pencil-sharpener. Normally, they would play together at recess, with the hostess and her bestfriend at the centre of the group, and the hostess' favourites supplanting the regular court. Normally, but? . . .

Ruth-Anne still has one more invitation to deliver: *Magda Lunt or Cecily Battersea?* Ruth-Anne is weary of power-mongering. She tosses Cecily her invitation and puts Magda on standby. She throws her brown envelope into the wastebasket.

Ruth-Anne Baltimore — all Room 6 can see it — is smooth-tummied after a lengthy delivery.

Ruth-Anne and Pandora take up their usual stance on the playground. The party group gathers around. This is no breech of security. Ruth-Anne's list, when peeled of its mystifications, turns out to be none other than the legitimate social order, reinforced by secrecy.

Pandora is, at last, disgusted. Commonsense has shredded her fantasy of goodness. She sees, with shameful clarity, exactly how mean she and Ruth-Anne have been.

She admits as much to Ruth-Anne last thing on Friday. "Yes," replies Ruth-Anne, her purple eyes as tranquil as paint-pots. "My party will be a time of specialness and joy, but the best thing is that no one will be hurt by it!"

Pandora, trudging homeward, ponders a question that will baffle her throughout her life: *How come the NICE people miss seeing so much?*

Pandora stops off at Arlene's. Arlene has chicken pox. Pandora is hoping to catch them. Introspection has dredged up a fact she was trying hard to forget: Pandora has her own humiliating reason for not wanting to go to Ruth-Anne's party.

"Please, mother. . . ."

"No."

"Ahh, *please*. . . ."

"I *said* no, and I *mean* it."

It is the shorthand of weary familiarity. Amplified, it means:

"*Please*, mother," begs Pandora, kneeling on her mother's footstool. "Just this once, let me take Ruth-Anne a *new* gift."

"No, Pandora," says Adelaide, drawing a hole-y sock over her darning-egg. "You'll have to choose something from the Gift Drawer."

"Ahhhh, mother. Those are *old ladies'* gifts."

"Nonsense! Little girls like Ruth-Anne *love* things that smell nice."

"Ahhh, mother. Georgia Brooks is giving her Princess Margaret Rose cutouts. Cecily Battersea is giving her a Sonja Henie doll!"

"It's nice they can afford it. We can't."

"It doesn't have to be *big*, mother. Just something that looks like it was bought for Ruth-Anne, and not something *you* got at Ladies' Aid and didn't like!"

"It isn't a matter of *not liking*," says Adelaide, picking sharply at the chewed wool. "Some things are just too extravagant to use. They're *meant* as gifts."

"Like Sweetpea *Toilet Water!*" jeers Pandora.

"That's just an expression, Pandora. It means *perfume*."

"It *says* Toilet Water, and it's the right colour!"

"Pandora! I will not put up with this disrespectful talk. Either take Ruth-Anne that lovely perfume, or a lovely hanky, or stay home."

"The perfume's half dried up!"

"Then we'll just add a little water. The smell's still there."

"Ahhhh, mother. Lend me a dollar . . . I'll pay you back."

"It would take ten weeks, and what would you spend in the meantime?"

"I won't put butter on my bread! I won't use brown sugar!"

"Don't talk rubbish, Pandora. You know your daddy and I never stint at table."

"Ruth-Anne is my bestfriend."

"Then she'll understand your position."

"She always gives *me* things! I'll look *cheap*."

"Not *cheap*, Pandora. *Modest*. When people have everything, why add to it? Save your generosity for those who need it."

"That's not what you said when you made me take Marjorie Maitland a War Savings stamp. *Then* you said the Maitlands don't have much. They'll appreciate what little we can do for them."

Adelaide bites her thread, with a resolute click. "It boils down to the same thing: We do what we can. It's the thought that counts, not the gift *or* its price."

"Then why does *father* always take Grandma Pearl's gifts back to see what Aunt Estelle paid for them? Why does he tell us the price of everything? Why does he —"

It is the usual embarrassment: Adelaide's moral precepts flung against the rock of Lyle's actual misdeeds. Beyond this point lie very dangerous waters: Pandora *daring* Adelaide to indict or defend her husband under her own stated principles. Adelaide insisting on the blind eye and the deaf ear. Adelaide discredited. Pandora resentful of her father and contemptuous of her mother, blaming her mother, imitating her father's fury. . . .

Adelaide rises: "I won't listen to any more of this badgering!" She adds plaintively: "You have *no idea* how much it costs just to keep food on the table, Pandora! Besides. . . ." Adelaide squares her shoulders. "It's the *principle* of the thing!"

Pandora clutches her mother's skirt. "It's *not* the principle! It's taking a horrible gift and having everyone snicker at it."

Adelaide feels Pandora's desperation tremble up her faded housedress, but . . . *over a party gift? over brown stockings? over cut hair?* These quarrels, which rage over ever-more-ridiculous ground, are a bafflement to Adelaide. To accept

Pandora's view of things — even to take it seriously — would be madness. There is a clear principle here. Her back stiff as a darning needle, Adelaide states it: "You are beginning to sound like a terrible snob, Pandora. Some families can afford to make a great display of gift-giving. We can't."

There is a broader principle behind the first. "Life is as it is, Pandora, and *you* can't change it. No point in kicking your heels. No point in forcing a few tears. You're *not* getting your own way, and that's final!"

Pandora has been trying hard not to cry: Since her tears are judged, out-of-hand, to be political, she has nothing to gain and her dignity to lose. She bites her lip. She holds her breath. The word "tears" is like a primer: Geysers gush from both eyes.

"Ha! Right on cue, I see!" exclaims Adelaide. "All right, Miss Hard-Done-By, turn off the waterworks or go up to bed. Honestly, Pandora, sometimes I don't think you have any *real* feelings!"

It is the old refrain: Pandora is goaded anew. To be told by her mother, who is coolly rolling a darning sock, that she is without feelings when she feels herself hysterical with them is a denial of her whole reality.

Pandora bangs her fists on the floor. She kicks her mother's sewing-basket across the room.

Adelaide is appalled.

Adelaide is relieved: Pandora has done the expected thing. She has kicked herself, with the sewing-basket, beyond the considerations of rational people. Adelaide's world stops oscillating: Heaven floats to the top where it belongs. Hell pitches to the bottom:

Children, obey thy parents.

Wives, honour thy husbands.

It is not difficult to separate Right from Wrong. It is just difficult to do it.

Pandora runs, crying, up the stairs.

Adelaide gets down on her hands and knees: She picks up pins, needles, bits of thread. Adel-Ada leave the cardtable, where they have been scoring $\frac{3}{4}$-inch lines down white pages. They pick up pins, needles, bits of thread.

"You two never minded taking gifts from the Gift Drawer, did you?!"

Adel-Ada do not affirm. They do not deny. Adelaide puts her hands on the twins' shoulders. "I don't know what I'd do without you two and your commonsense!"

Adel-Ada glow. Adel-Ada wince: The way of Righteousness is stiff and narrow. *Pandora has stolen all our badness. She doesn't leave us any!*

Pandora trudges along St. Charles Place, past St. Cecilia's Cripples' Home with its bleeding Jesus, wrapped in her khaki coat, the colour of dung or — take your choice — the colour of dying soldiers. Her head is turtled into her collar. Her eyes drag the gutters, as if looking for cigarette butts. The gritty November sidewalk pushes up through a hole in one of her scuffed brown shoes.

Pandora carries a white handkerchief, with a purple P re-embroidered as an R, tucked like a boil in her left armpit. It is wrapped in freshly-pressed tissue-paper that has known many Christmases. It is glued with a cornflower sticker, steamed from an IODE bingo prize. It is accompanied by an orchid card, first received by Rosie from a lovesick swain on the Thor Munitions' Bomber-gun line. Adelaide, once having determined it her Christian duty to separate Pandora from the deadly Sin of Pride, has outdone herself.

Pandora scowls up Baltic Avenue toward the Ventnor Theatre: She has ten cents, plus the hope of scrounging two cents in glass from someone's garbage-can.

"Pan-d*ooooo*-rah!"

It is Marjorie Maitland. She skips toward Pandora, the butterfly bow in her hair mating gracefully with the butterfly bow on her parcel.

"Waaaaaaaait!"

Pandora does so, stoically: All exits are now blocked.

Ruth-Anne's Georgian home has always impressed Pandora:

Today it intimidates her. The tatty parcel, under her arm, has worked as an evil talisman, reducing her to its size and meanness. She is Cinderella entering the ball, with pumpkins on her feet and rats in her hair, and no Fairy Godmother in sight.

Enid, the glowering coloured maid, takes Pandora's coat.

Ruth-Anne skips across the hall in her tapdance shoes: "Hi!" She is dressed in white lace, like a bride, with satin streamers in her naturally curly hair. Georgia Brooks is in puckered-pink velvet. Cecily Battersea is in tangerine taffeta. Marjorie Maitland is in orchid organdy: Pandora notices, with satisfaction, that it doesn't fit properly.

Pandora has on her stubborn navy-jumper, mended white blouse, poop stockings and hole-y shoes: She could have done better. Her mother said she should. The paltry handkerchief mesmerized Pandora into thinking nothing else mattered. Now, she sees — reflected in five mirrors — that it does.

Pandora steps into the whipped-cream living-room with its floating glass tables, heavy brocades, and silver bowls of yellow roses and roses and roses and . . .

"You?" mocks the Wicked Stepmother through yellow petal lips. *"You, all dusty and cindery, with poop on your legs and holes in your soul! You haven't a dress to wear and you can't dance."*

The guests pour through the glass doors.

"Let's play games!" sings Ruth-Anne. "For *prizes!*"

Her guests run briskly through the classics — Musical Sheraton Chairs. Pass the Pomegranate. Pin-the-Tail-on-the-Palomino. Guess-the-Beans-in-the-Silver-Salvo. Everyone wins, except for Pandora who is playing listlessly. Mrs. Baltimore — understated in oatmeal cashmere and cultured pearls — slips a hastily wrapped gift into Pandora's cold palm. "Just a little consolation. We seem to be one prize short."

Pandora opens it: *Two* lace handkerchiefs scented with yellow rosewater!

Ruth-Anne leads the triumphal march into the dining-room. It is transformed, for today only, into a pink circus tent.

186

"Ooooooooo! Isn't it beeeoootiful!"

Pink balloons! pink streamers! pink garlands! It is all there, as promised in the press-releases.

Ruth-Anne — pink-flushed — takes her place at the head of the table, Pandora on her right, Georgia on her left. There is a great fuss about finding placecards, though everyone knows from the order she received her invitation exactly where to look.

Pink crackers! pink hats! pink favours!

Dinner is served.

Pink bread! pink pop! pink *potato salad*!?

Ruth-Anne heaps Pandora's plate. "You're hardly eating a thing!"

Enid, scowling, brandishes a platter of icecream strawberries.

Fists snatch at the steamy bonbons. *Oooooooo.* Pink mouths fuse to the frigid fruit. *Ooowwwwww!* There is a vast, ten-second silence during which, *Eeeee-hee-heee,* Enid chuckles.

A rosebud mouth comes unglued: "Where's the cake?"

"Yes!" *Bring on the cake!*

On, it is splendid — three-tiers, as big as a wedding cake, with HAPPY BIRTHDAY, RUTH-ANNE DEAREST rococoed around the sides. On top is a pink carousel, mounted by seven pink candles: It plays, by terrible oversight, *Green-sleeves.*

"Make a wish! Make a wish!" yelps Lucy Ford.

Ruth-Anne puckers her face in concentration: *I wish for a palomino pony.* She blows out all the candles. They are relit for the photographer. Ruth-Anne blows them out again: *I wish for birthday cake for the starving War Orphans in Europe.*

Ruth-Anne cuts the cake: *I wish . . . palomino pony.*

Ruth-Anne re-cuts the cake: *I wish . . . starving War Orphans.*

The cake is pink all through, with maraschino cherries the size of quarters. Cecily Battersea breaks a tooth on a *real* quarter stuffed inside one. Georgia Brooks coughs up a real dime. A flutey sound emanates from the kitchen: *Enid, the cake-maker, is singing.*

"Presents!" shouts Marjorie Maitland, hysterical with good living. *"Pre-sents!"*

"No," reproves Ruth-Anne. "Presents come *last.*" She unbends a little. "There *is* one I'm curious about, though. Mummy, can I open *one* gift?"

Mrs. Baltimore smiles. "It's *your* party, darling."

Ruth-Anne investigates her pastel plenty. "It's just a *little* one . . . a white one."

Pandora's stomach flips, then flops. She bolts for the washroom. *Pink bread! pink pop! pink potato salad!*

Pandora rinses her sour mouth. She swabs her forehead with her Lest-We-Forget handkerchief. A white card flutters to the floor. She reads, in her mother's upright hand: "A Thought for Today — It is easier for a camel to go through the eye of a needle than for a rich man to enter the Kingdom of Heaven." Pandora flushes the Kingdom of Heaven down the eye of the Baltimores' sewage system. She returns to the living-room.

The gift Ruth-Anne has selected to open is from her mother and father. Mr. Baltimore lopes through the glass doors — a gaunt, handsome man, one-pinstripe wide. He pecks Ruth-Anne on the cheek. "Hi, Snooks! How's the birthday girl?"

"Jus' wun-ner-ful, dadd*eee*," lisps Ruth-Anne in a voice Pandora has never heard before.

Gilbert Baltimore positions himself behind Ruth-Anne and her mother, on their Hepplewhite loveseat. The bowl of his pipe rests against the lapel of his smoking-jacket. It is the same pose (art imitating nature? nature imitating art?) the artist has formalized in the pseudo-Gainsborough family portrait behind the Baltimores. It is an updated version of the Gormly Family in marble, to whom Roxanne Baltimore is related.

Ruth-Anne rips through the white paper and yellow roses. "Ohhh." She opens a gold box. "Ahhh." She withdraws a gold sweetheart locket. "Oooooo. . . ."

Ruth-Anne opens the locket. She finds . . . a heartshaped

miniature of the family portrait and . . . *"A palomino pony!"*

Gilbert Baltimore smiles a prosperous smile: "He'll be waiting for you next weekend at Gran's."

Ruth-Anne skips across the room in her tapdance shoes. "Oh, thank you, mumm*eee*! Thank you, dadd*eee*! I think I'll call him Frisk*eeee*!"

The locket is passed around the room, with Ruth-Anne holding the golden chain.

"Try it on!" she urges. She drops it around Pandora's throat. The silky chain tightens and *suddenly she is clothed in shimmering raiment so heavenly it must have been spun from rabbits' dreams. Her legs are cocooned in the finest gossamer. On her feet are holy crystal slippers. . . .*

Pandora stares sourly at the family portrait inside the locket. *This is what Ruth-Anne sees in HER mirror . . .* link-link-link, backwards and forwards into infinity. . . .

Pandora looks at the palomino pony. *"Mummeee! Daddeee!"* she cries, *gleefully trampling worms in her tapdance shoes. "I think I'll call him —"* oof! *she feels a sudden muscle-spasm "— Charlie-Horse!"*

Two tears, acidy with self-pity, burn at the corners of Pandora's eyes.

Ruth-Anne removes the locket.

Enid stands in the arch. "The Magician is here."

The Magician is dressed in pink tophat and tails, with a spangled vest.

Gazooks! He links and unlinks three solid silver rings.

Presto! He cuts one of Mr. Baltimore's ties, then magically re-knits it.

Abracadabra! He calls cards, by their names, from the deck.

The little girls sit, spellbound, on their damask chairs. Pandora clutches hers: *No! no! Not a pink rabbit! That would be well past the bearing.*

The Magician seems to be building to a bit of a climax. He twirls three silver rings around his left leg. He spins a plate on a stick with his right hand. The Union Jack rises on a flagpole from his left pocket. The Stars and Stripes rises on a flagpole from his right pocket. A dozen eggs fall, in quick succession, from his mouth. Geraniums sprout from both ears. He raises his hand to his pink tophat. He lifts it.

A pink rabbit!

The rabbit blinks its pink eyes. It twitches its pink nose. It hops to the floor on pink feet, leaving a single brown pellet on the Magician's perspiring head.

Pandora stares at the pink rabbit. The pink rabbit stares at Pandora. She knows now, if she ever doubted it. *The white hanky is not enough. My mother has betrayed me.*

"Presents!"

Yes, now it is time for presents.

Enid hauls them in on her back, by the hamperful, groaning the way she saw the slaves do it in Gone With the Wind, and flinching every time she passes the bewildered Master, as if struck by a cruel whip.

Oh, this is too much! Gilbert Baltimore makes a firm mental note to give Enid her notice the next day.

Oh, no you don't! Roxanne makes a firm mental note to rescind it. *God-damned war!*

Ruth-Anne sits crosslegged on the white broadloom, her lacy dress demurely covering her knees. The other girls sit around her, in a fairy circle. Pandora hands her her gifts, one at a time, from the pink hampers — yellow, green, purple, blue — bits of broken rainbow.

"Ohhhh, *thank* you, Lucy, for the lovely plastic dishes. I *needed* a new set!

"Ohhh, *thank* you! Blondie cutouts! They're just what I needed."

The gifts are passed around the circle to be assessed and admired. Pandora fondles a box of coloured pencils with leads as thick as gumdrops. She writes her name, in every colour, on a scrap of paper, the way she does at Woolworth's. Coloured pencils are the wealth of Room 6. *You can never have too many.* They are the only thing Pandora wants for Christmas.

Marjorie Maitland nudges her. "Wake up, Pandy! Ruth-Anne wants another present."

Pandora, distracted, digs into the hamper: She pulls out a modest gift wrapped in nicely pressed tissue.

Ruth-Anne turns it over. "Where's the card?"

"Here," says Marjorie. "It fell off."

Ruth-Anne unglues the re-glued flap. She pulls out a silvery card set with a satin orchid. "Oooooh, isn't it *luv*-ly." She reads: "Happy Birthday *Sweetheart?*" She wrinkles her nose. "It's from Pandora."

Cecily Battersea sniggers.

"I liked the *picture*," stammers Pandora. "I forgot to read it."

"I did that once," reassures Georgia. "I sent my sister a Dear *Grannie!*"

The little girls giggle, good-humouredly.

"It's the prettiest card I've got so far," says Ruthie. She tactfully refrains from reading aloud the intemperate verse.

Ruth-Anne unfolds, rather than tears, the white tissue: There is something about its gallant old age that inspires veneration. She lifts out a hanky rancid with sweetpea and mothballs. "Oooo, it's got my initial. *Thank* you, Pandora!"

The card and hanky are sent around the circle. They encounter a good deal of silence.

Lucy Ford examines the card. "It *is* pretty." She opens it to see how the satin is glued. "Ohhh...." She clamps her hand to her mouth. Cecily snatches the card. She reads: "Love to ya Rosie Rivetter from Sparkie on the Bomber-line."

Silence. Titters. A few outright guffaws. Pandora groans. She spews up *pink cake! pink icecream! pink marshmallows!* into the pink hamper. She bolts, screaming, for the bathroom. *It wasn't necessary! We aren't THAT poor!*

It is 7 p.m.

Fathers are called to pick up their daughters.

Guests, laden with *pink balloons! pink hats! pink favours!* exit noisily.

Pandora is coaxed from the bathroom.

"You couldn't help it, dear, if you weren't feeling well."

Ruth-Anne smiles her cherished smile: "I especially liked the handkerchief because you are my *best*friend!"

Pandora slogs down Boardwalk through air the texture of soggy kleenex. She turns up Baltic Avenue instead of crossing it.

Everyone else had fun at the party, why didn't I? Even Shelagh Stacey had fun, and she only brought bathsalts! Or did Shelagh only pretend to have fun? Do others see things I don't see? Do I see things they don't see? Has God put my eyes in backwards so all I can see is the meanness inside my own head? Was Ruth-Anne mean about the invitations, or was it just me? If Ruth-Anne is mean, why was she so nice about the hanky? Am I mean just because I know I'm mean? If I didn't know I was mean, would I be mean? If I'm mean, why don't the others think I'm mean the way they think Cecily is mean? Or do they think I'm mean, but pretend they don't? Or do they think I'm mean, and I can't see it? Does Cecily know everyone thinks she's mean?

The clammy sidewalk pokes up through the hole in Pandora's shoe. She looks at the shadow stuck to her feet. She watches it cringe into a dark dwarf, then shoot forward into a pale giant.

Why? Pandora asks the giant. But she gets the dwarf.

How come? Pandora asks the dwarf. But she gets the giant.

Crouch, spring . . . crouch, spring . . . as she passes from illumination to illumination, always concealing its true form. . . .

The drizzle hardens into raindrops. Pandora's party favours turn to pink porridge under her arm. She lifts a garbage lid and drops them in. Pandora notices the number of the house: 33 Baltic Avenue. *Magda's house.* Pandora sees a light in the window with three heads around a console radio: Magda and two of her brothers. They are listening to Truth or Consequences, and Magda is laughing her fool head off.

Ruth-Anne and her party guests collect in a knot on the playground.

"Do you remember? . . ."

"Wasn't it funny when? . . ."

At the edge of the group stands Dorothy Hunt: chin high, face flushed, eyes focussed in space; absorbing information but not reacting to it. Dorothy is with her bestfriend Shelagh Stacey. Shelagh was invited to the party. Dorothy was not. Dorothy is a "listener."

A listener is not a bystander: The regular bystanders stand in their usual covetous knot, five yards from the party group, with a few additional party castoffs. Sometimes Magda Lunt or Silly Lily attempts to creep close enough to eavesdrop: When that happens, all conversation stops.

No. In the Room 6 social glossary, a bystander is a girl preordained by God and her own inadequacies, real or imagined, to exist outside the main group until fluke reprieves her. By contrast, a listener is a girl of reasonable worth forced outside the group by flukish circumstances until normalcy reprieves her.

Though Dorothy is acceptable to the group, she was not invited to the party. The week before the party, she and her bestfriend Shelagh glossed over the situation as best they could. Now, at the first recess after the party, when the group meets for the only time without cover activity, there is no possibility of faking it. Shelagh was there. Dorothy was not.

What to do? If Dorothy goes off by herself, Shelagh is honourbound to follow. This not only deprives Shelagh of her post-party privileges but it is also a snub to Ruth-Anne.

Dorothy does the courageous thing: She accepts the position of listener, or privileged outcast. She does not, as an adult would, attempt to cover the dubiousness of her situation by acting as an appreciative audience: Room 6 is a barebones society. The participants know, in a way adults would not admit, that the point of this postpartum is to celebrate that there was a party to which they were all nice enough to be invited. Should Dorothy attempt to participate too fully, they would interpret it as a pushy attempt to pretend she was there.

No. Dorothy is doing the proper thing: dignified detachment. After a few embarrassed glances, the other girls talk past her, but loud enough for her to hear.

The whistle blows.

The party group breaks up, never to reassemble. Dorothy and Shelagh file back to class, hand-in-hand, babbling to each other in gratitude and relief.

Dorothy has earned the privilege of participating in the memory of the party: Henceforth, it will be openly referred to in her presence rather than behind-the-hand.

Ruth-Anne waits for Dorothy in the cloakroom. She delivers the highest accolade a listener can receive: "I'm sorry I didn't invite you, Dorothy. I didn't know you half as well then as I do now."

Opiates

Winter, 1944

Fat white moths nibble the red scarves, purple mitts, green parkas of pink-cheeked girls on their way to Thor Munitions. Pandora, in black snowsuit and helmet, watches from the slit in the storm-door. She crosses her fingers. She plunges. . . .

It is! "PAAAAAACK-ING snow!"

Arlene and Pandora roll the head and torso of a colossus too big to assemble. They suck icicles, pierced with sunlight. They dance, slowmotion, in air as clear as tinkling cymbals. They carve snowangels by the rocking chair of old Mr. Grandby who caught up to his season, turned cold, and died. . . .

They lie under an icebowl sky. The sun is a blurry pinwheel. Soft flakes weave a coverlet of deceptive warmth. Pandora rolls over and over in the snow, lacerating its gauzy whiteness with her tongue . . . *hot blood seeping through bandages.* . . .

When the onion skin is tough,

The coming winter will be . . . Capt. John Macintosh . . . Cpl. Mario Niobe . . . Brig. E. T. Weller. . . .

Pandora plummets down, down, down into infinite whiteness: "Ooooooooo." *Is this Always Was?*

Arlene and Pandora, adrift on their own flights of fantasy, have said "Ooooooooo!" at the same time. Laughing, they hook fingers.

"What goes up the chimney?"

"Smoke."

"What comes down?"

"Santa Claus."

"May your wish and my wish, never be broken."

Once I awoke and there was a golden teddy bear with eyes, like stars, at the bottom of my crib.

Once I awoke and I couldn't see. I said, "Oh, oh, I am blinded," but Adelaide says: "I think you're old enough to see things as they are, Pandora, and not as you would like them to be."

Lyle says: "The price of things these days is no joke."

"They give you perfectly good crayons at school. I don't see why you can't be content to use those the way Adel and Ada always have."

"It's not what you *get*, Pandora. It's the *spirit* of Christmas."

Pandora's head bends like a sapling under its winter-burden of self-pity. She says, with the stunning poise of a Ruth-Anne Baltimore, "Thank you, father, for the shoes. Thank you, mother, for the pyjamas. Thank you, Adel and Ada for the lovely Sweetpea Toilet Water. It is just what I always wanted."

And now, Lyle turns on the radio: *It is time for His Majesty the King to speak.*

And now, Adelaide turns on the oven: *It is time for His Excellency the Pope to get his nose roasted.*

"Deck the halls, with boughs of hol-ly. . . ."

Lyle devours breast, slathered in ketchup.

Estelle sops up heart, liver, gizzard with brown bread and giblet gravy.

Rosie gorges on thigh.

Pandora gnaws a drumstick.

Adelaide plucks a wing.

Adel-Ada divvy a neck, vertebrae turnabouts.

Other Grandmother looks at an eggwhite omelet, and gently turns it over.

The Tranquillity Rose dishes are washed, dried and put away.

Rosie displays the various flags and insignia staked about her person.

Thanks, Gino-Baby, in France, for the nifty Gruen wrist-watch!

Thanks, Joey-Lover, in Holland, for the super birthstone ring!

Thanks, Hank-Honey, in Belgium, for the swell gold anklet!

Rosie models the flare-back persian-paw coat she got from Sparkie on the Bomber-gun line, and a hat she bought for herself, in the cossack style made popular by Stalingrad. "The sales guy called it my *pièce de Résistance!*"

Adelaide strokes the crinkly fur. "It must be warm."

Estelle checks the label. "It must be expensive."

Rosie tosses her henna hair. "Yeah, kinda, but what the hell, maybe next year The War'll be over, and I'll be pounding the pavement. These good times aren't going to last forever!"

"You *could* get a job in an office," sniffs Estelle. "It might improve your language."

"And sharpen some guy's pencils? Nuts! They don't pay those girls enough to keep me in nailpolish!"

Rosie unbuttons her coat. "Here, Adelaide. Try it on." She drops it over Adelaide's shoulders, *and suddenly she was clothed in shimmering raiment so heavenly that . . .*

"No thanks. I'll get flour on it." Adelaide wipes her fingers on her apron. "I mustn't." She shrugs the fur coat from her shoulders. She returns to the kitchen, singing: "Clothed in the Radiance of Our Lord. . . ."

All the boys in Room 6 have new sweaters: Jessie Christie is red-checked instead of black-striped. Jason is white-cabled instead of yellow-crocheted. Roger Parker is blue-diamonded instead of green-circled.

Something resembling the Holy Grail shimmers in the centre of Ruth-Anne's desk. It has *five* drawers! *Ruth-Anne has a new pencilbox!*

Ruth-Anne systematically rifles the drawers: *ruby! emerald! sapphire! frankincense! myrrh! lapis lazuli!* She licks a lead or two. "You can borrow them sometimes, Pandora."

Pandora buries her fists in her green eyes. One more drawer in that bloody pencilbox and she would have become a socialist.

* * *

Pandora sits in a booth at the Mill City Malt Shop, with Arlene on her right and Ruth-Anne on her left. It is a tactful seating arrangement when you consider: Pandora is Ruth-Anne's classroom husband and Arlene's street wife.

Ruth-Anne opens the Mill City Clarion, flipping past interminable columns of grey type jazzed up with the maps, graphs, and boxscores that are the editors' way of coping with a World War that — like some World Series — has dragged on too long.

"Ahhhh, here. . . ." She smooths out a page. "Unfit to love, to marry, to be parents. WHY? Was their Sin ignorance? neglect? prudery? treachery? NO GREATER SIN — Dare you ignore it?"

"Where's that?"

"At the Uptown — Women Only."

"Any cartoon?"

"It doesn't say."

"That's a cheat!"

"Here's the Cap — 'What a man! Van Johnston BETWEEN TWO WOMEN. He's tall, tender and terrific! It's MGM's sizzling thrill-romance climaxed with a million kisses.' "

"Ooooo, I *love* Van Johnston!" enthuses Arlene. Pandora kicks her. "It sounds awfully *mushy*," Arlene amends. "What's on at the Grand?"

" 'FLIGHT FOR FREEDOM with Rosalind Russell and Fred MacMurray . . . So that we could blast the Japs out of the Pacific, this girl risked *everything*! Free popcorn for the first one hundred.' "

"I wish they'd give popcorn with a comedy," grumbles Pandora. "I hate War pictures. They're so *boring*." Arlene kicks her. Pandora amends brightly: "*Some* War pictures are boring."

Ruth-Anne checks her Mickey Mouse wristwatch. "I better read the rest fast: Ali Baba and the Forty Thieves. Jane Eyre. Lady in the Dark. Thousands Cheer."

"What's at the Ventnor?" asks Pandora, casually.

"Ummm . . . Rio Rita, with Abbott and Costello."

"They're a *riot!*" exclaims Arlene. She brakes herself. "Ah . . . that is, they're *pretty good*. What's on with it?"

Ruth-Anne wrinkles her nose: "Guerrilla Patrol. A boring *War* picture."

Arlene and Pandora have only twelve cents each, which is not enough for an uptown show.

"The Ventnor has a good Superman serial," prompts Pandora.

"And a Tom & Jerry cartoon," adds Arlene.

Ruth-Anne knows, now, it's a put-up job. "O.K. Let's go to the Ventnor." But her mother doesn't like her going to the tough neighbourhood theatres.

The line is halfway to the corner. Arlene saves places while Pandora and Ruth-Anne candy-shop. Ruth-Anne's bill comes to fifty-two cents. "Oof!" Arlene is scandalized. "You could have bought the same at the candy factory for thirty-one cents!" Pandora silences her with a pitying look: She was thinking exactly the same thing.

The three girls shift from one chilly foot to the other.

"We want in!" chants the line.

An usher, with skin like dirty snow, opens the door.

"Hurr-*aaaaaaaay!*"

The girls edge toward the bulb-encrusted marquee, designed, like the rest of the Ventnor Theatre, as a palliative to The Depression, and now never lit because of The War. They pass through a mirrored door, along a golden cord, under a cerulean ceiling frescoed in fat nymphets with flowered sexual parts, past a gaudy, fan-bearing Nubian slave to a baroque brass cage containing a bored, gum-chewing girl with badly-bleached hair who exchanges twelve cents, knotted in a hanky, for one orange ticket.

They turn right, down darkly carpeted stairs, past a marble

drinking-fountain recessed like a saint's grotto, through a se-
quined corridor of Next Attractions and Coming Soons to a
pair of soiled gloves that rips their tickets, then passes the ends
to a brass-braided youth with an adam's apple as large as his
flashlight. It is baffling: *How can all these people, with the
best jobs in the world, look so unhappy?*

Mottled lights slide across the velvet curtains. Unseen hands
play Roll Out the Barrel. Arlene and Pandora compare stubs
by the aisle light. *Rats!* But they never give up hoping.

The curtains part: *Hurrraaaaaaay!*

The Eyes and Ears of the World. *Booooooo!*

A Pete Smith Specialty. *Hurraaaaaay!*

Rio Rita . . . *Oh, what a riot!*

Guerrilla Patrol. "Ugh! A stupid War picture!"

There is, of course, no question of leaving.

"Don't go in there, Joe! It's a trap."

"Somebody's got to try it."

AKK-AKK-AKK. It was a trap.

"Pssst, Pandora. Pass the jujubes."

*"Ve haf vays und means uf dealink mit spies, even beeooooo-
tiful spies."*

"You can kill my body, but you can never kill my soul."

AKK-AKK-AKK. They kill her body.

"Isn't there any licorice whip?"

*"I know we'll be together again. Maybe not tomorrow, maybe
not this year, but. . . ."*

KA-BOOM. They fly apart, limb by limb.

"Here, *you* take the cinnamon hearts."

"No, I had the extra sherbet bag."

*The camera plays over the messy remains of hero and hero-
ine, a-twitch in final embrace.*

Pandora scrunches the candy bag.

*The camera plays over a bombed-out school. It focusses on a
dead child, cradling a doll with the head blown off.*

Pandora stops chewing jelly-baby. She clutches Arlene on
the right, and Ruth-Anne on the left. *"Loooook!"* She points
to the screen.

202

A fluffy kitten lies crumpled against a garbage-can, its silent white fur splattered with blood.

The lights come on. All three girls are sobbing. *War is Hell.*

Pandora does not forget. At the next Room 6 Red Cross meeting she delivers a powerful anti-War speech, denouncing both sides, and ending with a strongly-worded motion to divert all moneys from the Red Cross jar to the Humane Society jar. Ruth-Anne seconds the motion. It is carried, with only two dissenters: Miss Macintosh, who doesn't get the vote, and Jessie Christie, which proves what a good idea it is.

Room 6 is tired of War. They are tired of construction sets made of cardboard that bends, and off-brand chocolate bars that taste like brown wax. They are tired of collecting paper and baskets and gum cards with tanks on them. They are bored. *Every*one is, except for a few wives and widows, and Churchill.

Next Current Events, most of Room 6 passes up *Soviet Forces Massed to Storm Last Barrier* . . . for:

Caesar Is Dead . . . Honoured by Royalty and loved by children, Caesar the Big Dane, died Saturday of pneumonia. During the Royal Tour of 1939 the King and Queen stopped to pat him on the head while visiting the Children's Ward of Pacific Avenue Hospital, where he was a frequent guest . . .

The Humane Society jar is rattled and passed: Pandora drops in a dime, Ruth-Anne a quarter: *Je me souviens.*

Arlene and Pandora sit opposite each other at the Goodfellows' gateleg table, each with a slice of bread cut into three triangles. One is spread with honey, one with brown sugar, one with white sugar. That is the order in which Pandora likes them best. Arlene likes them in reverse order. They both intend to eat them in the *same* order: Arlene likes to have the best first, whereas Pandora likes to save the best till last.

Arlene and Pandora are writing letters on hand-lined paper. They are both writing to the *same* person, although he is at the top of Arlene's list and the bottom of Pandora's: All this is explained in the above paragraph.

Dear Mr. Johnston,
This is Pandora. I am in Miss Macintosh's room. You are my favourite. I saw you in (she consults the newspaper) BE-TWEEN TWO WOMEN, a sizzling thrill-romance. You were (she consults the paper again) tall, tender and terrific! Please send me a named picture. Colour would be best. I just like the heads.

Your friend,
Pandora Gothic (age 7½)

Dear Van,
You are my favourite because of your freckles! I have freckles too!!! I use lemon to squeeze them off. A friend of my mother's says milk and radishes work too.
Please send me a picture.
Well, I guess that is all to say for now.
Good-bye for now.

Your friend,
Arlene (9 years)

Pandora is jealous of Arlene's breezy nonchalance.
Arlene is jealous of Pandora's businesslike formality.
"Why would you tell him you like his freckles, and then tell him how to get rid of them?" criticizes Pandora.
"*Your* letter is full of lies!" exclaims Arlene. "He's not your favourite. He's your *last* favourite!"
Arlene goes to the kitchen to ask her mother whether it's radishes for removing freckles or *horse*radishes.
Pandora scrawls a postcript:
P.S. If a person calling herself Your friend Arlene sends you her freckle recipe, do not use it and send me a larger head as she has never faded a freckle in her whole life except when her skin fell off!

204

Pandora goes to the bathroom to wash honey from her fingers.

Arlene reads her postscript and writes:

P.P.S. If a person calling herself Your friend Pandora Gothic says you are tall and tender and terrific, do not send her anything as she is a Cornel Wilde fan not noted for truth-telling. Or to say it right out — a liar!!!!

Arlene and Pandora hand-line two more sheets of paper.

Pandora prints: "Dear Mr. Abbott. . . ."

Arlene prints: "Dear Mr. Costello. . . ."

Oh, it is painstaking work: *What choice have they?*

Dear Miss Grable,

Our name is Pandora, Arlene. You are our favourite. Please, send us two heads, no legs as there isn't room for them in our books. Colour will do nicely. . . .

Dear Dottie,

Our name is Arlene, Pandora. Is a sarong comfortable? How do you keep it up? If that's not too personal!!!!

Pandora borrows Miss Macintosh's jellypad. She and Arlene move into mass production:

Dear Miss or Mr. or Mrs. ....,

You are my favourite!!! I saw you in ....
and others too many to mention. Please send me two (2) large pictures personally named. Colour. Heads only, or factsmiley. No stamps! No substitutes!!!

Your friend,
Pandora Gothic (7½)
or
Arlene Goodfellow (9)

Pandora imprints her hands and feet in the fresh snow in front of Jung King Bros. Chinese laundry. She signs her name (or factsmiley):

PANDORA LAMOUR

Dorothy will have to change hers.

* * *

Pandora's clasped hands leave a sweaty heart on her desk: Of course. Today is Valentine's day.

All week the snug white box with the smug red hearts has been sitting by the door of Room 6. All week pupils have been gorging it with love ballots. Even Jessie Christie has posted eleven, rather fancifully inscribed: "Your friend, J. Christie."

Jill Peters, from last year's triumvirate, pokes her head around the doorframe. Grinning dually at Pandora and Ruth-Anne, she posts two cards. Pandora and Ruth-Anne drop their eyes like modest girls forced to listen to compliments about themselves. In fact, this is the payoff for a week's prudently retrieved friendship: the glamour of receiving foreign mail.

The bell rings.

Pandora, queasy with tension, closes the door. She knows she has power. She knows she has respect. But — even the great have their insecurities — *Am I loved?*

Miss Macintosh transfers the valentine box to her own desk. She lifts the lid, as if defusing a timebomb. "I guess we'll need some postmen."

Miss Macintosh doles out random handfuls of cards to random mailmen to be delivered at random. She encourages random chatter, even random movement. It is useless, of course. The results are anything but random. Pandora needs both arms to encircle her glut. She hears Cecily call to Ruth-Anne: "How many have you got?" She hears Ruth-Anne's self-assured reply: "I haven't had time to count."

Pandora glances across at Magda: Her lips are tightly drawn across her corncob teeth. She has four valentines, spread over her desk to make them look like more. All of them say, "Guess who?" which means they are from Miss Macintosh.

I should have sent Magda a card, but it's no joke, cutting out a couple dozen hearts and gluing the doors so they open. It isn't as if I could just buy them like Ruth-Anne.

Pandora considers erasing the name from one of hers, and re-posting it for Magda. *Maybe if I rub off 'Your friend, J. Christie' and mark it from myself?*

John Johnson drops a card on Magda's desk. He delivers a half-dozen more to Pandora and Ruth-Anne. *But what if Ruthie gets ONE more than me?*

Pandora hears a strange sound: *Splish splosh splish.*

She turns sideways: *Splittery, splosh-splosh.*

Magda is clutching her new valentine — a pink pig with "You Stink" written all over it in purple. Hot liquid sluices through the slit in Magda's seat. It spreads in a steamy starburst, the way horses do it on the road. . . .

Ooooooo, poor Magda! Pandora works very hard, then, erasing names from the backs of her valentines, but . . .

Thwonk! Magda's head hits her desk. *Ahhhhhhhggooooo!* Magda bawls out loud. *Splish-squish.* Magda lurches from the room, her red summer dirndl, worn out of hope, sloshing against her brown stockings.

"Oh *no!*" Miss Macintosh takes off after her.

What happened? . . .

What's wrong? . . .

No one at the back of the room can see. No one at the front wants to say. Bertie Brown stands on his seat: "*Ohhhh. . . .*"

Everyone gets up, then. They gather around Magda's desk, faces puckered in sorrow, but exaggerating it a little to conceal the relief of spectators at a catastrophe.

Pandora impulsively scoops the valentines from her own desk. She flings them onto Magda's desk.

"*Pandora!* What are you doing?" asks Ruth-Anne. She does the same. So does John Johnson. So does Candy Carter. So does everyone except for Jessie Christie, who didn't get any. Soon Magda's desk is buried under an avalanche of red, orange, yellow, blue protestations of love. They slop onto the floor. They sop up the puddle.

Miss Macintosh re-enters the room. She stares at Magda's

desk, garnished like a new grave. She studies the mourners — sad, but a little self-important. "If you *really* want to help Magda instead of just making yourselves feel better, you'll put right out of your minds the little accident we've had here today. You'll remember to be nice to Magda every day, and not just as something special."

Miss Macintosh starts stuffing valentines back into the broken white box.

"What are you going to do with them?" asks Ruth-Anne.

"Throw them *out*, I should think!" exclaims Miss Macintosh.

"Some aren't even opened," comments Cecily Battersea.

"Look! There's a Jack-in-the-box that jumps up!" exclaims Jason Green, pointing to one he recognizes as his own.

"They're awfully pretty," says Georgia.

"Yes, isn't it a shame to waste them," offers Bob Worth.

Miss Macintosh stops stuffing valentines. "O.K. kids, what do *you* want to do with them?"

Room 6 squirms: No one has the nerve to suggest they be given out all over again. Pandora squirms: She feels responsible.

"Miss Macintosh. . . ."

"Yes, Pandora. . . ."

"Miss Macintosh. . . ." *Oh, the pressure is terrible.* "Miss Macintosh. . . . Maybe we could paste the cards in a scrapbook. Maybe we could send them to a hospital the way my mother's Mission Circle does with Christmas cards to wounded soldiers. Maybe we could. . . ." *Oh, Pandora's mind is really churning* ". . . maybe we could send them to the Sand, to the people with T.B." *Sudden inspiration:* "I've got an Eskimo friend in the Sand. His name is Danny . . . Danny Lido. . . ."

"He's no Eskimo," jeers Jessie Christie. "He's a w - -"

"Jessie!" admonishes Miss Macintosh. "Pandora is making a suggestion. I think we should listen. Yes, Pandora?"

"Well, maybe he's not an Eskimo, but if he's got T.B. then he's got Eskimo friends." She thinks about mentioning the purple elbows but decides against it. "We could send the scrapbook from the whole class, and we wouldn't even have to rub out the names because they'd be pasted down. Except for Danny Ilson's cards. We could leave those turned up if they just have 'Danny' without the Ilson."

Miss Macintosh smiles: "That sounds like a good idea. How do the rest of you feel?"

"Yes!" shouts Room 6. *Anything to save our valentines!*

"Even if Danny Ilson's cards had 'Danny I.' on them we could change them to 'Danny L.'," says Pandora, expanding into an area of family expertise. "And even if Danny L. lifted up the corners and saw the other names it wouldn't matter because he'd know about the wounded soldiers getting cards with other peoples' names, and even if he didn't know, we could write him a letter and *tell* him."

"*You* could write the letter!" exclaims the loyal Ruth-Anne.

"Yes!" shout a half-dozen others: Pandora's jellypad correspondence with Rory Calhoun, Dame May Whitty, Lana Turner and Basil Rathbone is well known and much admired.

And so it is settled.

Miss Macintosh makes only one stipulation: "The scrapbook has to be finished today." That's to get it out of the way before Magda returns to school.

Flora Thwaite, the neatest person in the room (though fat), folds a white cover for the valentine scrapbook. Jessie Christie, the best artist in the room (though mean) draws a picture of Danny Lido inside a red heart that looks like a red noose. Danny Ilson, who possesses the most providential name in the class (though none too bright) selects valentines with suitable samples of it for display on the opening pages. Everyone else follows Danny's lead: Each sorts through the anonymous jumble for his own cards to be fondled, counted and exclaimed over before their consignment to charity.

Pandora writes the letter, using all her knowhow and frequently consulting her files:

Dear Mr. Danny Lido,

This is Pandora Gothic and Room 6. You are our favourite valentine!!! We saw you in Room 3 last year. Enclosed please find our valentine, which is really everybody's valentines glued by hand to the pages so that the moving parts still move. Don't worry about the wrong names as that is like the wounded soldiers get on the backs of their old Christmas cards, and every one really has your name on it the moment it is glued down.

I was wondering, do you have freckles? If so, try milk and horseradish. If not, maybe radishes. If this doesn't work then don't worry as some say freckles are tall, tender and terrific!!!

Please send us one (1) large picture, personally named, head only, or factsmiley. No stamps! No substitutes! We will hang it on our Humane Society Board.

Your friend,
Pandora Gothic
or
Room 6

Magda does not return to class the following day. A note comes, via one of her brothers, saying she is in bed with "sniffles."

Everyone is disappointed: How can Room 6 show Magda how completely it has forgotten she piddled on the floor if she isn't there to see it? Everyone treats Magda's desk with consideration, even deference. Pandora sharpens Magda's pencils. Ruth-Anne replaces the grubby Canada Bread cover on her reader with a silver one. Silly Lily Brill (who wasn't so silly as to neglect to send herself eleven pseudononymous valentines) drops a plastic four-leaf clover into Magda's inkwell.

On the following Monday, a hangdog Magda thrusts her wet nose around the doorframe.

Pandora smiles toothily: *Hi Magda!*

Ruth-Anne smiles toothily.

Jason Green smiles toothily.

John Johnson smiles toothily.

Magda risks a self-conscious grin, which looks rather like a mutt barring its teeth.

"Let's start with a little grammar today, please. . . ."

At recess, Magda is rushed like a debutante. Pandora is the

lucky one. Magda hooks an arm through hers for the walk to the playground. She wrings Pandora's hand. She picks imaginary lint from Pandora's coat, the maddening way Pandora's mother does it. She runs her greasy comb through Pandora's hair.

Pandora and Ruth-Anne avoid exchanging rueful looks — by a scant half-inch.

"What'ull we play?" mumbles Pandora.

Magda beams. "Let's play hopscotch."

Nobody plays hopscotch in winter. "O.K.," says Pandora. "Let's play hopscotch."

Ruth-Anne and Georgia tamp a hopscotch in fresh snow near the Downstairs Girl/Boy dividing line. Magda tosses her plastic four-leaf clover (for which she persists in thanking Pandora) toward square No. 1. It lands on a line: Magda doesn't mind. The other girls pretend not to notice. Magda hops heavily up and down the hopscotch, botching its delicate webbing: Magda doesn't mind. The other girls pretend not to notice.

Jessie Christie, prancing down the Boys' side of the line, yells: "Hey, Magda! Smell-eeee!" Magda minds. The other girls pretend not to notice. Magda bends to pick up her talisman. Jessie tosses a snowball up her skirt. "Wet pants! *Wets-her-pants!*"

Magda cries: The other girls are forced to notice. "Shut up Jessie!" shouts Pandora, dutifully.

"Smelly pants! Wets-her-pants!"

"Shut *up*!"

"Who's gonna make me?"

"I'm gonna make you." *Me, the Big Billy Goat Gruff!*

"How? Gonna tell Macky? *Smelly-pants and tattletale-tit!*"

Pandora, her own honour impunged, is now thoroughly engaged. She confronts Jessie, head thrust forward, eyes blazing, over the playground line.

"I'm *warning* you, Jessie. Shut up or —"

"Or what?"

Pandora hesitates. This is *not* the street. *Inspiration!* She smiles triumphantly. "I'll *thank* you for the *beoooootiful* valentine. *Thank* you, Jessie for the *luv*elly *luv*elly valentine. It was just what I always wanted!"

Jessie grabs Pandora's hair. Miss Horowitz blows her whistle. Jessie spins around. Miss Horowitz reprimands two boys throwing snowballs. Jessie spins back. Too late. Pandora brings down her fist between his shoulderblades. Jessie crumples.

The end-of-recess whistle blows. Pandora runs back to the girls. Ruth-Anne is shocked: "Pandora! You should be *ashamed!*" Magda is thrilled. "Oooh, thank you Pan-d*ee!*" She puts a proprietary hand on Pandora's arm. Pandora, still shooting adrenalin, snatches it away. She controls a murderous urge to smack Magda's hurt-idiot's face: *Phaw!* To have earned the princess and be offered the scullery-maid!

Pandora links her arm through Ruth-Anne's. "I think me and my friend will go back together *for a change!*"

Magda, head down, runs to her old spot at the end of the line.

Pandora and Ruth-Anne giggle their way back to class, with Pandora reciting a soothing litany of Magda's offences: *Magda wets her pants. Magda's nose drips. Magda has germy teeth....*

Cecily Battersea is, for once, supportive: "PHheeoooey! that Magda stinks of rotten fish!"

Pandora winces. *No. Magda stinks of fear. I have smelled it on myself.*

A letter arrives for Pandora Gothic or Room 6: It is from Danny Lido. He is thrilled with the valentines and encloses one (1) named picture, head only, with the rest scissored off. He doesn't have freckles. It is cold in the Sand. He sleeps on an open porch, and at night they bring hot stones for his bed.

Room 6 pins Danny's picture to the Humane Society board, inside a large heart, and when strangers come to Room 6 they are introduced to it as "Our Friend, Danny Lido in the Sand," and the children of Room 6 treat this picture with as much deference as they treated Magda's desk before she came back and sat in it.

Crime & Punishment

Inspector Jasper of the Mill City police and Father Flinton of St. Peter's Cathedral visit Laura Secord Public School: the one is massive and beetle-browed; the other is porcine, with a cornsilk halo. Inspector Jasper is the plumply haloed one.

They confer with Col. Burns in his second-floor office. Their escort — four priests and four policemen — wait in a bunch outside the door. Upstairs pupils can see the bulge of Bibles and guns in their cassocks and holsters. Downstairs pupils imagine they can see the bulge of their feet through the floor.

Col. Burns paces his office on high grasshopper legs, drilling his fingers through his polished hair. He dispatches the priests and policemen, in pairs, to rooms 24, 23, 22 to begin a boy-by-boy interrogation of Laura Secord Public School. Any boy found insufficient in his answers is to be escorted to the colonel's office for a more formal grilling.

Clearly, a crime has been committed.

A crime offensive to school, church and state.

A crime so awful only a BOY could think of it!

All morning, Downstairs pupils hear the measured tramp of footsteps in the halls above. A sober air of Crime and Punishment hangs over Laura Secord School. Everyone feels it. Coloured pencils, borrowed weeks before, are fished out of desks and returned. Stolen chalk finds its way back into troughs.

Lucy Ford blurts out to Candy Carter that she was the one who spilled ink on her natural-science chart. Beth Shay admits cheating over Dorothy Hunt's shoulder. Cecily Battersea belligerently confesses: *"I* sent Magda the 'You Stink' valentine. *So what?"*

The boys talk with bravado about the strap.

"If they hit you on the *wrist* you can get them fired."

"I know one guy pulled his hand back, and old Burnsie *set fire to matches in his pocket!*"

Recess for Upper School is cancelled. Downstairs pupils file, two-by-two, around the border of Upper School's playground, staring at the untrampled snow: *What is it? Who did it? What did they do?*

Noon hour does little to dispel the mystery: The questioning, though thorough, has been slyly circumspect.

"My sister's boyfriend says it was a 'profane' crime on 'sacred' property," whispers Georgia Brooks.

"Golly!" whispers Ruth-Anne.

"Gee!" whispers Candy.

"That must be why the priest's here," says Pandora.

"Maybe," says Marjorie Maitland, "but if it's a *horrible* crime, and a *Catholic* did it, they might bring in a priest so the boy won't burn in perkatory."

The 1:30 bell rings.

The girls scurry to their seats.

Miss Macintosh is not yet in the room.

Pandora mounts guard.

She hears the heavy tramp of footsteps coming down the stairs. She sees — *hola!* — blue serge! black robes! "It's *the police!"* Pandora dashes to her seat. *"They're coming DOWN-STAIRS!"*

Miss Macintosh strides into the room, three yards behind Pandora. She slams the door; opens it; then recloses it with icy calm. "We may have *visitors* this afternoon. Don't be concerned. Just answer all questions as fully as possible. . . ."

A knock on the door. A whey-faced room-runner thrusts a white paper into Miss Macintosh's hands. "Recess has been *repealed,"* she announces, in a voice bladed with sarcasm.

It is difficult for Room 6 to concentrate: The words slide

around their readers like letters in alphabet soup. Now the footsteps march up and down, back and forth *right outside our own door!* Bert Brown cracks his knuckles. Lily Brill hiccups. John Johnson has a sneeze fit.

The footsteps halt. *OUR room! Us! Room 6! They're HERE!* A long procedural delay. A radiator explodes. Room 6 rises, as one, to the ceiling.

Miss Macintosh yanks open the door. A priest and a policeman stand ready to pound. "Our *visitors*," she announces, with a scornful flourish.

They fill the doorway. *They fill the room!* The priest is wearing rimless glasses, a ring and a crucifix. The policeman is wearing a badge, a buckle and two rows of brass buttons. These shiny points of authority collect, and reflect, the sunlight. The priest and policeman stand over Pandora's desk. She can smell their uniforms. She can't see their faces for glint. Pandora feels a queer twist of hysteria. Before, she felt only her proper share of the anonymous guilt. Now, confronted, she feels a very personal sense of calling.

The priest and policeman install themselves at chairs and a table in the cloakroom. As each boy hears his name, he is to enter by way of the entrance. As each boy completes his interrogation, he is to leave by the exit.

"Bertrand Brown," intones the priest through the plaster.

Bert gulps. Stands. Shuffles to the cloakroom.

The girls stare pityingly, accusingly, at the boys: *What did you do?* The boys stare pityingly, defiantly, at each other: *What did we do?*

Five minutes pass. Bert emerges, numbed but relieved.

"Jason Green."

As each name is called, Room 6 sucks noisily inward. As each boy emerges, Room 6 exhales breathily. Pandora stares, in escalating terror, at the cloakroom where she knows the interlocutors are sitting. She imagines she can see rays of policeman's brass and crucifix silver, *right through the plaster!* She imagines the priest and policeman can see back down these piercing rays, *right into my own head!* She imagines they can see the evil thoughts, cringing like rats in the sewers of her mind. She imagines they are calling forth her rats. *"Come! Come! Come!"* They are calling them by name. *"Come, Filthy! Come, Rotten! Come, Stinker!"* She feels her rats *scuttle-scamper, blink-blink* . . . dragging their slime-tails into the sunlight.

Pandora binds herself to the scrollwork of her desk with sweaty links of flesh. She fights the giddy urge to fling herself at the feet of the uniformed men and to confess.

Confess to what?

Confesssssssss!

I didn't do it! I don't even know its name!

"Jessie Christie."

The interrogations have settled into four-minute rituals. As more and more boys emerge, unscathed, from the cloak-room, Room 6 begins to relax. Curiosity replaces fear. There is a shift in the balance of power: The girls, once superior in their innocence, are now inferior through lack of participation. The boys, once impotent in the face of authority, are now initiates in a secret society bonded by risk.

Jessie Christie swaggers to the entrance. Smirks all around. He tips an imaginary hat, and disappears inside. The minutes tick by.

"Almost *ten* minutes!" whispers Ruth-Anne, shaking her Mickey Mouse wristwatch. Room 6 fidgets. The boys mouth reassurances: *Ole Jessie must really be giving them a story!*

Ole Jess saunters from the cloakroom — *with the priest!* The policeman says a few words to Miss Macintosh. Priest and police escort Jessie Christie from the room.

Room 6 is electrified.

"Settle down, children, please! I know this is a distraction, but it doesn't mean much."

The recess bell rings. Room 6 hears Upper School shuffle out to the playground. Room 6 hears Upper School whoop it up on the playground. *Not fair! Not fair! The bell! We're supposed to be out! The bell!*

Miss Macintosh reads in a low, sing-songy voice, weaving a

net across the panicky gap in ritual.

There is a knock on the door. *The policeman!* Miss Macintosh talks to him in the hall. She re-enters the room. Frowning, she whispers to Jason. "They want to see *you*, again, dear."

The freckles leap off Jason's nose.

"Just go with them a few minutes, and get this thing cleared up."

Now, Miss Macintosh is not so calm. Twice, she loses her place. Once, she re-reads a whole paragraph. Finally, she breaks off. She scribbles a note so ferociously she snaps a lead:

"Sarah — The Great Manhunt has ended in MY room! Could you put your class on monitors and look after mine? I don't dare leave them! — Tillie."

Miss Wills is tall, waspish and imperial, with diction as precise as her marcelled hair. "Listen to these instructions, for I shall not repeat them:

"Take one lined sheet of foolscap. Draw a one-and-one-quarter-inch margin down the left side.

"Now, divide the remainder in half, lengthwise.

"Print your name, legibly, in the top right corner.

"Print your room and number in the top left corner.

"Centre the word 'Spelling' on the first blue line.

"Leave one line space.

"Print the digits 1 to 25, vertically, inside the lefthand margin.

"Put a dot after each.

"Print the digits 26 to 50, vertically, to the left of the centre line.

"Put a dot after each."

Miss Wills checks her wristwatch: It is not a Mickey Mouse one. "I shall give you exactly two-minutes fifteen-seconds to complete this task. Then I shall begin deducting marks."

A surprise spelling test! For marks! Room 6 is almost too appalled to think about profane acts on sacred property.

Miss Macintosh returns as Room 6 is rounding the top of the page to No. 26. She takes over the dictation, biting off each letter as crisply as Miss Wills, but now it is with fury.

At No. 37, Jason sticks his head around the doorframe. His face is bloated. He is having difficulty with the doorknob. His hands are . . .

Pandora shoves her head into her desk. She laughs with the guilty hysteria of someone who ducks a knife then turns to see it sticking into a friend. She is sick with shame. She stuffs her mouth with blotting paper, terrified someone will hear.

Miss Macintosh hands Jason his coat, then closes the door. She says, very quietly: "I suppose it's pointless for me to ask you not to talk about this after all the fuss that's been made. Just remember: People *do* make mistakes. Even people with titles and uniforms. *Especially* people with titles and uniforms because sometimes they think they can't go wrong."

The bell rings.

Room 6 shoves toward the fire-escape door. Room 6 *explodes* onto the playground. *What happened? Where's Jason? What did he do?*

Jason Green is nowhere in sight.

Jessie Christie is standing at homeplate, on the Big Diamond, flanked by Godfrey Trumps and Horace Ghostie.

Room 6 runs towards him, then falls back, reluctant to approach such a hostile citadel on the apex of playground authority.

"Hey, Jess!" calls Bert Brown, advancing on his own. "What happened? Was it Jason?"

Jessie nods. "Yeah, it was *him*, O.K." Room 6 shuffles forward. "They caught him practically red-handed. *He* was the one!"

"What'd he do, Jess?"

"Old Burnsie was going to give the whole school detention!" fumes Jessie. "For a month!"

"Yeah? What did Jason —"

"He was going to *strap* all the boys! Even the *little* kids!"

"Jessie *had* to tell," interrupts Godfrey, getting rid of this problem early. "Jessie did it for *all* of us."

"But *what* did Jason *do?*"

Jessie is very solemn, very stern. "Jason did a *sacrilege.* . . . Jason broke into St. Pete's!"

"The cathedral?"

"Yeah."

"To steal?"

"Nahh. . . ." Jessie is clearly repelled. "To do a *profane.*"

"*WHAT? Come on, Jess! TELL! What did he do?*"

Jessie can hardly keep a straight face, the crime is so terrible. "Jason Green put goldfish in the Holy Baptismal Fount!"

Room 6 is stunned. *No! Gosh! . . . Jason? That's awful!*

Bert Brown, and a couple of others, burst out laughing. Jessie, Godfrey, Horace turn on him in unutterable scorn. Bert, startled, wipes the smile from his face. "Gee, no kidding!" He looks from one to the other to make sure there isn't a joke. "*No kidding!*"

The Big Three indulge in a tricorner smile.

"That's not all," continues Jessie. "That wasn't the *only* thing Jason did." He lowers his voice, dramatically. Room 6 shuffles forward. "Jason buttered the Holy Communion bread. He reached under the altar and buttered the Hostie! *Jason buttered the Body of Christ!*"

Gasps from the girls.

"*Why* would Jason *do* a thing like that?" demands Ruth-Anne.

"Don't ask *me*. All *I* know is I *saw* him."

"What? You *saw* him butter . . ." Ruth-Anne can't even say it.

Jessie is scathing. "No! I saw him go into St. Pete's with *a pound of butter* in one hand, and *a package shaped like three goldfish* in the other."

"We saw him leave," insists Horace. "Godfrey and me saw Jason *running away* from St. Pete's with *buttered paper* in one hand and a package shaped like three *missing* goldfish in the other." He nudges Godfrey. "Inspector Jasper called it 'corroborative evidence.' "

The Big Boys burst into raucous laughter: It feeds a certain skeptical backwash.

"*Bull!*" scoffs Thomas Dunn. "You're just shooting off."

"Bull, eh?" Jessie is very cool, very sarcastic. "You *saw* the priest, didn't you? You *saw* the police? You *saw* Jason? He *did* get the strap, didn't he? You *saw* his hands."

A sober question hangs over Room 6: *Can school, church and state ALL be wrong?*

There is another consideration: Jessie is, after all, the only source of information.

"Did *you* see Jason get it?" asks Bob Worth, respectfully.

"Yeah."

"How many did he get?"

"Ten."

"On each?"

"Yeah."

"Eleven, on one hand!" pipes a girl from Room 12. "We counted them out loud as they landed. Col. Burns was *really* mad! He came for Miss Wills' strap. He ripped the lock right off the drawer!"

"*That's* because Macintosh came busting in!" says Jessie. "She shouts, 'Is this *bullying* what you call *justice*?' Old Burnsie shouts back, 'What right do *you* have in here?' Tillie shouts, 'What right do *you* have to strap an innocent boy?'

"*That's* when Burnsie decided he *would* strap Jason. *Before* that he was just going to call his old man. Then Tillie really lights up. She shouts, 'You strike that boy, and I'm filing a report to the Board.' He hollers, 'You get the fuck out of here or —' "

"Oh — he wouldn't say F.U.!" protests the punctilious Thomas Dunn. "Burnsie wouldn't say F.U. in front of the priest!"

"Well," drawls Jessie. "Maybe he didn't *say* F.U., but he sure-the-fuck *meant* F.U.! He said, 'You get the *hell* out of here, or *I'll* tell the Board what goes on *with you and Foukes* behind the blowers, *not* to mention in the broom closet at high noon!' "

What? WHAT?

Jessie rolls his eyes to heaven, unwilling to take responsibility for what he is, afterall, just reporting. "Old Tillie just stood there, sputtering and pooping her pants, right down her legs, and it was coming out her shoes, and —"

That's a lie, Jessie Christie! Liar! LI-AR!

"A lie? A lie?" Jessie is just warming up. "Who's a liar? Scouts Honour! She pooped her pants. Right there on the floor. Didn't she Horace? Didn't she Godfrey?"

Horace and Godfrey nod in unison. *Corroborative evidence! Corroborative evidence!*

Jessie catches Pandora's horrified eye. "You've seen her red pants? *You've* seen the poop on them? Well? *Well!* She pooped her pants, then she stepped right out of them, and Burnsie stuck his hand up her skirt, and she giggled, 'OOOoooo! That's *wonderful,* colonel! Do it again!' and then Jason, blubbering, grabs a tit, and —"

The girls of Room 6 run screeching, hands over ears, to their own side of the playground: *GIVE US BARABBAS!*

Jason Green never returns to Laura Secord Public School.

Col. Burns hands in his resignation: It is rejected.

Miss Macintosh is asked to resign, effective at the end of June.

"My *sister* says, her *boyfriend* says, *Horace Ghostie* says, it was *Jessie* who put the goldfish in the Holy Water," whispers Georgia. "He did it for *dares* to get into their Satan Club. They sneak out at night. They do terrible things. Everybody says it: 'They do terrible things.' "

What do they do? What do they do?

Nobody knows.

A guilty sense of the miscarriage of justice hangs *heavy heavy heavy* over Laura Secord Public School.

As for Pandora. . . . She can't get her rats to go back into their holes. She feels them forcing their way, like vomit, up her throat. She hears them clawing and squealing inside her skull. They have heard the Pied Piper. They are dancing to his tune. . . .

"Does anyone know what a peacock's tail is for?" asks Miss Macintosh.

"For making hats!" exclaims Ruth-Anne. "My grandmother has one."

"That's what *people* use it for," smiles Miss Macintosh. "What does the peacock do with it?"

"He sweeps the barnyard," says Bertie Brown.

"He balances himself like a cat," says Pandora.

"He keeps off flies," says Candy Carter.

"The peacock uses his tail for courting," replies Miss Macintosh. "Do you know how peacocks dance? They put out their tails, and they puff out their chests, and they jut out their heads, and they rustle and rattle their feathers. Then they hop. Sometimes they peck each other, but mostly it's bluff. The peacock that bluffs the most wins. The loser collapses his tail and runs."

"Cats do that," says Pandora.

"So do people!" exclaims Ruth-Anne. "I've seen them on the playground."

Magda Lunt flips an envelope, twisted into a corkscrew, onto Pandora's desk.

Miss Macintosh holds up another picture from her Natural Science file. "Who's this staid-looking fellow?"

"He's a penguin, Miss Macintosh. He looks like my brother when he goes to a dance."

"Yes, Lucy. But when *our* Mr. Penguin goes courting, he doesn't take flowers. He takes a white stone that the lady penguin can use to make her nest. *If* she decides to pick it up. Even lady penguins can be coy."

Pandora eyes the twisted envelope. It is from Jessie Christie.

Miss Macintosh holds up another picture. "What's this?"

"It's a bird!" exclaims Magda, triumphantly.

"Yes, Magda, but what kind? Have you seen this chap strutting along the beach? He's a tern. He eats fish. Sometimes when he finds a tasty one, he takes it to a lady tern, and they have a picnic."

"I wouldn't catch a fish for any stupid girl!" scoffs Roger Parker.

Miss Macintosh smiles: "You might be surprised, Roger."

Pandora picks up the envelope. She feels it.

"What do you suppose this is?" asks Miss Macintosh.

"Oohhh! It's a spider!" says Flora.

"It's an ugly hairy spider!" exclaims Georgia.

Ha! It's a black widow spider! decides Pandora.

"Yes," affirms Miss Macintosh. "It's a black widow spider."

Pandora runs her thumb down a ridge: *THAT will be the stick with the elastic wound round it.* When you untwist the envelope, the elastic is supposed to unwind, making a whirry sound. You're supposed to scream, thinking it's something horrible, like a black widow spider. She tosses Jessie a scornful look. *That's an old trick.*

"Most spiders aren't dangerous," reassures Miss Macintosh. "You just have to recognize the few that are."

Pandora pins the "black widow" to keep it from untwirling. She untwists the envelope.

"What does the black widow do?" asks John Johnson. "Does she bite?"

"Yes. She's quite nasty and unpredictable. Even to her mate. *Even* after he's brought her a juicy fly wrapped in cobweb."

Pandora looks inside the envelope. She looks for a long time, without seeming to react.

"If the black widow isn't satisfied with her gift, she's likely to gobble up the giver for dessert. It isn't wise to tamper with a black widow spider."

"OOOoooo!" exclaims Marjorie Maitland. "That's terrible!"

"It's the worst thing I ever heard," agrees Ruth-Anne.

Pandora puts the envelope, and its contents, into her desk. She folds her hands on top. Jessie Christie is disappointed. He had expected more — much more.

225

"So you see," concludes Miss Macintosh, "life isn't easy to predict. You can expect to get one reaction, and get another. . . . It's the same with people. You can do something you think is right and have it turn out badly. Or you can do something mean, and have that backfire. The important thing is to do your best, and not to lose faith in yourself or in others. . . . You see, animals act by *instinct*. They don't know the difference between cruelty and kindness so they can't be held to account. Humans do. Humans have *intelligence*. Humans *must* be held to account for what they do, even for their mistakes. . . . Now, let's try a few arithmetic sums."

Pandora spreads the March 1 Mill City Clarion on her patchwork quilt. She forces herself to read.

Pet Tortured, Burned.

The mutilated body of a white kitten was found yesterday in an alley behind Baltic Avenue. It had been tortured with knives, then drenched in gasoline and set aflame.

J. R. Severn of Baltic Avenue was returning home from work when he saw the fire. "I used my cap to put out the flames. I thought it was just a pile of rags. Then I saw that other thing."

"That other thing" was the kitten's severed head, impaled on a rake handle.

"I'd like to have given chase, but which way? Whoever done it got clean away!"

Mrs. Mable Hanson of Baltic Avenue, owner of the kitten, was heartsick. "She was the sweetest little thing you could imagine. We called her Happy. She had a purr on her that would like to drowned out a steam engine. The mind that would do such a thing. . . . Well, it doesn't seem human, does it? Now I worry about the children. Someone should put a stop to him before he does more evil."

Pandora opens the twisted envelope. She takes out a white cat's tail smelling of gasoline and caked with blood.

It is dark but it is not late: These winter days are stingy with their light. *In the midst of life we are in death:* The night has strangled the day.

Pandora climbs, fully clothed, from her bed. She creeps down two flights of stairs. She pauses in the shadows, outside the living-room. She sees her mother on the chesterfield, crocheting a doily, *round and round* in smaller and smaller circles. She sees her father playing Monopoly at the lame-legged cardtable: Tonight he is making a fool of J. Paul Getty. She sees Adel-Ada practising their penmanship: *round and round and round and* . . . They are arced by light from the tri-light. They are woven with laughter from the radio: They are listening to The Aldrich Family, occasionally punctuating its canned laughter with a little of their own.

Pandora darts past the living-room into the pantry. She opens the trapdoor. The pit is very black. She holds her breath. She plunges.

Pandora fumbles her way past her mother's glass fruit-crypts. She smells the carbon cloud over the coal bin. She sees the mouth of her father's furnace, outlined in Flame Henna. She sees the stiff rubber lips of her mother's wash-machine.

Pandora sticks her hands into the icy gut of the dirty-clothes hamper. She feels . . . Adel's shivery *right* stocking, Ada's slithery *left* stocking, her mother's silk drawers. *Ahh* . . . her fingers scrape it. Her father's butcher's apron, smeared with blood. She puts it on.

Pandora piles King Cola cases into a slivery staircase. She climbs it. She runs her fingers along cold porcelain trays. She selects her father's meat-cleaver.

Pandora climbs down the King Cola staircase. She lifts the lid of her mother's washtub. She takes out her khaki coat and her "Hi, Sweetheart" pillowcase. She pulls a hangman's noose, made from Cecily Battersea's skipping-rope, out of the "Hi, Sweetheart" pillowcase. She knots the meat-cleaver around her waist. She puts on her khaki coat. She slings the pillowcase over her shoulder. Now she is ready: *I am going to kill Jessie Christie.*

Pandora unlatches the cellar door. She crawls into the earth vestibule, smelling of mould, fungus and decay. She pushes up the storm door: It creaks like a coffin lid.

The air is foggy.

Pandora darts down her backyard, blending her body with the skeletons of dead shrubs. She turns right, into the alley. The rays of her flashlight penetrate only a few feet before bending back, turning the super-saturated air around her into liquid light. Pandora glides through the night in a chariot of quicksilver. She does not know it is being pulled by — *hi ho, my lovelies* — her sleek-footed team of rats!

Pandora turns right onto States Avenue, then left onto the railway tracks. She hears nothing. She sees no one. She is not afraid. Nothing is real. If she shut off her light, she knows she would disappear.

The railway shack sits in a tangle of garbage lightly covered with snow. It is early Dogpatch — skinny, peaked, on stilts, like a skyrocket someone forgot to set off. Pandora leaps from garbage-floe to garbage-floe. She pushes against the door of the shack. It sticks, then gives. She shines her flashlight over . . . a busted carseat, a rusted stove, a wicker chair, two new folding chairs like the kind you'd steal from a church basement, a ricketty table, an orangecrate stuffed with rags . . . paint . . . candles . . . gasoline. The walls are decorated with swastikas. There is a picture of Hitler saluting himself; a photo of a Russian soldier hanging from a streetlight; a nude calendar, mutilated. *Oh, it is their club, all right.* The only key Pandora needed was Jessie Christie's braggart's tongue.

Pandora roots herself on the wicker chair. Now it is safe to turn off her flashlight. She balances her meat-cleaver on her lap. *I'll get Jessie as soon as he opens the door. Splish-splosh! I'll wack his head right off!*

Pandora waits.

She is confident Jessie will come. She has divined the mystic relationship between Victor and Victim — that each has the need to play both roles. She is here as a compulsive actor in two dramas. She is here as a Victor-Avenger. Pandora knows a crime has been committed, a terrible crime, for which she alone possesses the evidence: She will punish.

She is here as a Victim-Penitent. Pandora belongs to that group of potential criminals for whom guilt precedes the crime, and is its chief motivating force. She is plagued by a ratpack of anonymous guilts which she must collect into a single crime for which there can be punishment, suffering, and expiation or destruction. All she knows of this second subterranean drama is . . . *On, Filthy! On, Rotten! On, Dandruff! On, Vixen!* . . . She can see, feel, hear, smell the rats.

Pandora waits.

It does not occur to her that Godfrey Trumps or Horace Ghostie might come through the door first: It is Jessie with whom she has performed her mating-dance of mutual self-hate and destruction. He is the other half of her Victor/Victim. He is the other half of her murder/suicide. She has travelled, as if by radarbeam, to rendezvous with him at this time, in this place. Can Jessie himself do less?

Pandora waits.

The temperature falls. The wind rises. It whips the chilled air into creamy snowflakes. She looks out the window. The fog is lifting. She can see the railway tracks. She can see boxcars and trees and fences. Pandora fidgets: The broken wicker cuts into her legs. She is cold. She can smell mould and gasoline and . . . dried blood. Pandora wants to go home.

Jessie isn't coming.

Pandora attacks the clubhouse with her meat-cleaver. She slashes the carseat and the wicker chair as best she can. She rips down the posters. She overturns the orangecrates. She smears everything with red paint. She pours on gasoline.

Pandora draws a match. *No.* The fog has lifted. The world is too real. She puts away her match.

Pandora signs her collage with the last of her fiery justification: a cat face made from her hangman's noose, with a joke-poop nose, and a Cheshire grin twisted from a severed cat-tail.

Pandora slings her "Hi Sweetheart" pillowcase over her shoulder.

She runs home.

She jumps into bed.

She falls asleep: She does not dream. She has already had one nightmare. There is another coming.

In the midst of life we are in death. . . . *After a lengthy ill-ness, at her residence . . . beloved mother of . . . beloved sister of . . . beloved grandmother of. . . .* As it must to all of us.

Adel shakes Pandora by the right arm. "You're supposed to get up!"

Ada shakes Pandora by the left leg. "We've got to get an early start."

"Grandma Pearl is dead," says Adel.

"She died in her sleep."

Lyle brushes his black suit. He knots his black tie. He creases his black fedora. He buttons his black glove. He drives Adelaide, Adel-Ada, Rosalind and Pandora, in a black car to the place in the country without a name, down the aisle of dead elms, to dead Other Grandma. . . .

They file through the vestibule: Lyle, Rosalind, Adelaide, Adel-Ada, Pandora. They file into the parlour, opened, aired and dusted.

Other Grandmother is up three steps in a metal box, set with lilies in silver vases — Other Grandmother, with marble-white arms and porcelain-white cheeks and frost-white hair and tomb-white teeth and crystallized eyes too cloudy to suck. Other Grandma, wound in white lace, yards and years of white lace, adrift on ice coffin. . . .

Lyle goes up the three white steps.

Rosalind goes up the three white steps.

Adelaide goes up the three white steps.

Adel-Ada go up the three white steps.

Pandora does not go up the three white steps.

Pandora darts into the heart of a jet-curtain, tied with a golden cord.

The death of Other Grandma has slipped between Pandora's crime and its discovery, leaving her with a martyr's need for alternate suffering-purification-atonement.

Pandora parts the black curtains. She sees . . . Other Grandmother's coffin, gleaming like an altar. She feels guilt spew up from deep inside her. She clings to the black curtains. She cowers under the golden cord. She tries to control her terror by naming it. She tries to call it by something she can understand, and hence ward off.

Pandora remembers another coffin, and another grandma, now a long way off. . . . *A chocolate coffin, trimmed with chocolate rosebuds. Pandora nibbles one of the rosebuds. Aunt Estelle slaps it from her hands. She attacks her with a pair of sugar tongs: "Nasty! Filthy! Rotten! Greedy!"*

Pandora opens her eyes. She fixes them, courageously, on Other Grandma's silver coffin. *If I get dirty fingers on Grandma's box, Aunt Estelle will scold me! She will beat me!* That makes Pandora feel a lot better because: *If I DON'T touch Grandma's box, Aunt Estelle WON'T beat me!*

Pandora rocks back and forth on her haunches, with her hands in tight fists, reassuring herself: *Mustn't touch! Mustn't touch!*

It is hot inside the black curtains.

It is dusty.

The death room empties. . . .

Mustn't! Mustn't! Mustn't!

Pandora feels the gold cord slide down the curtains, around her neck. She chokes. She feels dizzy. The room starts to get away from Pandora. . . . Chairs and tables float off into space. Grandma Pearl's coffin undulates in the candlelight. It melts into puddles of quicksilver. It sways, as if it were going to topple. The lace and candles and lilies s-l-i-d-e. . . .

Pandora runs to the coffin. She lays both palms *touch! touch! touch!* on the side of Other Grandma's coffin. *Ohh. . . .* Her hands freeze. *Ahhhhh. . . .*

Aunt Estelle finds Pandora sobbing, on her knees, with her

palms stuck to Grandma Pearl's coffin. Aunt Estelle draws the cringing Pandora to her feet. Aunt Estelle is not angry. Aunt Estelle does not scold. Aunt Estelle does not beat.

"Come. . . ." Aunt Estelle is touched by the depth of Pandora's sorrow. Aunt Estelle rewards Pandora: "I will lift you so you can kiss Grandma Pearl good-bye."

Kissssssssssssss?

The air leaves Pandora's body in a long, incredulous stream.

Kissssssssssssssss? Oh, the penance is too hard!

Pandora feels herself tumbling head-over-heels, in space, through air the texture of hot syrup, away from the room, away from Aunt Estelle, with reality slipping in a long thin wire through her fingers. . . .

Time wobbles. . . . Time gets away from Pandora, the way space has done. She moves into stretched time, as experienced by the mad, the drowning, the dreaming, the dying. *T-i-c Toooo-c* . . .

Many hallucinated moments pass from the time Pandora's foot leaves her body till the time it arrives on the first coffin step. She is forced to s-t-r-e-t-ch her leg, like Plastic Man, to pass through all that space. She sees Other Grandma's silver winding-sheet a l-o-n-g way off, undulating in the candlelight. She thinks for the first time: *Other Grandmother is in it!*

Now the wire slips very quickly through Pandora's fingers. She closes her eyes. Aunt Estelle's iron hands draw her up the side of the coffin. The edge of the coffin bites her legs. Aunt Estelle lowers Pandora into the coffin. Pandora smells corpse. Pandora opens her eyes. *Oohhhhhhhhhhh!* That is a mistake. *Other Grandmother isn't white any more!* Her eyes are black. Her cheeks are hollow. Her arms are crossed like pirates bones. *She is the poison mask on the iodine bottle. Other Grandmother is yellow.* Jaundice yellow.

Pandora screams — a deep exhalation of breath, struggling to become sound. Pandora screams — a wisp of spittle, soaring a full half-inch before drowning in its own sputter.

Pandora screams — playing out the wire, very quickly, through her fingers, not wanting to hold it any longer, wishing to come to the end and *forever and ever and* . . . Pandora screams — once more — AND IS HEARD!

A hand — hard, warm — digs deep into her neck-tremble. It yanks her *bump bump bump* from the side of the coffin. Pandora lies at the base of two worsted treetrunks. A tingle of feeling spreads through her body, in the shape of a hand.

Pandora hears voices: a man's voice . . . a woman's. . . .

"Why?"

". . . . . Death? . . .

". . . *out!"*

". . . . . for lightning to strike. . . ."

". . . *please* . . . you can't. . . ."

". . . . . she know?"

"Fool!"

". . . . ahh . . . a long lost brother. . . ."

Pandora's eyes travel up the treetrunks: cloven chin . . . tombstone teeth . . . black-wire hair . . bristle moustache. . . . *The shape is of the Devil.* She embraces the treetrunks. *The act was of God!*

It is raining.

Mud sucks *plock! plock!* at Pandora's feet. Mud — the colour of dying soldiers. Mud — the colour of dead Other Grandma.

The snow died the night Other Grandma died. The world was white, and it turned to iodine-uck. Other Grandma was white, and she turned to iodine-uck. . . . The night I stole my daddy's meat-cleaver.

Pandora lies down in the mud in her father's ruined victory garden. She makes *plick-plock* angels in the *uck-guck* iodine muck. She rolls over and over and over in her black slicker . . . feeling the rats fall out of her ears, whistling the tune of the Pied Piper, drowning the rats in a sea of mud. *Ashes to ashes, and mud to mud. . . .*

Rubber wheels swish through the bloated gutter: *The grownups are home from the cemetery*. The silent black feet are spattered with mud.

Jessie Christie runs toward Pandora, fist shaking, mouth foaming, eyes blazing. He cudgels her with sexual insult: *"Tit! Fuck-er! Shit! Bug-ger!"*

Pandora passes the infuriated Jessie without seeming to notice. Jessie sprints ahead. *"Bug-ger! Fuck-er! Tit!"* Pandora passes the hysterical Jessie Christie without seeming to notice.

Now they are crossing the railway tracks. Jessie jumps, hot-footed, up and over the glinty rails. The sun dances madly in his glasses. His tongue wags like the red crossing-signal. He puffs up his brass-buttoned chest, juts out his chin, ruffles and rattles his feathers. Pandora passes the unshriven Jessie Christie without seeming to notice.

Jessie loses his cock-a-hoop. He is no match for the morally rearmed Pandora. His feet founder. His arms flail. Jessie runs beside Pandora, in the gutter, offering up himself as Victim. "Sorry, sorry. . . . Don't tell the police . . . not my fault. . . . My father would . . . Wasn't there. . . ."

Pandora looks through Jessie without bothering to change her sightlines: *Jessie Christie is dead.*

Love

Spring, 1945

"Look! Up in the sky!"
"It's a bird!" says Ruth-Anne.
"It's a plane!" says Roger.
"No!" says Miss Macintosh. "It's Pandora*!"*
 Ruth-Anne and Roger and Cecily and Georgia can't believe it at first, but Pandora loop-de-loop-de-loops right in the middle of 3 x 2, fluttering all their sweaty papers, poxed with wrong numbers.
 All of Room 6 converges on the windowboxes, but Pandora has no time! no time! Three turns around the reproving IODE flagpole, then up, up, up . . .
 And God put on his sky-blue spectacles: "Bless my soul! Roll out the golden streets! Serve up the tutti-frutti icecream! Here comes PANDORA!!"

It is spring.
All up and down Oriental Avenue families have switched from Red River porridge to Rice Krispies. The first robin has been sighted, and eaten, by the Stintons' Persian cat. Davey Clay, the newsboy, no longer has to look for puddles to pitch his papers into. Mrs. Newton's orange-plastic flamingoes are out: ditto her birdbath, green frogs, seven dwarfs, darkie lantern-holder and petunia windowboxes.
 The baker has hot-cross buns. The vegetableman has overripe strawberries, veiled like whores in red netting. The girls of Thor Munitions offer up their painted calves and sweatered

bosoms to the fantasies of Oriental men, dourly calculating the cost of grass-seed. The junkman returns from Florida. The popcorn man switches to his summer schedule. Mrs. Spittal is once more scatologically active on behalf of her rosebushes. Mrs. Newton has several extra hours of daylight behind her venetian blinds. The Clays have a new baby, and a fresh set of headcolds. Mrs. Niobe has another Regret-to-inform-you telegram.

Lyle Gothic moves his wicker chair from his living-room to his front porch: *Thousands of dirty, unshaven Germans shuffle through Brandenburg to lay down their arms where Nazis once goose-stepped in triumph. "Where can we go? The Russians are coming!"*

All this as well as the more publicized signs of spring — burbling brooks! bumbling bees! rainbows! sun! shadow! showers! buttercups! and love!

Yes, love.

Pandora is in love, and this time it is *real.*

She is in love with her Uncle Damon: He buys her licorice cigars. He lets her drive his red convertible.

Pandora, puffing furiously on a licorice cigar, turns the wheel while Uncle Damon pushes the pedals.

"Hi, Mrs. Newton!"

"Hi, Stinky!"

All the way down Oriental Avenue.

Pandora's father gets mad when Pandora drives Uncle Damon's car; when Adelaide glows at a Damon compliment; when Adel-Ada giggle at a Damon joke; when Aunt Estelle makes a payment on Uncle Damon's red convertible.

Aunt Estelle gets mad when Uncle Damon takes Rosie for a ride in the red convertible: Well, so does Pandora.

The red convertible pulls up in front of 13 Oriental Avenue.

Aunt Rosie is in the front beside a grinning Uncle Damon. She draws the seat forward so Pandora and Adel-Ada can squeeze in behind. Pandora thinks that's mean: *There was room for me in front. I could have turned the wheel.*

But it is impossible to stay miffed. They are going on a picnic to Zoo Farm! They are going to eat twelve-inch hotdogs
and suck Mel-O-Rol icecream cones!

Rosie looks very pretty in a white sundress with a halter top.
Her red hair is rolled in a neat June Allyson pageboy, her nails
are discreetly blushed. Aunt Rosie works in an office now.
Uncle Damon calls her Ros-a-lind.

Rosalind turns on the radio. She and Uncle Damon laugh a
lot over the warm gush of romantic ballads — a honey soprano
and a molasses bass, blended to warm taffy.

The wind pounds against Pandora in the backseat. At first
she pretends she is Wonder Woman flying into a tornado.
Then, admitting vincibility, she huddles on the floor, with
Adel-Ada, wrapped in a black car-robe.

Now she hears Rosalind and Damon laugh through the car
seat. The wind blows away their frivolous notes, leaving a hot
whine of hysteria that twists through the seat coils. It reminds
Pandora of the high-pitched whine she sometimes hears in
her own head . . . caressed by a muffled drum.

Hola! Zoo Farm is the best place Pandora has ever been. She
rides a donkey named Ethel. She throws a carrot to a billy goat
with a beard like old Mr. *R.I.P.* Grandby. She throws a fish to
a seal with a moustache like . . . *Uncle Damon! He and Aunt
Rosie are missing all the fun.*

Pandora runs back to the picnic park where they had lunch.
Rosie and Damon are nowhere in sight. She sees Aunt Rosie's
white scarf, snagged to the entrance of a cedar maze. Pandora
wraps the scarf around her wrist and skips into the labyrinth,
round and round and . . .

Pandora stops: She hears voices, one high, one low, whorled
like the shoots of a new leaf. She peeks through the last cedar
hedge.

Pandora sees Rosalind and Damon lying together, under a
quaking aspen, wrapped in Uncle Damon's black car-robe, as
if it were cold. Their heads are very close together. Pandora
tries to hear what they are saying, but the trembling aspen
obliterates each syllable as it is formed.

Rosalind's hair is tousled. Her face is puffy. Damon is eating a pickled onion, peeling it gravely, layer by layer, and looking at each one, the way Pandora investigates a blackball.

Pandora, in an expansive mood, is unwilling to accept the evidence of sorrow. She looks from Rosalind's red eyes to Uncle Damon's pickled onion: *Oh well, my mother always cries when she peels onions!*

Pandora wraps Rosalind's white scarf around her eyes, and gropes her way out of the labyrinth, *round and round and round and* . . . counting on the bright thread of happiness she wove on the way in to guide her back into the sunlight. . . .

* * *

It is the hottest day so far.

Arlene and Pandora lie in the spicy shadow of the Binder-Twine Company, sucking honey from phlox florets, and retrieving a friendship that has lapsed a little over the winter.

"What's your favourite flower, Arlene?"

"Ummm. . . ." Arlene considers her answer. It is important to know your friend's favourite colour, favourite number, favourite tree. "Hollyhocks, I guess. Because they look like ladies in skirts."

Pandora nods: *Yes. That's a good answer.* "I like bleeding hearts because you can split off the red case and still have the white heart inside. That's how I made my valentines this year, remember?" She lowers her eyes with the mock modesty of her mother showing off a cleverly-turned doily. "So *many* asked for the pattern!"

"Truth to tell!" exclaims Arlene, just the way her mother would say it. "I like sweet peas *second* best because of the way the pods pop, but I guess my *absolute* favourite is Jack-in-the-pulpit." Arlene adds shyly, "I *used* to think they were sea-horses on stems!"

"Ho!" says Pandora, missing Arlene's self-consciousness, and trying to go her one better. "*I* think of them as *unicorns*." She points up into the sky. "What does that cloud remind you of?"

"Which one?"

"The big puffy one."

Arlene finger-frames the cloud. "It looks like —" she giggles "— a cow's bag with five taps!"

"*Arlene!*" scolds Pandora. "That's *dirty!*"

Arlene pleads factual justification: "Well, it does!"

Arlene, still giggling, breaks off a dandelion and twists it into a ring. She slides it onto Pandora's finger. "Now we're engaged."

Pandora picks a phlox floret. She sucks the shaft, spreading the purple petals over her lips. She pouts at Arlene.

Arlene makes a matching set of beestung lips. She picks a brier rose. The two girls press its scarlet petals onto their fingertips. They practise sultry Hedy Lamarr glances, over Dragon Lady talons.

Arlene and Pandora lie down in a patch of sun. Fire-straws suck the moisture from their skin. Fire-needles hemorrhage their eyelids. Arlene picks a buttercup. "Do you like butter?" She leans impudently across Pandora's chest, her hair gleaming like a copper halo. She squishes the buttercup into Pandora's cloven chin. "Yup. You like butter."

Arlene's moist palm is making a bog of Pandora's sunsuit. She twitches irritably. Arlene whispers: "Do you know where babies come from?"

Pandora's cheeks flare. "Uhhh . . . yah. . . ."

"From *where?*"

Pandora hesitates: It is important not to call down the derision of Arlene's extra two years. "From your mother's *belly*." She is gripped by uncertainty. *Should I have said stomach?*

"*How* does the baby get in your mother's belly?"

Pandora lemon-twists her face: "Your *father* puts it there!"

"*How* does your father put it there?"

Pandora has just dropped off her precipice of knowledge: "I don't know." She amends hastily: "I'm not *sure*."

Arlene, giggling, presses her lips into Pandora's ear: "Your father shoves his *thing* into your mother in the dark!"

Pandora is incredulous. She is about to blurt, *That's not true!* but she knows, suddenly, that it *is* true, and . . . *I knew it all along!* Something overheard? Murky knowledge present but refused?

"*I* knew that!" scoffs Pandora, half-truthfully.

Arlene is skeptical: "*How* did you know?"

Stalling: "What *you* said!"

"*Who* said?"

Pandora can never resist an elaborate prevarication where a simple lie might do. "Amy Walker told me, in Junior Choir. . . . A lady came in with a big belly when we were singing Hallelujah. Amy said, 'She's got a baby in there.' I said, 'Who put it in?' and she said, 'Mr. Collick,' and I said, 'How did he put it in?' and she said. . . . She said what *you* said."

"*What* did she say?"

Pandora closes her ears so as not to hear her lips say it: "She said, 'Your father shoves his *thing* into your mother in the dark!' "

Arlene smirks: "Did she say *how*?"

"Uhhh. . . ." Pandora sweats vinegar. "She . . . uh . . . Amy drew a picture. She drew it on her church program. I remember because Mr. Thwaite gave us a dirty look. Amy had to eat her program. She had to eat the whole thing — *four extra pages* because there was a special Easter service!"

Arlene is entirely won over: Who would go to all this trouble unless they were telling the truth? She nods, approvingly, then relaxes in the gone-wild phlox, her skinny arms angled like the limbs of a praying mantis. She seems about to go to sleep.

Hey! That's not fair. "How did *you* find out?"

Ho hum, Arlene fairly yawns her sophistication. "In a book."

"*What* book?"

"A book my mother got me."

"National Geographics, I'll bet!"

"Naaaaaahh. . . . A book you send away for. They send it in plain wrapper. You have to be over sixteen."

"*You're* not sixteen!"

"My *mother* is, numbskull!"

"Can I see the book?"

"My mother took it back. She says I can't show it to anyone unless their mother phones up first. Especially if they're *younger*."

Pandora winces, on two accounts: "Can you draw me a picture?"

"I thought Amy Walker drew you one."

"She's not a very good drawer. Not like *you*, Arlene."

Arlene giggles: "They *don't* do it the way *dogs* do it!"

The way dogs do it? Dogs?! Pandora is hopelessly addled. "That's what Amy Walker said! She said, 'They don't do it like dogs. Not like dogs at all. They do it . . .' "

Arlene's shadow changes Pandora's eye-soup from blood to ink. "Your father climbs on your mother and . . ." Arlene creeps on top of Pandora, still festooned in flowers. "Arlene! Get *off*! That's *dirty*!"

They roll in the gone-wild phlox.

"Ar-lene! Get OFF!"

"What's the matter, *cry*baby! I'm not *hurt*ing you!"

"I've rolled on a *bee*! I'm *stung*! You rolled me onto a bee!"

It is a point of honour that Pandora never cries over a bee-sting, seldom over a hornet-sting, and only rarely over a wasp-sting. Now, however, she is eager for a safe cause of grievance. "*OO*hhh, my back. It bu*uuuuuuurrrrrns*!"

"Here. . . . Let me see." Arlene, falling easily into her nurse's role, draws aside Pandora's sunsuit straps. She examines the wound. She announces very coolly: "The spot's all swelly. I'll have to suck out the poison."

Arlene gives Pandora a phlox floret to suck. She takes one herself. She surrounds the swollen tissue with her purple lips. She prods the bee-prick with her tongue-tip. She licks the poison mound, round and round and . . .

Arlene spirals outward with her tongue: round and round and . . . *undulating waves of saliva . . . curls, whorls . . . round and round and round*, until she is tasting the whole of Pandora's back, sucking up the sun from the golden pores, arranging the tawny hairs in indolent patterns like a mother cat at its kitten.

"Ar-*lene*!"

It is Mrs. Goodfellow.

"Ar-*lene*!"

She is standing — ham-hands on hock-hips — in the back-door.

"Oh,oh." Arlene leaps up. "Co-*ming*!" She sprints up the yard, leaving her bee-stung lips still plastered to Pandora's bee-stung back.

Pandora cringes in the purple stubble. *Hola!*

She bellies into a clump of ferns. She adjusts her calico sun-suit. She discards her gaudy petals. She crawls out the other side, guilelessly chewing a catkin.

Arlene, shaking with laughter, sprints back from the house. "My - mother - says - we're - not - to - do - whatever - we're - doing - because - it - doesn't - look - good - to - the - neighbours!" She catches her breath. "Let's go climb the rotten apple."

Arlene and Pandora play recklessly, exuberantly, conspicuously, up the rotten apple.

"I'm tired," says Pandora.

"Let's go play at the Pollywog Pond."

Pandora picks a brier rose. She snags it behind her ear. Arlene helps her over the wire fence. They stroll, hand in hand, down the tracks. They do not scrounge for a frog jar.

The heat has ruined the perspective of the tracks. The rails shimmer giddily over the cinderbed, then bend upward at the horizon instead of down. The steel-and-cinder crust of the earth seems to slide over its molten core.

It is cool at the Pollywog Pond.

Arlene and Pandora sit in their favourite spot, under the weeping willow, with their feet in the brook. The water is cold. They wade. The pebbles are hard.

They travel upstream, to the pond itself — over yellow-green felt-mats, that squish under their feet; through rubbery brown tangles, that scratch their ankles; through red filaments, that blood-vein their calves; through blue-green jelly-clouds, that smear their thighs.

The water has become soupy, the pond itself, furtive. Its

bottom is lost in shifting layers of muck, ooze, slime, silt. Its shore, in massings of reed and rice grass.

A spongy island — half-animal, half-vegetable — rises from a clump of bullrushes. Arlene and Pandora pull themselves up onto it. They wipe muck from their legs, with water shamrock. They lie, chins cupped, in a bed of adders' tongues, staring into the water, watching mud particles spiral down stems to greater and greater depth. The re-negotiated bottom appears once more, strewn with hairy rocks and glutinous egg masses.

There is just room for two on their tenuous island. Arlene whispers that honied seduction known to children everywhere: "If . . ."

Pandora does not say yes. Pandora does not say no. Silence incriminates her as it has so many others.

Arlene undoes Pandora's sunsuit. She pulls it off. She pulls off her pants. Pandora sinks, nakedly, into the moss. A breeze curls through flesh unused to exposure. Pandora shivers with the helpless vulnerability of a shucked oyster who sees a Walrus and a Carpenter strolling *tum-tee-tuddle-dee-dum* down the beach towards her. Arlene parts Pandora's legs and *tum-tee-tuddle-dee* gazes upward with lively curiosity, and *tum-tee . . . golly!* experiences all the humiliating uncertainty of a cartographer confused by real landscape. The burden of her two extra years weighs heavily. She is forced, out of pride, to come to some conclusions.

"This," she announces, probing at random, "is your bathroom place." This —" another scientific questionable "— is your bedroom place."

Pandora, mortified, buries her head in the moss in an attempt to sever it from the rest of her body. Arlene, quite unself-conscious, peels off her shorts and T-shirt. She lies beside Pandora, in the adders' tongues. "This —" she is less scientific now "— is what your father does to your mother. He crawls on top of her, and he sticks his thing into her, *right between her legs*. Then he squirts his juice. It has wriggly things in it, like pollywogs, and they swim up into your mother's belly, and

245

they eat her eggs, and they grow fat, like babies, in her belly.
. . . They do it at night, in the dark. We hear the bed squeak.
Sydney turns up his hearing-aid. He lets me listen. I hear. . . ."

Arlene, delighted more by fantasy than present realities,
pours out her erotic gleanings: *hot toilet seats! squishing taps!
tiptoeing feet! creaks! groans! and THINGS that go bump in
the night!*

Shockwaves pound Pandora's psychic breakwaters: *My
mother? My father?* Familiar-unfamiliar bodies copulate gro-
tesquely. . . .

"What's that?"

They listen, heads up, necks taut.

Someone is whistling the Whiffenpoof Song over by the
willow tree.

Pandora leaps into the water, with a terrible *kerplunk*. Arlene dives after her.

The Whiffenpoof continues unabated.

Arlene peeks through the bullrushes. "It's only Sydney!"
She shouts: "Syyyyyd-*neee!*"

Pandora is appalled: It is an old quarrel, this business with
Sydney. She clamps her hand over Arlene's mouth. Arlene
bites it. "SYYYYYYYYYYYYYYD-*NEEEEEEEEEEE!*"

Sydney turns their way, but he has his hearing-aid off, and
silence makes him vague with his other senses.

Pandora yanks Arlene back into the bullrushes. They grapple, angrily. Arlene tries to shove Pandora under. Pandora
drags Arlene down by the hair. They re-surface sputtering.
Their hands slither over each other's greasy bodies. They
trample gelatinous egg masses. They pelt each other with frogs
and swamp dung.

Arlene hits Pandora with a bullrush. Pandora grabs the
swollen cap: It bursts. Honied seedlings spout in an endless
stream. They stick to Pandora's mud slicker.

Pandora thwacks Arlene with another bullrush: It bursts.
They giggle, two bratlings wallowing in primordial stew.

They haul themselves onto their island. They sink back
into its poachy contours. They embrace, trailing strands of

albumen. They feel each other's beating hearts. They press their bodies in mutual exploration. . . . Lips, their juice and flexibility. Cheeks, their comfort and contour. Chests, their budded mystery. Bellies, their warmth. Hands, their infinite variety. Thighs, their power. Genitals, their vulnerability. They explore their mirror-images: Narcissus embracing his reflection.

Sydney whistles the last melancholy strains of the Whiffen-poof Song: *What a dull place. Smelly. Infested. For children with frog bottles. What a boring life. Nothing to do. No one to do it with.*

Sydney kicks a stone, without noticing it is really a running-shoe. He wanders down the tracks, feeling very, very lonely. . . .

"Good-riddance!" giggles Arlene, with the cruelty of the satiated lover. "He's probably gone to catch butterflies!"

Arlene and Pandora wrap their clothes in lily pads, and, balancing them on their heads the way bare-breasted women do it in National Geographics, they wade back to their willow-tree — through blue-green jelly-clouds, feathery red filaments, rubbery brown tangles, yellow-green felt-mats. The water evolves from sludgy to clear, from soupy to cool, from quiet to rippling. They slither, paddle, crawl, scrubbing off impurities and hiding their nakedness. They leap, upright, onto dry land. They dress, fastidiously, behind separate bushes.

A quarrel breaks out.

"You're peeking," complains Pandora in a lispy baby-voice that attempts to fob off responsibility on Arlene, her seducer.

"How could *you* tell, unless *you* were peeking," replies Arlene, in her blameless voice of scientific detachment.

They wave good-bye and — in the tradition of the tryst — head in opposite directions down the track.

It is the long way round for Pandora, which is just as well. She needs the extra time to think up an implausible reason for her matted hair and tainted sunsuit. Arlene simply intends to say she fell in.

Pandora nit-picks her hair: She is afraid she has frogspawn in it. Pandora wriggles the length and breadth of her calico sunsuit. She is afraid she has pollywogs inside that will hatch into toads in her belly.

*　*　*

Adel-Ada sit on a wood bench in Other Grandma's vestibule, their braids stuck out from their heads as if electrified. Pandora sits on the spongy bench, opposite. Rain slashes against the vestibule window. Lightning forks. Thunder crashes. The dead elms snap and snarl like witches quarrelling in the wind.

Pandora keeps one eye on the storm, and the other on the door at the end of the hall. *They* are also quarrelling: Lyle, Aunt Estelle, Uncle Damon. Tongues flash, like lightning. Fists pound, like thunder. Hysteria slides in a puddle under the door.

Aunt Rosie screams.

Uncle Damon hurtles through the vestibule, out into the storm. He red-clefts the aisle of dead elms, with the wind whistling through his cloven chin at 90 miles per hour.

"Ten-twenny-thurdy-fordy. . . ."
Pandora hides in Mrs. Niobe's bridal-wreath bushes: No point in being inventive. Lucy Spittal is "it."
"Fifty-sixty-eighdy-sevendy. . . ."
Sydney Goodfellow pokes his head into Mrs. Niobe's bridal-wreath bushes.
"Gw'an, Sydney. *I'm* here."
"There's plenty room."
"Go-on!"
"Ready-er-not,
Mus-be-cot!"
Lucy squints down Oriental Avenue. Lucy squints up Oriental Avenue. She shuffles toward Mrs. Niobe's bridal-wreath bushes.
Sydney edges toward Pandora.
"Get *out*!"

Sydney leers, familiarly. It is then Pandora knows for sure: *Arlene TOLD, the bugger!*

"I'm *warning* you!"

But Pandora has no more moral authority than any other Fallen Woman: Sydney edges closer. He squeezes Pandora's knee. Almost whining for acceptance, he kisses her: *Mush-ugh! teeth-click!*

Pandora is incensed: She crashes her fist into Sydney's face. She feels his nose mush under her knuckles.

Sydney runs, crying, from the bridal-wreath bushes. Pandora crawls out after him. She is confetti'd in petals. She is dripping with blood. . . .

"Shame! Shame! Shame!" chants Lucy, who knows a thing or two when she sees it. "Shame! Shame! Shame!"

Pandora takes each step of the apartment fire-escape as a separate challenge, planting two feet on one tread before attempting the next, clutching the outer rail in one hand while chesting a jar of peach preserves with the other.

The peach preserves are for Aunt Rosalind who has been ill since Uncle Damon went away.

Aunt Rosalind lives on the fifth floor. Pandora keeps her eyes high as she climbs. That is to prevent them from smashing, like two white eggs, through the iron webbing onto the pavement below. She could have gone up the inside stairs, but the fire-escape, rickracking down an outside seam of the apartment, feeds Pandora's spooky sense of participating in a tragedy in which only one shoe has fallen.

Pandora pauses on the fourth floor. She looks up at Rosie's landing, one floor above. She sees something white flutter through the iron rail. It looks like . . . a white nightgown, blowing in the wind.

Pandora starts up the last flight of stairs. Rosalind passes her on the way down. She passes her in a hurry. She passes her with her nightgown luffing around her *flap! flap! flap!* like a parachute that fails to open. She plummets past Pandora, down down down, past the tops of the quaking aspens, down

down down, through Joe-the-barber's awning, with her red-tipped fingers clutching at straw-thoughts as they slide through the candystriped hole.

Pandora drops her jam-jar. It spatters to peach-pulp on the pavement below. It oozes, like treacle, along the cracks.

Pandora screams. Her scream tears other people, from other apartments: They converge on the mess below.

Two men-in-white scalpel-scrape Rosalind from the sidewalk. They spatula her onto a stretcher. Pandora runs down the fire-escape. It beats under her feet like an open heart.

Pandora lies in the terror-dark, on a bed of her own hell-make, and she counts her ghosts. *Baby Victor Choke-Rope . . . Auntie Cora Tissue-Kiss . . . Grannie Locust Parchment-Crumble . . . Other Grandma Iodine Uck-Muck. . . .*

Hark! What's that? Is that Bubble-Ooze? Is that Aunt Rosalind trickling like treacle under the cubbyhole door? Is that Auntie (the Rivetter) Rosie smelling of peach-preserves?

Round and round and round and . . . Pandora travels through white corridors, to a white room, with a white bed, containing a white mummy-never, strung up to the ceiling with butcher's twine. It is tapping out messages — *yes, no, yes, no* — with one red-chipped finger through a mousehole in its plaster.

Aunt Estelle sits at the head of Rosalind's bed. Uncle Damon stands at the foot. He wraps a red curl *round and round and round* his finger. Aunt Estelle makes lace, inches and weeks of black lace, *round and round and round and* . . . Their black-wire heads are bent. Their cloven chins are buried. They are crying like two black angels.

Pandora sees Aunt Rosalind once more in her life. She is with Uncle Damon in the red convertible, with two pieces of rawhide luggage. She is carrying the red Chinese box, inlaid with a mother-of-pearl dragon.

Rosalind is dressed in black. She is heavily trussed and veiled. She waves from the car, with difficulty.

A capricious wind lifts Rosalind's veil: Her face is a mosaic of broken mirror bits. . . . Aunt Rosie's hair is as white as snow. . . .

＊　＊　＊

Pandora sits in her gable window, in the eye of the frog, on her three-legged stool, covered with patches of Grannie Cragg's dead children, in that intense silence that sometimes precedes great events. *Tomorrow is the last day of school. Tomorrow is the last day of Room 6!*

It has been raining.

The stars hang on constellations across the fresh-scrubbed sky. The moon drips like a silver dollar Aunt Estelle has just washed.

Pandora searches the western horizon. She is looking for *her* stars. *Her* Leo-lion, with a golden mane. *Her* stars because Grannie Cragg gave them to her. *Her* stars because of her birth date.

Pandora finds Leo stretching lazily, yet powerfully, over the smokestacks of Mill City, with his tail raised in a zestful question-mark, and his triangle head snoozing on his paws. (Astronomers see Leo the other way round, but then, astronomers have never known a cat like Charlie-puss.)

Pandora wishes on Regulus, Leo's brightest star:

"Star light,
Star bright,
Nicest star I see tonight. . . ."

She does not wish for a five-drawer pencilbox, or for a skip-rope with ends that won't unravel. Pandora wishes a new wish, a secret wish, a grownup wish. Pandora wishes for Another Sort of Life.

Her mother told her about it.

They were sitting on a hickory bench at the bank, which is as bad as a church pew for not fitting your behind, when her mother drew a wad of money, wrapped in elastic bands, from her purse, and asked, in a hushed voice Pandora could tell was serious: "Do you know what this is?"

Pandora nods. "Sure. It's money."

"It's money, all right, my girl! It's *three hundred dollars!* The most money I've ever held in my hands! It's your daddy's money, from Grandma Pearl."

Adelaide wraps her fingers around the money. "Pandora. . . . Your daddy and I . . . we've been talking about you. We think maybe you should be educated, like your Grandma Pearl. We think . . . and especially, your daddy thinks. . . . Well, we're putting this money in the bank for you, and we're hoping to add to it from time to time. We can't *promise,* but . . ." Adelaide breaks off. She adds brusquely, almost fiercely, "There's *one* sort of life, Pandora, and I suppose, if you're *lucky,* there's Another Sort of Life. You don't seem very happy with the sort we can provide. Maybe —" Adelaide strides over to the girl in the brass-cage and hands over her *most-ever* money.

Pandora stares after her mother. She wraps her fingers around the edge of the bench. *Another Sort of Life?* She thinks about Grandma Pearl. She thinks about the box of poetry! . . . the monkey cape! . . . the trunks with the labels — *Paris! India! Japan!* She chants the magic words over and over, possessing them, being possessed by them: *Another Sort of Life. Another Sort of Life.*

Adelaide beckons Pandora — suddenly shy with the terrible weight and joy of this new responsibility. They continue up New York Avenue, through crowds of bargain-hunters with dull eyes and sharp elbows. Pandora is jostled between shopping bags. She is trampled under bunioned feet. She smells armpit. She smells pant-soil. She hums in a dull monotone, and then in sprightly fashion: *Another Sort . . . Another Sort . . .*

Adelaide stops at a counter where a sale of rayon substandard stockings, 39 cents a pair, is in anarchy. She moves past. Stops. Sighs. Returns. Frowns. Bites her lip. Plunges into chaos. She emerges, ten minutes later, with three pair of stockings held high, a fat wheezy lady on the end of two, and an expression of intense humiliation. The fat lady makes a prolonged fuss. Adelaide gives up one pair. She joins the crush to the cash-register.

"All right, Pandora." Adelaide's voice is heavy with resignation. "Let's go and buy your running shoes."

Pandora is suddenly overwhelmed with love for her mother. She wants to take her mother's hand. She wants to tell her mother that she understands, and appreciates, her particular quality of magic: about the twelve eggs, which turn into thirteen, when you run your fingers thriftily inside every shell; about the enchanted potatoes which, in their transformations from boiled to fried to salad, lead more lives than Merlin's cat; about the hole-y socks which, when pricked thirty-three times one way, and thirty-three times the other, magically become whole; about hoarded pennies which alchemize to nickel and then to silver and then into running shoes.

Pandora wants to take her mother's hand, to cling to it possibly, and therein lies her dilemma: She is afraid she will stick to it, glued at the end, like Adel-Ada. She is afraid she will never get to know *Another Sort . . . Another Sort. . . .* Or maybe her mother will take her hand away?

Pandora folds her arms across her chest, securing it, and she stuffs her fists into her armpits. She binds the pieces of her face into an expression that, if examined carefully, would not seem sullen. She trots behind her mother to the shoe department. . . . It is very difficult to keep from crying.

Lyle Gothic sits on the porch in his wicker chair, reading about the collapse of The War on one continent, and its intensification on another; erasing the Union Jack from the boats and planes of his loyalty, and replacing it with the Stars and Stripes; shrinking the enemy from blond giants to black-haired dwarfs, raising their voices from guttural to super-sing-song-sonic; moving from the trenches to the jungle trees; keeping his airpower; amassing his fleets, and then, of course, preparing to make that switch in psychology from The Rocket to The Bomb.

Pandora shuffles around her father's chair, *round and round and* . . . trying to break through his wicker defences, trying to find the words to thank him. *Round and round and* . . .

Lyle looks up, once, from under war, inflation and the bristling denial of his own inadequacies with a fierce expression which, if examined carefully, would not seem angry.

It is impossible, of course. *Impossible, impossible* . . . Pandora skips across the street, in her new running shoes, tossing and catching her own possibilities like a bright golden ball up, up into the sunlight. . . . *Another Sort . . . Another Sort . . .*

Now, Pandora looks up at her stars, and then — ooh! *below!* right in her own backyard! Fireflies — like star-sparks — dart about the garden.

Pandora steals downstairs, outside, into the balmy night. She runs, barefoot, through the squishy-grass. She drinks rainsplash from the throat of a lily. She dances, white nightie, under the rain-splayed stars, following the fireflies as they make fire-love, in checkmarks, to her mother's mimosa; seeing them illumine her father's cabbages to at least the status of pumpkins.

Pandora leaps high under the head/tail of Leo, the two-way lion. *Aha!* She nips a firefly by the tail-light. She makes her wish. . . . *Another Sort . . . Another Sort. . . .*

What Sort?

It is enough to know, for now, that such a life exists.

Everyone passes — including Magda.

Pandora comes first, Ruth-Anne, second. They will not be in the same room next year: Pandora is going to skip Grade 3. Ruth-Anne is going to private school.

Miss Macintosh won't be back either: Miss Macintosh and Janitor Foukes are getting married!

2 Y's U R
2 Y's U B
I C U R
2 Y's 4 me.

Till we meet again,
Ruth-Anne Baltimore, Room 6

If all the boys lived across the sea,
What a good swimmer Pandora would be.
Cecily Battersea, Age 8

Roses are red,
Violets are blue,
When I see something pretty,
I think of my best friend, YOU
Your friend,
Magda   XXX

Yours till Niagara Falls. . . .
Yours till the kitchen sinks. . . .
Yours till my breath comes in pants. . . .

Good-bye! Good-bye! Good-bye! Ruth-Anne gives Pandora her five-drawer pencilbox: Pandora bursts into tears. She blows her nose on her Lest-We-Forget hanky.

Good-bye! Good-bye! Good-bye! Room 6 runs off in forty-one directions.